Why the Germans Do it Better

'A rich guide to modern Germany.'
Guardian

'A revelation of a book . . . with insights based on painstaking research and evidence gleaned from months crisscrossing the country . . . Kampfner's analysis is simply peerless.'
Literary Review

'A nuanced but compelling account.'
New Statesman

'Authoritative, timely and courageous.'
Philippe Sands

'Smart, provocative and entertaining.'
Kay Burley

'Kampfner's clear and unanswerable argument should be compulsory reading for every politician, civil servant and commentator in Britain.'
John Simpson

JOHN KAMPFNER is an award-winning author, broad-caster and foreign-affairs commentator. He began his career reporting from East Berlin (during the fall of the Wall) and Moscow (during the collapse of communism) for the *Telegraph*. After covering British politics for the *Financial Times* and BBC, he edited the *New Statesman*. He is a regular TV and radio pundit, documentary maker and author of five previous books, including the bestselling *Blair's Wars*.

Why the Germans Do it Better

Notes from a Grown-Up Country

JOHN KAMPFNER

Atlantic Books
London

First published in hardback in Great Britain in 2020 by
Atlantic Books, an imprint of Atlantic Books Ltd.

This paperback edition published in 2021

14

A CIP catalogue record for this book
is available from the British Library.

Paperback ISBN: 978 1 78649 978 3
E-book ISBN: 978 1 78649 977 6

Germany map © Laura Mcfarlane

Printed and bound by CPI Group (UK) Ltd, Croydon, CR0 4YY

Atlantic Books
An imprint of Atlantic Books Ltd
Ormond House
26–27 Boswell Street
London
WC1N 3JZ

www.atlantic-books.co.uk

*To my late parents, Betty and Fred, who, in their
different ways, saw Germany at its worst during the War*

Contents

Preface to the
Paperback Edition

When this book first came out in August 2020, I hoped that it might trigger a new conversation in the UK, and further afield, about Germany. I also hoped that it might prompt Germans to begin looking at themselves in a different, more confident light. I didn't dare imagine it would strike a chord with quite so many people. But something happened to lend my arguments a greater resonance. I suspect that something was COVID-19.

The pandemic said much about the organization of society and capacity of the state. Invariably, Angela Merkel was cited as an exemplar, alongside Jacinda Ardern of New Zealand, the leaders of Taiwan, Finland and elsewhere. The fact that they were all women may well have played a part. People have their own views on that. But what matters far more in Merkel's case is her science background and her character. She believes in facts not grandiloquence.

Throughout 2020, Britain's response to the pandemic was a study in failure. Every development was hailed by Boris Johnson as 'world beating', only to fall apart. The contrast with Germany's relative success made it all the more painful for Brits who are often frightened to look at their own country through a clear lens. To say this is to risk being accused of declinism. I would argue the opposite. It is only by taking a cold, hard look at itself that a people can prepare itself for the future. Instead, many people on *die Insel* – the island – as Germans have taken to calling us, wallow in self-delusion, clinging to past glories as balm. When I read a review by the conservative commentator Simon Heffer in my old paper, the *Telegraph*, fulminating at the slightest suggestion that the Great British nation had any reason to change, I was more convinced than ever of the wider purpose of the book.

Alongside the public debate came many private messages. People young and old, Germans and Brits, with long memories and short, were keen to add their thoughts about the relationship. Compared to America, compared to France even, Germany receives far less coverage in Britain. I hope the attention this book received is a sign that things are changing.

As the UK hurtled into an uncertain future with the flimsiest of Brexit deals, as trade suffered, goods became scarcer and costlier, as the health service suffered from the exodus of European workers, Johnson and his ministers rallied behind the flag. Even though ministers spoke of a fresh 'special relationship' with the EU, their first instinct was to pick fights with these supposed new friends. Asked in an interview why the British had early access to the COVID-19 vaccines (a few weeks earlier than France, Belgium, America and other countries), the Education Secretary, Gavin Williamson, came up with an ingenious response. Rather than saying that regulators had pushed approval through more quickly, he asserted: 'That doesn't surprise me at all because we're a much better country than every single one of them, aren't we?' Germans are no longer shocked or even disappointed by Britain. It did not take long after the UK's departure from the EU for them to move on. They were no longer intrigued by the buffoonery of the prime minister or the accompanying Brexit turmoil. Studied indifference became their *modus operandi*.

For all the brickbats and attempted jokes, a concerted effort is being made in both countries' foreign offices to rediscover what Germany and Britain have in common – a considerable amount. That is a noble endeavour, which deserves support. It has to be recognized, though, that what matters far more to Germany now is the future of the EU, and particularly its bilateral relationship with France, alongside managing the many threats posed by China and Russia. But top of its list of priorities is its relationship with the country that post-war Germany depended on: the United States.

Shortly before the presidential election, ARD, Germany's channel one, aired a documentary in prime time. Called 'Frenzy. An American catastrophe', it opened with dramatic pictures of pitched street battles, police officers beating up protesters of colour, and members of the Proud Boys vowing to make America great again. What, the narrator asked, had happened to the land of the free? The programme was designed to shock, but it was only a foretaste of what was to come two months later.

The assault in January 2021 on Capitol Hill, the citadel of democracy as Americans (and many Europeans) like to see it, was, with hindsight, not surprising. It was the logical endpoint of the Trump era, the manipulation of grievance and truth. But it was still deeply shocking. Joe Biden's socially distanced inauguration two weeks later came as an enormous relief, but Germans in particular would not lull themselves into a false sense of security. Beyond Donald Trump's histrionics and his refusal to acknowledge defeat, the most disconcerting aspect of the election was the narrowness of the verdict itself. Yes, Biden won a record tally of votes – the turnout far exceeded previous elections. But Trump did well too – in spite of everything: the vitriol, divisiveness and the terrible handling of the pandemic. Imagine, Germans asked themselves, what would the world be like if America was run from 2024 onwards by someone as extreme as Trump, but far cleverer? They have never been more aware of the fragility of democracy.

Locked down, like pretty much everyone else in Europe, Germans went into 2021 with trepidation. The relative consensus on dealing with the pandemic frayed. COVID-deniers and anti-vaxxers mounted vocal, if small, demonstrations. The government responded with less precision than earlier in the crisis. Some of the regions became more fractious. Rules were not adhered to as strongly as they should have been.

Shortly before finishing this preface, the European Commission got into a fierce argument with pharmaceutical companies, complaining that vaccines were reaching member countries far more slowly than the UK. The Commission was trying to off-set blame for its own failure to order enough supplies. Britain, alongside Israel and even the US, had been faster and smarter. It was the first instance of the Johnson government doing anything right during the pandemic.

Many Germans were furious with the Commission and its (German) president, Ursula von der Leyen. After all, the successful trial the previous November of the first vaccine, Pfizer/BioNTech, had been heralded as a very German success story. They were bewildered by the turn of events. Much of the British media went into instant 'told you so' mode over Brexit. Who needs solidarity when you can be nimble? Might Johnson emerge the 'victor', some wondered? Might he 'get away with' whatever criticisms a public inquiry on the pandemic might throw at him. After all, hadn't his team scored the winning goal in the final minute of the game?

Politics reduced to sport or a game. A very British way of looking at things.

In winter 2020 and spring 2021, Brits were being vaccinated at an impressively rapid rate. It was a tremendous achievement. However, the verdict on how nations dealt with the COVID crisis will not be written for several years. Will the jabs be effective against all the various mutations? How quickly will the world recover once lockdowns are eased? Only three days before the vaccines row, I watched Johnson announce the grim milestone of 100,000 deaths in Britain. It was 'hard to compute the sorrow contained in that grim statistic', he said. His head hung low, he couldn't answer the question why Britain's death rate was so much higher than any equivalent country and twice as high as Germany's.

It was a rare and unconvincing display of humility. It didn't last long. Even after the pandemic, will Britain, I wonder, ever be big enough to learn from others? As the Germans try to do.

John Kampfner
February 2021

Introduction – Them and Us

In January 2021, Germany turned 150 years old, but its people barely marked the milestone. Germany from the time of Bismarck to that of Hitler is synonymous with militarism, war, the Holocaust and division. No country has caused so much harm in so little time.

And yet, two nearby anniversaries tell a different history. In November 2019, millions celebrated thirty years since the Berlin Wall came down. In October 2020, three decades had passed since reunification. Half of modern Germany's lifespan has been a tale of horror, war and dictatorship. The other half is a remarkable tale of atonement, stability and maturity. No country has achieved so much good in so little time.

As much of the contemporary world succumbs to authoritarianism, as democracy is undermined from its heart by an out-of-control American president, a powerful China and a vengeful Russia, one country – Germany – stands as a bulwark for decency and stability.

This is the other Germany. This is the story I wish to tell.

Those with longer memories struggle to accept the notion of Germany as a moral and political beacon. I want to compare all parts of this society with others, particularly my own, Britain. It will discomfort those still obsessed with Churchill and the

Blitz spirit. Germany's constitution is strong; political debate is more grown-up; economic performance has for much of the post-war era been unrivalled.

Which other nation could have absorbed a poor cousin with so little trauma? Which other nation would have allowed in more than a million of the world's most destitute?

Germany faces many problems. The refugee influx has exacerbated cultural divide. Faith in established political parties is waning. Many, particularly in the East, have turned to the simple slogans of the extremes. The economy has slowed, weighed down by an excessive focus on exports, particularly to China, an ageing population and worsening infrastructure. At a time when Europe and the democratic world desperately needs leadership, Germany has been reluctant to meet its foreign-policy responsibilities.

And then the country was hit by another crisis. In early 2020, COVID-19 came to Europe, a pandemic that killed several million around the world, shattered economies and destroyed millions of lives and livelihoods. It also forced people around the world – locked down wherever they lived – to reassess their priorities and to look again at the role of the state and society. As people impatiently pondered a return to normal, after a year of fear, uncertainty and grief, it became axiomatic to ask: what is the new normal?

So why the confidence, why the faith? The measure of a country – or an institution or individual for that matter – is not the difficulties they face, but how they surmount them. On that test, contemporary Germany is a country to be envied. It has developed a maturity that few others can match. It has done so not because of a preordained disposition. It has learnt the hard way.

Coronavirus provided the ultimate test of leadership. Angela

Merkel, after 15 years in office, rose to the challenge. Empathetic, dogged, she told Germans in precise detail the sacrifices they would have to make and the emergency laws her government would have to impose – something that was extraordinarily sensitive in light of the country's history. She told citizens what she, her ministers and scientists knew and what they didn't. She never blagged. She never boasted. Most of the decisions she was forced to take went against everything modern Germany stood for. The closing of borders showed how easily the great dream of free travel across the continent might end. A people fearful of giving their information to the state was asked to sign up to being tracked and traced. Yet Merkel knew she had no choice.

On the other hand, Britain provided a case-study of how not to deal with a crisis. The bombast of the recently-elected prime minister was in inverse proportion to his government's competence. Boris Johnson was slow to grasp the seriousness of the problem. Even though a pandemic was listed as one of the highest-priority dangers facing the country in the UK government's 2015 National Strategic Defence and Security Review, almost no preparations had been made. With a mixture of libertarianism and English exceptionalism, the prime minister declared that with good old-fashioned pluck, Britain would get through it. However, despite witnessing the tragic advance of the virus in Italy, societal restrictions were slow to be implemented. The British also faced a crisis in their provision of testing and personal protective equipment (PPE). All in all, the UK could not have alighted upon a leader less qualified to deal with a situation that required methodical attention to detail. Johnson had engineered his ascent to power through a flexible relationship with the truth and a reliance on bluster.

It was desperately sad but no surprise that so many died. Care homes became death traps. By May 2020, Britain found itself in the ignominious position of having the highest death toll in Europe and one of the highest in the world. That sorry statistic remained consistent throughout the many months of the pandemic. Meanwhile, the economy contracted at a far higher rate than others.

This British tragedy did not come in isolation. Some of the mistakes related specifically to healthcare decisions. But most of the problem was more deeply embedded in the fabric of government. Germans watched in horror as a country they admired for its pragmatism and *sangfroid* fell into pseudo-Churchillian self-delusion. For most Germans I have spoken to, Britain's recent travails have been the object of sadness and sympathy. So many conversations began with the same question: 'What has happened to you, my British friends?' They hope that, one day, good sense will return.

The post-war Federal Republic of Germany has had only eight leaders, most of them of considerable stature. Konrad Adenauer embedded democracy and anchored West Germany in the transatlantic alliance; Willy Brandt helped engineer detente at the height of the Cold War; Helmut Kohl steered reunification with determination and dexterity; Gerhard Schröder introduced radical economic reforms, albeit at great cost to his party. He was replaced in 2005 by Angela Merkel, the woman around whom so much of contemporary Germany has revolved. She has already overtaken Adenauer in terms of time in office. If she survives until December 2021, she will have outlasted Kohl and become the longest-serving chancellor of modern times. I first met her when she was an unassuming adviser to the man who would become East Germany's first and only democratically elected leader, Lothar de Maizière. She and I sat and drank coffee in the Palast der Republik, the parliament building in East

Berlin that was a popular meeting point. I was struck by her poise, restraint and calm when all around was chaos. If only I had known . . .

Four key years have defined Germany since the war: 1949, 1968, 1989 and 2015. I will look at the effects of these great moments on all areas of life, thematically rather than chronologically. Each has left a deep imprint on society. Each has made Germany what it is today. From 1945 to 1949, a devastated and occupied land had to be rebuilt. Almost all towns and cities were damaged, while many were destroyed. Millions of people were displaced. The trauma of total defeat dominated the national consciousness. The Allies, particularly the Americans, enabled the country to get back on its feet. At the heart of all public life in Germany is the *Grundgesetz* (Basic Law), approved in 1949. It is an extraordinary document, one of the greatest achievements of its post-war reconstruction and rehabilitation. It has managed to be both robust and able to change with the times. It has been amended more than sixty times (a two-thirds majority of both houses is required), without endangering the principles that underpin it. Compared with the alternatives elsewhere it has been a masterstroke. The US Constitution is weighed down by provisions that might have suited the eighteenth century (such as the Second Amendment, granting the right to bear arms); France's Fourth Republic, enshrined around the same time as Germany's, lasted a mere twelve years. Spain's post-Franco constitution of 1978 is creaking under the dispute between the central government and Catalonia. Post-war Italy and Belgium struggle to produce functioning governments. Britain makes it up as it goes along, ever confident that it will muddle through.

The creation of West Germany's post-war political architecture is one of the great triumphs of liberal democracy. The

British played their part in that. They helped devise a constitution so successful that it is cited by Germans as their object of greatest pride.

Why did we not think of creating something similar back home, instead of continuing to encumber ourselves with our embarrassingly atrophied political structures?

Germany rebuilt its economy with staggering success but the atonement, the historical reckoning, did not take place in the immediate post-war years. It took until the rebellions of 1968, the second key event, for Germany's younger generation to confront their parents about the past. They were no longer prepared to accept silence, half-truths or untruths. They wanted answers about the horror that they knew many older people had taken part in or turned a blind eye to. A few years later, the spirit of 1968 took on a violent and ugly hue with the terrorism of the Baader–Meinhof Group. The country was in peril again. Germany stared at another abyss and came through, its democracy strengthened.

The third moment was, of course, the fall of the Wall and reunification. Not long before those heady events in Berlin, Kohl had welcomed East German leader Erich Honecker to Bonn with full military honours. The German Democratic Republic (GDR) had finally received the recognition it craved. Yet his militarized state was beginning to crumble. I lived through those dramatic years, 1989 and 1990, as the *Telegraph*'s correspondent in East Germany. I remember in Leipzig and East Berlin being among the civil society activists and church congregations calling for reform, knowing that police and army units were outside and ready to fire on them. The protests took place shortly after the massacre at Tiananmen Square. What happened next was not inevitable. It did not have to end peacefully. Reunification was not preordained.

Germany became a stable state with settled borders for the first time in its history.

In the years since, many have chewed over the mistakes that were made. Could more of the East German economy have been preserved? Was it all done too quickly? Were the *Wessis*, West Germans, arrogant and insensitive? Why were the one or two better aspects of East German life, not least the more emancipated role of women, not absorbed into the new country? These are legitimate questions. Yet I defy anyone to name another country that could have done what Germany did with so little collateral damage.

The fourth and final upheaval was the refugee crisis of 2015. Charities, security services and the military were reporting that the tide of migrants from the Middle East and North Africa into the EU's southernmost ports was becoming unsustainable. Merkel, preoccupied with the Greek debt crisis at the time, was slow to appreciate what was happening. Yet her eventual response was remarkable. To the consternation of its neighbours, Germany opened its doors to a human stream not seen in Europe since the end of the war. She paid a big price politically. Social wounds were reopened. The far right, anti-immigration Alternative für Deutschland (AfD) surged. Germany is still reeling from her decision, but it was right and it was good. What else, the chancellor would say as the criticism mounted, was a German supposed to do? Build camps?

As the Merkel era comes to an end, Germany faces a greater test than any equivalent country. Why? As Thomas Bagger, an adviser to current German president Frank-Walter Steinmeier, points out, the nation depends entirely for its identity, stability and self-worth on the liberal democratic post-war settlement, on the rule of law. The year 1945 was *Stunde Null*, Zero Hour. Germany started again. Unlike Russia and France, with their military symbols, the US with the story of its founding fathers, or the UK, with its Rule Britannia teaching of history and *Dad's Army* war obsessions, Germany has nothing else to fall back on. That is why it cares so passionately about process, about getting it right, not playing fast and loose. Germany has few positive reference points from history. That is why it refuses to look back. That is why it sees every challenge to democracy as an existential threat. That is why I, like many who have a complicated relationship with the country, so fulsomely admire the seriousness with which it has set about its task since 1945. Most of all, it is about the power of memory.

My journey goes back vicariously to the 1930s. My Jewish father, Fred, fled Bratislava, his home town, as Hitler's army was marching the other way into Czechoslovakia. His father and mother smuggled the three of them in train carriages and cars back across Germany and out. They were nearly caught several times but escaped by the skin of their teeth and by individual acts of kindness. Many of their extended family died in the concentration camps. He made his life in England, via a fifteen-year stint in Singapore, where he met my mother, a nurse from Kent of solid Christian working-class stock, on the ward of the British Army hospital.

My childhood in London in the 1960s and 1970s contained the usual fare of war songs, jokes and TV shows at the expense of the Krauts. The dirty Germans crossed the Rhine, parlez vous. Hitler only had one ball, the other was in the Albert Hall. I would play in the bomb shelter in the garden of my grandmother's north Oxford house. I would read le Carré and Forsyth, watch *Colditz* and *The Dam Busters*, and a few years later would collapse in uproarious laughter over *Fawlty Towers* and 'Don't Mention the War'. Occasionally, the mould was broken. *Auf*

Wiedersehen, Pet, a TV drama about brickies from the North East of England looking for casual labour in northern Germany, showed a more human and complex side to the relationship with Germany. Most of the time, though, popular culture was confined to tabloid insults and jokes about beach towels and sunloungers.

I was a bit young for Vincent Mulchrone's commentary in the *Daily Mail* on the morning of the 1966 World Cup final: 'West Germany may beat us at our national sport today, but that would be only fair. We beat them twice at theirs.'[1] As we all know, England won 4–2, courtesy of a dodgy goal. A new chant was born: two world wars and one World Cup. Even in 1996, as football, we hoped, was coming home after thirty years of hurt, as Cool Britannia was emerging on the eve of the Blair era, we couldn't help ourselves. 'Achtung Surrender!' screamed the front page of the *Mirror*. 'For You Fritz ze Euro Championship is Over.'[2] The jokes were a laugh – for some. The magazine *Der Spiegel* wrote in 2002: 'For many English, the Second World War will never end. It is just too much fun to taunt the Germans.'[3]

It changed for me at the age of fifteen. I started to study the language and fell in love with it. I was exposed to Goethe, Brecht, Max Frisch – and Nina Hagen. In my early twenties, I jumped at the opportunity to work in Germany, as a cub reporter in Bonn, the *Bundesdorf*, or federal-village as it was known. In April 1986, nearly fifty years on from his escape, my father came to visit me. He had not been back since his extraordinary journey across the country to freedom. On the phone before his departure, he was apprehensive. His nerves weren't improved when Lufthansa lost his bags on arrival. Perhaps the Germans aren't that efficient after all, he joked. His overriding impression, including a journey along the transit motorway that took you down a protected road to West Berlin, was of a country at ease with itself and effortlessly polite to a man whose German revived almost immediately, albeit with a Viennese vernacular stuck in the 1930s.

Apart from my dad's visit, I was seldom required to think about the war during my time in placid Bonn. My friends in the office and various students I had met at the university were, I felt, not dissimilar to my peers at home. It wasn't the past that bothered me. It was the present, and Germany's obsession with rules. I recall sitting on the balcony of my apartment one sunny Sunday lunchtime listening to the local rock music station on the radio. When the pips came on for the news, my German girlfriend at the time switched it off. I asked her to switch it back on. She refused. Didn't I know it was the *quiet hour*? During the quiet hour you have to show consideration to your elderly neighbours. That set me off. You don't need rules for that kind of thing, I said. Oh yes you do, she retorted. I fell into stereotyping the herd mentality that leads, ahem, to evil as well as good. She accused me of being a selfish Thatcherite who cares only for myself. I often think about that conversation and who was wrong and who was right.

Some of the day-to-day annoyances of living in Germany were clichés, but they were no less true for that. I was once fined by the police who spotted me crossing the road when the fabled red man was showing, at four o'clock in the morning. When I suggested to the officer that another car was unlikely to come down this quiet lane for hours, I only made matters worse. Rules are rules. Bureaucracy must be respected, even if logic suggests otherwise. Once I received a beautifully embossed envelope on the windscreen of my car. 'Dear neighbour,' it read, 'please would you clean your car as it is bringing down the reputation of the street.' Some rules have been relaxed in the intervening years; others have simply been replaced by newer ones. Woe betide a pedestrian who edges onto the cycle lane. When does punctuality go too far? A friend recently gave me a lift to Sunday lunch at someone's home in Berlin's suburbs, and we arrived at our destination at seven minutes to one. 'Now we can relax and chat,' she said triumphantly. At one on the dot, she declared: 'We can go in now.'

Many Germans understand the frustrations; they attempt several explanations or excuses. First comes 'Every country has its quirks.' The second is a war-weary 'We need rules in order to keep ourselves in check.' The third is the most intriguing. German society is based on a sense of mutual obligation, shared endeavour and a belief that a rules-based order is benign. An ageing former punk I met in Leipzig, who would hang out with Malcom McLaren and the Sex Pistols in London back in the day, explained that everyone's worst fear is a *Rechtsfreier Raum*. A space with no rules is where the powerful exploit the weak. He points out of his window. People shouldn't be allowed to build extensions that block out the light for their neighbours. People shouldn't make noise after a certain time, because old people will struggle to sleep. This from a former punk musician. He is unrepentant. In a democratic society, he insists, the role of the state should be to help the weak take on the strong: to rebalance between rich and poor.

The culture war of the past five or so years, and the twin shocks of Trump and Brexit, shook Germany to the core. As did the often-violent demonstrations in France by the *gilets jaunes*, the yellow vests. Most of all, Germans watched the four years of Britain's Brexit torment with stunned disbelief. They could not understand how the Mother of Parliaments, a country synonymous with stability and predictability, could have descended into such chaos. The referendum result came as a shock – they realized that the Brits were sceptical of the European project (as even some Germans are), but they couldn't imagine that this would be followed by a collective loss of nerve. Infantile and improvised were two of the most common descriptions of British politics during this period.

They were bewildered by the absence of rules. Which held precedence – a one-off referendum or representative democracy? That, I mumbled, was murky. How could you have a system in which your speaker and prime minister made it up as they went along? I would respond with a shrug of the shoulders that comes from having to explain the failings of your own country knowing that there is no credible explanation. The dismay was offset by very German attempts at humour, not least impersonations of Speaker John Bercow bellowing 'Order! Order!' One Berliner told me, in all seriousness, that she had given up her Netflix subscription because she got all the entertainment she needed watching Britain's Parliament channel.

In December 2018, when Theresa May's attempted deal suffered its first setback, the *Heute Show* (Germany's equivalent of America's *Daily Show*) awarded its annual 'golden dumbass' prize to the UK . . . alongside Donald Trump and Crown Prince of Saudi Arabia Mohammed bin Salman. Over pictures of Merkel waiting awkwardly outside the Chancellery as the door of the British prime minister's limo failed to open, host Oliver Welke described how May 'can't get out of the EU and can't get out of her bloody car!'. He then showed a cartoon of a caricature British gentleman in a bowler hat and pinstriped suit repeatedly burning his hand on a hot stove, then stabbing his eye with a fork. The audience fell about laughing. 'Hard Brexit, soft Brexit, liquid Brexit, just fog off,' Welke yelled. It was painful to watch. Britain: the butt of global mirth. Yet as the prime minister of the state of Brandenburg, Dietmar Woidke, put it at a gathering of policymakers: 'Brexit is not a comedy show. It is a real-life drama in many acts.'[4]

The general election victory secured by Johnson in December 2019 drove a further wedge. Germany might have been relieved that it no longer had to deal with Brexit uncertainty, but instead it had to navigate a new-found populism on its doorstep, borrowed and developed from Johnson's 'friend' Donald Trump. How could the British have elected a man known for making up stories about the EU when he was a journalist in Brussels, a man who likes to play the clown? Johnson is to many Germans the antithesis of what a politician should represent.

Brexit is not the cause of Britain's psychodrama. It is a symptom. We are trapped by a moribund political system and delusions of grandeur. When the former US secretary of state Dean Acheson noted back in 1962 that Britain had lost an empire and not yet found a role, he would not have thought that sixty years on we would still be floundering. We have never got over winning the war. We flock to see films such as *Dunkirk* and *Darkest Hour*; we continue to set our cultural and historical parameters around events that took place seventy-five years ago. Most of our media has spent decades portraying European integration as a plot by the Germans and the French designed to undermine English values. The language is of victory and surrender, collaborator and traitor.

Immediately after the war, Britain didn't have the economic or military power of the Americans. We didn't devise the Marshall Plan. We did, however, play a major role in keeping Berlin free, in keeping Germany secure thanks to the British Army on the Rhine, and helping to develop a free media and respected political institutions, for which Germans remain immensely grateful.

Britain has never been comfortable with the European

Union. During that first referendum in 1975, those campaigning against remaining in the EEC likened the Treaty of Accession to Chamberlain's Munich Agreement and appeasement. In 1974, as he was preparing to address the Labour Party conference, Helmut Schmidt asked his cabinet what he might say in his speech that would help convince voters to stay in the EEC. One of his ministers, who had just met her British counterpart, Barbara Castle, told him: 'The only way to keep Britain in the European Community is not to remind it that it is already in.'[5]

This memo formed part of an exhibition at the German House of History in Bonn in 2019 entitled *Very British: A German Point of View*. This was, as curator Peter Hoffmann pointed out to me, one of the museum's most popular shows. It had been devised before the referendum. The contents were amended to include a room focused on Brexit. Hoffmann admitted Germans' fixation with Britain's travails had boosted visitor numbers. The show is funny, informative – and painful. It is about an unrequited love.

Germans have devoured British subculture, pop music, TV shows (they too found *Fawlty Towers* funny in a self-deprecating way), the glamour of Emma Peel and the Avengers, to the present day. Many Germans can recount holidays to Cornwall, Scotland and the Lake District in their camper vans. They are glued to Premier League football. They obsess about the royal family (Germans, from Hanover, they like to note). They love English traditions, even when they make them up. Every New Year's Eve, the entire country, young and old, watches an English-language film called 'Dinner for One'. Black and white, lasting only twenty minutes, it was first aired in 1963. It is the most repeated TV programme in history, the ninetieth-birthday dinner of Miss Sophie, a bejewelled English aristocrat. Every year, she invites the same four gentlemen around. The trouble is they are now all dead. Undeterred, the butler lays the table and goes through the same ritual: a four-course meal, including mulligatawny soup, washed down with dry sherry, wine and champagne. Germans know every gag. The line that has them collapsing in laughter is when the butler asks Miss Sophie: 'The same procedure as last year?'

The fall of the Berlin Wall could and should have been a great moment for celebrating Britain's role in the rebirth of democratic Germany. An oppressive communist system was dismantled with extraordinary success. Margaret Thatcher, alongside Ronald Reagan and Mikhail Gorbachev, had an important part to play. Yet all she saw was danger. A month after the incredible scenes in Berlin, she told EU leaders at a dinner in Strasbourg: 'Twice we beat the Germans. Now they are there again.' Pulling out maps of Silesia, Pomerania and East Prussia from her handbag, she intoned to French president François Mitterrand: 'They'll take all of that, and Czechoslovakia too.'[6]

Weeks later, the Thatcherite Bruges Group heard the following from one of her favourite economists, Kenneth Minogue: 'The European institutions were attempting to create a European Union, in the tradition of the medieval popes, Charlemagne, Napoleon, the Kaiser and Adolf Hitler.'[7] One of her most trusted cabinet ministers, Nicholas Ridley, famously told the *Spectator* magazine that the European Exchange Rate Mechanism (the precursor to the Euro) was 'all a German racket designed to take over the whole of Europe [. . .] I'm not against giving up sovereignty in principle, but not to this lot. You might as well give it to Adolf Hitler frankly.'[8] He was forced to resign, but he was only saying what a lot of Brits, a certain type of Brit, were thinking.

Thatcher saw it as her mission to push back, until she realized she had no one on her side. She tried to lobby Gorbachev privately. The Soviet leader had not for a moment suspected that his political reforms would lead to the collapse of communism across the whole bloc. His was the most pivotal role and yet he agreed not just to the reunification of Germany, but to a Western-leaning Germany in NATO, and to the Soviet Union pulling back its military front line. Thatcher's pleading with him fell on deaf ears. Mitterrand too had reservations about the new German project. The French had many historical reasons to fear a strengthened and united Germany. A weakened and divided Germany had served them well. As the French writer and resistance figure François Mauriac quipped in 1952: 'I love Germany so much that I rejoice there are two of them.'[9] Yet Mitterrand knew that he could not stand in the way of history.

The Two Plus Four process gave journalists a ringside view of the dynamics – Kohl, Thatcher, Mitterrand, Gorbachev and George Bush senior (who had taken over from Reagan at the start of 1989) negotiating a treaty that would create a single Germany and a new European architecture. East Germany's notional leader, de Maizière, had a walk-on part. Thatcher never concealed her animus towards Kohl, a reaction that was rooted in the psyche of war, not politics. Kohl kept a bust of Churchill in his office in the Chancellery. He was an avowed Anglophile, seeing Britain's influence in Europe as a good. And yet, no matter how hard he tried, he couldn't win her around. In March 1990, the two had agreed to attend the fortieth Königswinter, an Anglo-German conference, in Cambridge. The organizers decided it was too risky to put them next to each other. That evening Thatcher gave her dinner neighbour, a veteran German diplomat, the benefit of her musings. It would, she said, be 'at least another 40 years before the British could trust the Germans again'.[10]

To her credit, she admitted in her memoirs only three years

later that she had got it wrong: 'If there is one instance in which a foreign policy I pursued met with unambiguous failure, it was my policy on German reunification.'[11]

Even now Britain doesn't quite seem to know what it wants of Germany. When its economy struggles, as it did in the mid-eighties and mid-nineties, it is derided as the 'sick man of Europe', over-regulated and hidebound. When Deutschland AG corners global markets, it is over-weaning and rapacious. Now that its economy is slowing again, the gloating has resumed. The British don't want Germany to throw its weight around the world, yet they do want it to pull its weight.

The millennium and 2000s, when Tony Blair and Gerhard Schröder were talking about a common European home, brought a brief interlude. It all came crashing down with Brexit. The arrival of Johnson as Foreign Secretary in 2016 ushered in a new era of crassness towards Germany. His officials despaired of his language. Leaving the EU, Johnson told the Munich Security Conference, would be a *liberation*, pronouncing the word in French, to the consternation of his audience. The wannabe historian and now prime minister who models himself on Churchill has borrowed much from the Thatcher lexicon. This rhetoric has always played well among the Conservative core – and it still does. One minister who served under Theresa May recalls a party stalwart spluttering at a recent constituency evening: 'We didn't win the war in order to be told what to do by the Germans.' He was loudly cheered.

Britain may be the global leader in wartime obsessions, but it is not alone. Germany still feels it cannot do anything right. When it clamped down on Greece in the debt crisis (the rights and wrongs of which are discussed later in this book), placards of Merkel went up in Athens with a Hitler moustache painted on her.

*

Mercifully, there is another story about Germany. The lived experience, in business, tech and arts, has demystified Germany to a new generation of Brits. The 'poor but sexy' (the phrase used by the mayor in 2003) capital became a magnet for tourists. Teenage and twenty-something clubbers flock on weekend breaks to Berlin, Hamburg and Leipzig. Germany now has the fourth-largest contingent of Brits in Europe, after Spain, France and Ireland. According to a joint study by the organizations Oxford in Berlin and the Berlin Social Science Centre (WZB),[12] the number of Britons receiving German citizenship rose tenfold in the three years after the referendum, with predictions for subsequent years to be higher still. Among many younger Brits, Germany is a source of hope and opportunity.

Over the last decade or two, Germans have become a little less reluctant to talk up their country. Some put this down to the popular hosting of the 2006 World Cup. Others insist there was no turning point, more a gradual passage of time. But they still remain hesitant. The seventieth anniversary of the *Grundgesetz* was quietly marked in 2019, with exhibitions, television documentaries and commemorative stands in high streets. Around the same time, the Open Society Foundation conducted a detailed survey about patriotism, a vexed subject for Germans. It pointed out that consistently, over decades, the most important source of national pride has been the Basic Law. The one form of patriotism that many Germans embrace is called constitutional patriotism. The pride they feel in their country is not of the small-island, flag-waving variety. Instead, they hope they are setting a good example for the world through a clear set of democratic rules.

I was keen to test all of this for myself – if only anecdotally. One summer's day in 2019 in Prenzlauer Berg, the now-hipster area of East Berlin where I had witnessed the Church protests against the communist regime thirty years earlier, I carried out a set of video interviews for Cari and Januscz, friends who run a German-language course called Easy German. The question I was asked to pop to everyone was: 'What do the Germans do well?' Most passers-by were shocked at being asked, struggling to think of anything. Sometimes seriously, sometimes ironically, they would proffer the following: punctuality, correctness, thoroughness. One went so far as to say: 'We are tough, but honest and direct. We are good to our word.' Many sought sanctuary in 'bread' or 'beer'.

It made me wonder, though, what *do* the Germans do better, and what lessons do they actually have to teach, or rather have they learnt? In posing these questions, I hope to spark a different kind of debate about the country, not to suggest superiority but to redress the balance of recent history. Look around your local bookshop, in any country, and how many books are there about Germany that are *not* about the two world wars? There have been some admirable ones in recent years, but they are few and far between.

Why write this book now? Germany is coming out of a sustained period of economic growth and entering a time of heightened uncertainty. My year-long road trip and series of interviews have not made me starry-eyed or blind to the country's faults. I include them all here. The Germans I interviewed for this book, from prominent politicians and CEOs of multinationals, to artists, volunteers helping refugees, old mates and ordinary folk met at random, all recoiled at the thesis and the title of the book. Without a single exception. 'You can't say that,' they would exclaim with a shriek or awkward laugh. They then embarked on a long list of troubles that the country faces and things that it gets wrong. Everywhere they look, Germans feel anxious. They see all that they hold dear being threatened. They see a world in which democracy is openly mocked by populists and strongmen – from Donald Trump to Vladimir Putin, from Turkey's Recep Tayyip Erdoğan to Brazil's Jair Bolsonaro. At home, they see the AfD everywhere and mainstream politicians struggling to cope. They, like everyone, see the climate emergency before their eyes.

What better time to test their country's resilience than now? Most Germans, let alone foreigners, see only dark times ahead for their country. I passionately disagree, although of course there are many problems ahead. What gives me cause for hope is their self-questioning, their almost morbid re-stoking of memory. Germans cannot bring themselves to praise their country. This refusal to see good is hardwired. And yet, particularly when compared with the alternatives on offer in Europe and beyond, they have much to be proud of. As the American commentator George Will wrote early in 2019: 'Today's Germany is the best Germany the world has seen.'[13] More hubristic countries like my own would be wise to learn from it.

1

Rebuilding and Remembering

The pain of the post-war years

Weimar is the city of Goethe and Schiller, of Bach and Liszt, of the Renaissance painter Cranach the Elder. It is where the woman of letters and salon queen Madame de Staël fell in love with the culture of Germany, and where the Bauhaus art school had its beginnings.

Outside my hotel, the no. 6 bus takes you the short distance from Goethe Square to the Buchenwald concentration camp. You don't need to go far in Germany to be confronted by its terrible history. In Munich, it takes just over half an hour to travel from the S-Bahn no. 2's central station to its end stop, Dachau. In Berlin, it's a little more complicated to reach Sachsenhausen by public transport, but the trip north of the city can be done in just over an hour.

For the past half-century Germany has engaged in an act of atonement that has dominated all aspects of life, with everything referenced back to the Nazi era. Germans' high state of moral alert, even after all these years, still dictates much of what they do. The historian Fritz Stern talks of 'the Germans' wish to believe' in Hitler, 'in their voluntary choice of Nazism'.[1] Stern spent his long career seeking to answer the question 'Why and how did the universal human potential for evil become an actuality in Germany?'[2] Or, as the British historian A. J. P. Taylor contended, writing in the closing months of the war: 'The history of the Germans is a history of extremes. It contains everything except moderation, and in the course of a thousand years the Germans have experienced everything except normality.'[3]

An entire phraseology has been built up around the need to remember: *Vergangenheitsbewältigung* (coming to terms with history); *Vergangenheitsaufarbeitung* (processing history); *Erinnerungskultur* (culture of remembrance); and most controversially, *Kollektivschuld* (collective guilt).

German history, even pre-twentieth century, is seen through this lens. Unlike France or Britain or many other countries around the world, there are no grand national day ceremonies, although the recently inaugurated Day of German Unity (on 3 October) is now tentatively being marked. Those who died in military service to their country rarely receive public commemorations. The only parades are local folkloric or cultural ones. There is little pageantry – which could account for Germans' obsession with royalty and celebrity elsewhere.

Which other country would build a monument to its own shame – and right next to its two most famous landmarks? The Memorial to the Murdered Jews of Europe sits close to the Brandenburg Gate and the Reichstag in the heart of Berlin. Containing 2,711 rectangular concrete slabs, each resembling a coffin, it was inaugurated in 2005. School groups descend on it from all parts of the country, children warned to be quiet at all times. To watch their faces as they leave is instructive. Some historians and architects have criticized it as too abstract, cold even. I see it as chilling and in the appropriate sense. This is now the most famous site of remembrance to the Holocaust within modern Germany and the territory of the former Third Reich, but it is only one of many.

In 1992, the artist Gunter Demnig came up with an idea. Three decades on, there are more than 70,000 *Stolpersteine* in 20 languages in 120 towns and cities in 24 countries across Europe. These are small symmetrical stones, literally stumbling stones, 10 centimetres by 10, with brass plaques bearing the names of people exterminated in the concentration camps and other victims of National Socialism. They are located outside the last known home of the victims, mainly but not exclusively Jews. Some are Roma, others are homosexuals or disabled. The inscription on each stone begins 'Here lived', followed by the victim's name, date of birth and fate: internment, suicide, exile or, in the vast majority of cases, deportation and murder. Most are located in Germany.[4]

These acts of remembrance did not come easily, and they did not come quickly. Indeed, it took the best part of two decades after the war for Germans to really confront the unvarnished truth of the Holocaust and other horrors. From the mid-1940s, the prevailing mood was of shocked humiliation. The Allies' tactic of breaking civilian morale by firebombing cities into oblivion may have brought forward the end of the war. It also allowed a sense of victimhood to take root, usually silently; in the views of some, there was a sense of moral equivalence between Nazi crimes and Allied excesses.

Initially, the process of rebuilding took only physical form. The image of the *Trümmerfrauen*, the rubble women, is writ large on the German psyche. Immediately on the Nazis' surrender, the Allies enlisted all able-bodied women aged between fifteen and fifty to clear buildings brick by brick, using sledgehammers and picks. The streets were cleared of rubble. Many of these women were traumatized from war. But they were deemed capable of manual work, nine hours per day for a few coins and a ration card. Many men were crippled or in prisoner-of-war camps. Eight million people had been killed or were missing, more than 10 per cent of the population. Around 150 towns and cities lay in ruins. Nearly half the roads, railways, gas, electricity and water supplies were destroyed. George Orwell described what he found in Cologne in March 1945: 'The master race are all around you, threading their way on their bicycles between the piles of rubble or rushing off with jugs and buckets to meet the water cart.'[5] His caustic fury was typical of its time.

As Neil MacGregor writes, 'The pathos of the handcart is powerful and real.'[6] An already impoverished country was required to house and feed twelve million people driven out from the eastern lands by the Russian advance, increasing the population by a fifth at a time when there was barely any food to go round. This was possibly the biggest forced population movement in history. Many people had nowhere to go, nowhere warm to shelter, pushing a few ragged belongings with them. The winter of 1946–47 was particularly harsh. Money was worthless. Barter was the currency of choice. The most sought-after commodities were cigarettes and chocolate. Food rationing prescribed a mere 1,000–1,500 calories per day. American food supplies – a sixth of Germany's total food production at the time – saved tens of thousands from starvation.

To this day, few families do not have someone, or know of someone, who was scarred by the post-war collapse. This was for a long time an under-commemorated and under-studied aspect of German history. Is this, MacGregor wonders, 'because Germans consider these events as just retribution for evil deeds? When a state has done so much wrong, how are we to respond to the suffering its citizens endure as a result? If we assert a communal guilt, can we nonetheless plead for individual compassion?'[7]

In a book published in 2008 called *The Cold Homeland*, the historian Andreas Kossert examines the treatment of these destitute people from the east. They were not welcomed with open arms by their countrymen – something that has always been, and remains, an awkward subject that requires sensitive handling. 'Seventy years after the end of the war, almost every family in Germany is affected by it,' writes Kossert. 'But it is only gradually becoming a topic of collective memory in Germany, because until very recently the issue was associated with a right-wing, revisionist position. [. . .] In many families there was a total silence and not a word about the loss, the mourning of parents or grandparents.'[8]

Occupying forces promoted the idea that through denazification, demilitarization and reconstruction, Germany could reset the clock. It began to be used in everyday parlance. Roberto Rossellini's film *Germany, Year Zero*, which was shot on location in 1947 and screened in German and English the following year, may have helped spread the use of the term. Zero, rubbing everything out, was convenient. Most Germans in that period chose to see themselves as either victims or unwitting participants. A truly honest debate about the nature of participation and guilt would take two decades to materialize. As the war reporter Martha Gellhorn wrote mockingly during her travels across the defeated lands: 'No one is a Nazi. No one ever was. There may have been some Nazis in the next village . . . there weren't many Jews in this neighbourhood . . . we have nothing against the Jews; we always got on well with them.' She added: 'It should be set to music.'[9]

For the Allies, the situation required pragmatism. With the

Soviet threat increasing, they desperately needed Germany back on its feet. They needed it stable. The first sign of a shift away from punishment came during a visit by US secretary of state James Byrnes in September 1946. He visited a number of destroyed cities, giving a speech in Stuttgart which he entitled a 'Restatement of Policy'; it was anything but. Two processes were set in motion: economic assistance and a decision to focus more on the dangers of communism than the crimes of fascism. 'The American government has supported and will continue to support the necessary measures to denazify and demilitarize Germany, but it does not follow that large armies of foreign soldiers or alien bureaucrats, however well motivated and disciplined, are in the long run the most reliable guardians of another country's democracy,' Byrnes said. 'The United States cannot relieve Germany from the hardships inflicted upon her by the war her leaders started. But the United States has no desire to increase those hardships or to deny the German people an opportunity to work their way out of those hardships so long as they respect human freedom and cling to the paths of peace.'[10]

President Harry Truman concluded that without a massive injection, Europe would not get back on its feet. As his secretary of state George Marshall (who had succeeded Byrnes), put it: 'It is logical that the United States should do whatever it is able to do to assist in the return of normal economic health to the world, without which there can be no political stability and no assured peace.'[11] The European Recovery Program, or Marshall Plan, provided $12 billion to eighteen European nations (the equivalent of more than $100 billion in today's prices). Britain and France received the most, followed by Germany. The USSR refused money for itself and for the new Eastern European bloc that had come under its wing.

Many middle- and even some higher-ranking Nazis were restored to their positions. Denazification certifications – dubbed *Persilscheine*, 'Persil notes' – were easy to obtain. Suspicions of Nazi complicity could be washed away with some historical detergent. Suspected Nazi offenders could be exonerated by statements of good reputation. People talked about being washed clean or walking in with a brown shirt and coming out with a white one. A few years later, the new Bundestag passed Article 131, formalizing the process. This allowed public servants, including politicians, judges, military officers, teachers and doctors, to be automatically reinstated if they had passed denazification tests. Retirement benefits were restored. A number of business leaders were able to take up their posts at the helm of companies that had been complicit.

The memory of war guilt has not receded with time. I am struck by how many Germans, particularly the young to middle-aged, bring it up unprompted. They do so less to dwell on the past, important though that is, but to check that the lessons have been learnt. In these times of increasing authoritarianism, nationalism and incivility in Europe and around the world, they are talking about the crimes of the Third Reich more than they have ever done. In Munich, I meet Matthias Mühling, director of the Lenbachhaus, one of Munich's most important galleries. As we look out from the museum onto the neoclassical splendour of Königsplatz, the square that was at the heart of Nazi power, he points out to me the Central Institute for Art History. Soon after the war, the Americans set up a team there to investigate the thousands of looted works of art. The episode featured in a 2014 Hollywood hit, *The Monuments Men*, starring George Clooney. As Mühling tells the story, he becomes ever more impassioned. The ease with which many ex-Nazis returned to prominent positions in culture, and other parts of society, rankles with him. He talks of 'everyone's grandfathers and possibly fathers being Nazis – and still getting away with it'. He points out that the Lenbachhaus, unlike pretty much all its rivals, did not become a cheerleader for Hitler. Many museum directors who had enthusiastically complied with instructions to rid themselves of 'degenerate Jewish' art were co-opted by the US forces to help find missing works. 'I suppose that was obvious,' Mühling says. 'They knew where it had gone.' What matters more? The fact that many senior people got away with it? Or the fact that many of the present generation in public life are still angry that they did?

In the mid to late 1940s, apart from the most egregious war criminals, there was little interest in pursuing smaller fry. Only twenty-four top Nazis were put on trial at the Palace of Justice in Nuremberg. Twelve were sentenced to death, and ten of them were hanged on the same day, 16 October 1946, in the building's gymnasium. It was a public manifestation of guilt, but at the same time it was part of a narrative that the war chapter had been closed. Institutions were forced to recant. One of the first was the Protestant Church, which acknowledged its collaboration with the Nazis in what was called the Stuttgart Confession in October 1945. 'Through us infinite wrong was brought over many peoples and countries,' it declared. 'That which we often testified to in our communities, we express now in the name of the whole Church: we did fight for long years in the name of Jesus Christ against the mentality that found its awful expression in the National Socialist regime of violence; but we accuse ourselves for not standing to our beliefs more courageously, for not praying more faithfully, for not believing more joyously, and for not loving more ardently.'[12] Even this half-apology, half-non-apology was regarded as too much by many at the time.

*

The Iron Curtain had descended. The Soviets were steadily increasing their stranglehold on their occupied sector. The US and the British decided to consolidate their two occupied sectors, at least economically. After a difficult beginning, the Bizone proved a success. (It took the French two years to join, briefly creating a Trizone.) This became the nucleus of the future West Germany. Between February and June 1948, the three Allies, alongside the Netherlands, Belgium and Luxembourg, convened in London to discuss how to restore self-rule to the vanquished state. They were desperate to be rid of the task of governing German lands, given the twin requirements of rebuilding their own countries and tackling the rapidly growing communist threat.

All the attention of Germany's first governments was on the economic task at hand. Theodor Heuss, West Germany's first post-war president, declared: 'We have practically only one chance – and that is work.' Two politicians were instrumental in Germany's rapid recovery, for laying the foundations of the *Wirtschaftswunder*, the Economic Miracle. In 1948, as director of economics under the American and British Bizone, Ludwig Erhard abolished the existing currency overnight. Ten Reichsmarks would be exchanged for one new Deutschmark. Some 90 per cent of public debt was instantly wiped away (as were any private savings in Reichsmarks). Even more daringly, within a week he abolished rationing and price controls which had been introduced by the Nazis, and production limits which had been imposed by the Allies. Erhard was a rare commodity for his time, an original thinker and an optimist. Towards the end of the war, his essays on public finances had reached US intelligence. Occupying forces sought him out. Once Germany did surrender, he was immediately appointed finance minister of Bavaria before taking responsibility for the entire occupied western half of Germany. He was still answerable, in principle, to the Allies. Erhard took a huge risk. He had not cleared his reforms with the occupiers. He was summoned to the office of the commanding officer, US general Lucius Clay, who gave him a dressing down. He told Erhard that his advisers had informed him that the new policies would be a terrible mistake. Erhard famously responded: 'Herr General, pay no attention to them. My advisers tell me the same thing.'[13] In the end, the Allies did not stand in his way. They were already preparing for the restoration of sovereignty and were pleased to see German officials and politicians taking over responsibilities. Work on the new constitution was well under way.

The status of Berlin, though, was increasingly precarious. On 24 June 1948, Soviet troops closed all road and rail connections to the Western sectors. Within a few days, shipping on the Spree and Havel rivers was halted; electric power, which had been supplied to West Berlin by plants in the Soviet Zone, was cut off; and supplies of fresh food from the surrounding countryside were suddenly unavailable. The Four Power status of Berlin, agreed upon by the Allied victors, had not included any provisions regarding traffic by land to and from Berlin through the Soviet Zone. It had, however, established three air corridors from the Western Zones to the city. The three Western powers acted swiftly: an airlift of unprecedented dimensions was organized to supply the 2.5 million inhabitants of the Western sectors of Berlin with what they needed to survive. Some 230 US and 150 British planes were deployed. Up to ten thousand tons of supplies were flown in daily, including coal and other heating fuels for the winter. Altogether, about 275,000 flights succeeded in keeping West Berliners alive for nearly a year.

The Soviet blockade crystallized thinking among the Allies. Their two main preoccupations were to ensure that Germany (or at least the three sectors that they occupied) could never again fall into the hands of a dictatorship, and to embed it strategically in the West. In July 1948, the Allies handed over a number of documents to nine prime ministers and two mayors of the Western Zones of Occupation, with a series of recommendations. These were to be called the Frankfurt Documents.

Bonn, Beethoven's birthplace on the Rhine, was chosen ahead of Frankfurt as the seat of government. By opting for this relatively small city, the new leadership sought to emphasize the provisional nature of the arrangements and the importance of decentralizing power. Berlin was still the notional capital. Over time, parliamentarians and those around them got used to the serene, orderly and high quality of life that Bonn afforded. The Bonn Republic assumed its own persona in the image of the city.

The 'temporary' Basic Law was approved on 8 May 1949, coming into force two weeks later. This was the moment when a new Germany was born. It is one of the greatest constitutional achievements of any country anywhere in the world. British and American lawyers played a prominent role in drawing up the provisions. The document borrowed aspects from other constitutions, including from the Weimar Republic, although each provision was stress-tested for its durability. The first nineteen articles set out human rights. Article 20 makes clear that the Federal Republic of Germany 'is a democratic and social federal state. All state authority is derived from the people.' Further sections set out the relationship between the federal government and the regions, or *Länder*, between the two houses of parliament, and between legislature and executive. Any and all areas of dispute would be arbitrated by a Constitutional Court, based in the unheralded city of Karlsruhe. The judges are figures of considerable respect. They are not pressurized or denounced as 'enemies of the people', as their equivalents have been in the UK

– a habit that is now being copied with impunity by hard-line regimes in Hungary, Poland and elsewhere.

The post-war German constitution laid down the parameters of political engagement. New parties were created, with statutory responsibilities. Article 21 stipulated that parties must 'work together to develop political consciousness and strengthen democracy'. It established a framework for preventing anti-constitutional activity, and for cooperating in the conduct of parliamentary and governmental business. Three political strands were identified – a centre-right grouping under the Christian Democrats, left-wing Social Democrats and the Free Democrats representing a liberal tradition. These were designated *Volksparteien*, people's parties, broad enough to encompass as much of the populace as possible. With a 5 per cent threshold for representation in federal and state parliaments, extreme forces would be drowned out. The voting system (a mix of direct constituency mandates and proportional top-ups) ensured that coalitions would be the norm, but that they would also last.

In the post-war years, Christian Democracy proved an instant hit across Europe. In all but ten of the past seventy-five years, the Christian Democratic Union (CDU) has been the largest party in Germany; it has provided the chancellor for all but twenty. After supporting or acquiescing to authoritarian and fascist movements in large numbers, Europe's middle classes converged around these new forces of the centre-right, which embraced the rule of law and accepted parliamentary structures. The CDU and its Bavarian sister grouping, the Christian Social Union (CSU), have their roots in a belief in community and traditional notions of the family. Faith was also a central plank. The party's architects believed that divisions between Catholics and Protestants were in part responsible for the rise of Hitler and that both denominations should be equally represented. Alongside these founding beliefs was a particular view about capitalism, an insistence that markets should always be tempered by the needs of society. Hans Schlange-Schöningen, one of the founders of the CDU (and later a German ambassador in London), said in 1946: 'What we understand as Christians [today] is a great declaration of war against materialism.'[14]

The only party with pre-war roots was the Social Democratic Party (SDP), the oldest party of its type in continental Europe. Founded in 1863, the SPD has outlived kaisers and National Socialism. It was a Social Democrat, Friedrich Ebert, who was the country's first democratically elected head of state. At the end of the 1950s, the SPD dispensed with Marxist-influenced socialism to embrace a market economy.

When Germans are asked to rank their most important leader since the war, Konrad Adenauer is invariably put at the top. His credentials during the Third Reich were about as good as they got for a public official. A conservative Catholic from the Rhine, deeply suspicious of the bombast of Bavarians and Prussians, Adenauer was mayor of Cologne when Hitler was bidding for power. He refused to meet him or allow the National Socialists to hang their banners in his city. He quickly fled when the Nazis took over, spending much of the next decade in hiding. At the end of the war he was restored to his former position, only to be sacked by the British. The young British officers in charge of this foreign city did not appreciate the attitude of a German man in his seventies who knew his mind. Undaunted, Adenauer set about his task of turning the Christian Democrats into a major political force. For the Allies, he was a reliable choice to be Germany's first post-war chancellor. And yet this staunch opponent of Hitler held a determination not to probe deeply into his country's recent past.

The philosopher Hermann Lübbe wondered whether a devastated Germany could have rebuilt without what he calls 'communicative silence'.[15] The prevailing mood was not to defend the legacy of the Third Reich, but to try to bury it. The French-Israeli historian Saul Friedländer describes it as 'a constant see-saw between remembering and forgetting'.[16] The hounding of exiles was a case in point. Having refused Nazi blandishments and renounced her German citizenship in 1939, Marlene Dietrich became a darling of Allied servicemen and was one of the first public figures to sell war bonds. She made more than five hundred appearances before Allied troops. When she returned to Germany in 1960, she played to packed-out auditoria but was also booed, harried, had stink bombs thrown at her and was spat at. 'Marlene, Go Home' was a popular banner. The press response was vicious in places. One paper denounced her for 'traitorously wearing the uniform of the enemy'. She never returned, but she retained mixed emotions. On one occasion, she said: 'When I die, I would like to be buried in Paris. I would leave my heart to England, and to Germany nothing.'[17] On another, she admitted: 'America took me into her bosom when I no longer had a native country worthy of the name, but in my heart I am German – German in my soul.' On her death in 1992 she was laid to rest in a humble plot close to her original Berlin home in Schöneberg. In 2001, on the 100th anniversary of her birth, the city issued a formal apology to her.

The Allies introduced bans that were swiftly incorporated into German law. The wearing of Nazi symbols or propagation of related literature was forbidden. Holocaust denial was introduced into the Criminal Code. Measures such as these ran up against guarantees of freedom of expression. It was in adjudicating arguments such as these that the Constitutional Court would prove so effective. Control of the rights to *Mein Kampf* was given by the Allies to the state of Bavaria straight after the war. Publication of the book was illegal and research copies were extremely tightly monitored. The ban was required by law to last for seventy years and was due to run out in January 2016. As the clock counted down to that moment, politicians, academics and others were in a state about what to do. The prevailing view was not to interfere. Germany could take it. The Institute of Contemporary History of Munich (IfZ) issued three thousand new copies for sale. Such was the interest that it ended up doing six print runs, selling 85,000 in the first year. 'It turned out that the fear the publication would promote Hitler's ideology or even make it socially acceptable and give neo-Nazis a new propaganda platform was totally unfounded,' Andreas Wirsching, director of the IfZ, said. 'To the contrary, the debate about Hitler's world view and his approach to propaganda offered a chance to look at the causes and consequences of totalitarian ideologies, at a time in which authoritarian political views and right-wing slogans are gaining ground.'[18]

Even into the 1960s, German academic research on war crimes was tentative. The first comprehensive study of the Nazi genocide, *The Destruction of the European Jews*, was written by the Austrian-Jewish historian Raul Hilberg. He fled Vienna in 1939, ending up in Brooklyn. When stationed with the US Army in 1944 in southern Germany, he became so alarmed at reports of death camps that he asked to be assigned straight after the war to a unit in charge of documentation. He completed the book in 1961. But amid a stream of rejections it took him two years to find a publisher, a small house in Chicago. In Germany, the reluctance was even greater. It was only in 1982 that it was published by a small Berlin company, Olle & Wolter. From that point, Hilberg became a popular presence on the German academic circuit and in 2006 was awarded the Knight Commander's Cross of the Order of Merit, the highest honour given to non-citizens.

One of the most prominent Nazis to evade immediate post-war justice was Adolf Eichmann, one of the architects and over-seers of the Final Solution. Eichmann's flight from American detention and capture by Israeli intelligence in Argentina fifteen years later is one of the totems by which Nazi war crimes are judged. Several survivors of the Holocaust had dedicated themselves to finding him; among them was Jewish Nazi-hunter Simon Wiesenthal. During the trial, Eichmann did not deny the Holocaust or his role in organizing it. He used the familiar defence of the *Führerprinzip* – he, like others, was merely following orders handed down in a vertical military structure. He was found guilty on all of the charges and hanged on 1 June 1962.

The trial was one of the first great global televized events. Reports and analysis of the courtroom proceedings were relayed back for programming in thirty-eight countries. Since television broadcasting did not yet exist in 1961 in Israel, the government contracted an independent company from the US to provide the images. Audiences around the world were gripped to their screens and to newspaper coverage. Controversy surrounded one particular account – by the historian Hannah Arendt. A celebrity of her time, Arendt had been commissioned by the *New Yorker* magazine to cover the trial in Jerusalem. In her article, published in 1963, she said: 'The trouble with Eichmann was precisely that there were so many like him, and that the many were neither perverted nor sadistic but were, and still are, terribly normal.'[19] Eichmann, she said, had acted only to advance his career, not realizing what he was doing due to a cognitive distance from his victims. 'The banality of evil' became a stock phrase in the debate. Arendt was attacked by many of her peers for 'psychologizing' what were clear moral choices.

The Eichmann case left its mark for decades after. CIA

documents declassified in 2006 caused shock and embarrassment in the US and Germany. They showed that American and
West German intelligence had known about Eichmann's whereabouts for at least two years before he was seized by the Israelis.
They had kept it secret, not wanting to destabilize a key partner
at a time of heightened tension with Moscow. This was the era of
the Berlin Wall going up and the Bay of Pigs crisis in Cuba. The
documents described Adenauer's fear that Eichmann's evidence
would incriminate senior figures in his government. He had
one particular reason for concern: his chief of staff of ten years,
the man who made the Chancellery tick, was a certain Hans
Globke. Globke had written the legal statutes for Hitler's notorious Nuremberg Race Laws. One of these was the Law for the
Protection of German Blood and German Honour, which for-
bade marriages and extramarital intercourse between Jews and
Germans and prohibited the employment of German females
aged under forty-five in Jewish households. Globke had also
been responsible for drafting the Reich Citizenship Law, which
declared that only those of German blood were eligible for German citizenship. In spite of that, he was taken into the heart of
the new post-war government.

The West German government was so worried that it tasked
the BND, the foreign intelligence service, to get intelligence in
advance about the evidence that might be produced in the Eichmann trial. The defence minister at the time, Franz Josef Strauss,
who had negotiated a series of sales of tanks and submarines
personally with David Ben-Gurion, warned the Israelis that if
they failed to protect German interests, the arms deals would
be in jeopardy. Strauss's formulation was telling: 'I have told my
contacts that it is a matter of course that if the Federal Republic supports the security of Israel, it will not be held collectively
liable, morally, politically or journalistically, for the crimes of

a past generation in connection with the Eichmann trial.'[20] The trial did not incriminate Globke, and a few months later Adenauer approved a fresh consignment of military aid.

The West Germany of that era was still conservative and hidebound, but it was recovering. Cities had been rebuilt; creature comforts had returned to families. The Deutschmark had become a dependable currency. Car production was booming. The first foreign holidays to Italy and Spain were being taken. When abroad, many Germans either stuck together or pretended they were Scandinavian – anything to avoid hostile looks.

As the war generation grew into old age, their children began to ask questions of their parents and wider society. Across the Western world, the sixties were influenced by music, sexual liberation and political radicalism. Some of the characteristics were shared across continents, such as antipathy towards the United States and the war in Vietnam. University campuses were often the focal points for demonstrations against capitalism, consumerism and imperialism. In Paris, the student rising briefly drove Charles de Gaulle to flee the Élysée Palace. In Germany, protest was guided by similar political passion, but it was also personal. It was laced with anger towards an elite that, to many of those coming of age, had not even begun to address, let alone atone for the past. The election of Kurt Georg Kiesinger as chancellor was seen as provocative. Kiesinger had been in charge of the radio department of Joseph Goebbels's Propaganda Ministry (although after the war he was absolved of any crimes). Everywhere you looked, someone in a high position had been involved in something.

The protests continued for two years. The flashpoint came in April 1968 when the de facto leader of the student movement, Rudi Dutschke, was shot in the head and wounded by a young anti-communist painter and decorator. Activists blamed the Springer media group for encouraging the assassination attempt. *Bild*, the main tabloid newspaper, had mounted a campaign against Dutschke, at one point urging readers to 'eliminate the trouble-makers'. In response to the attempt on Dutschke's life, thousands of students marched from the Free University to Springer HQ, next to the still-new Berlin Wall, and tried to ransack the building. Dutschke, who was badly injured by the shooting, was invited by Cambridge University to finish his studies and recuperate in the UK. He was then expelled in 1971 by the Conservative government of Edward Heath, which feared that he would foment trouble. He moved to Denmark and then back to Germany, but he never fully recovered from his injuries and died in 1979, aged thirty-nine.

The immediate challenges of the student movement were seen off. The government introduced emergency legislation, reinforcing security. But the influence of the *Achtundsechziger*, the 68-ers, remains strong to this day, stronger in Germany than in any other country. Almost instantly, a more questioning and less deferential society was born. There were two sides to the generational challenge: this, the positive non-violent one, and a much darker terrorist one. They shared a common analysis of the state of German society but employed very different methods.

From 1970 to 1977, Germany was rocked by terrorist violence. The Baader–Meinhof Gang (officially, the Red Army Faction) mounted a series of bombings, kidnappings, assassinations and robberies. And the massacre at the 1972 Munich Olympics, in which eleven Israeli athletes were taken hostage and killed by a Palestinian group, Black September, was a devastating blow to Germany's attempts at rehabilitation. The Olympics were supposed to be the antidote to the Nazi propaganda games of 1936.

Instead, they became synonymous with tragedy, exposing shoddy security, and giving rise to countless conspiracy theories. An article in 2012 by *Der Spiegel* alleged a cover-up. The magazine reported that successive governments had hidden nearly four thousand files that gave details of how officials had bungled the hostage crisis. The magazine also wrote that the German authorities had been told three weeks before the massacre that Palestinians were planning an 'incident' at the Olympics, but they failed to take the necessary security measures. These facts, it said, had gone missing from the official documents.

In all, thirty-four people, including several prominent figures from public life, were killed in three waves of attacks by the Red Army Faction. These culminated in the so-called German Autumn of 1977. This included the hijacking of a Lufthansa plane, which was diverted to Mogadishu, Somalia, where it was stormed by German special forces. On the same day came the murder of Hanns Martin Schleyer, a typical 'establishment' figure who personified everything that the radicals despised. Schleyer, like many business leaders of that time, had baggage. While studying at the University of Heidelberg in the mid-1930s, he accused his classmates of lacking National Socialist spirit. He was an avid Nazi, becoming an economic adviser to the German administration of occupied Bohemia (in Czechoslovakia). He spent three years at a prisoner-of-war camp, where he understated his rank in the SS. By 1948, he had received his 'Persil' ticket, and a year later was in charge of the Chamber of Commerce in Baden-Baden. He became president of the BDI, the Federation of German Industries. For the Red Army Faction and its supporters, Mr Economic Miracle and War Apologist was considered fair game. In September 1977, they ambushed his car in Cologne, killing four members of his security detail. The government refused to negotiate for his release. His kidnappers eventually killed him and dumped his body in a car in eastern France. As part of the battle for public opinion, the Red Army Faction kidnappers put Schleyer on trial in a 'people's prison'. But they didn't have a clue what to ask him about the war. They, like the rest of their student friends, had not been taught the details.

By the end of 1977, all the main Baader–Meinhof figures had been rounded up or killed. A new high-security wing at Stammheim prison in Stuttgart was built, guarded by GSG 9 special forces. The violence of this era has been hotly debated and heavily researched ever since. The editor of *Der Spiegel*, Stefan Aust, wrote perhaps the definitive account. *The Baader–Meinhof Complex*, published in 1985 and later adapted into a film, quotes one of its members as saying: 'We were the first generation since the war, and we were asking our parents questions. Due to the Nazi past, everything bad was compared to the Third Reich. If you heard about police brutality, that was said to be just like the SS. The moment you see your own country as the continuation of a fascist state, you give yourself permission to do almost anything against it. You see your action as the resistance that your parents did not put up.'[21]

If you ask any German of that generation, people who are now in their sixties or so, what transformed their understanding of the war, they might offer these three following examples: the first is the *Kniefall*, the moment when Willy Brandt fell on his knees at the monument to the Warsaw Ghetto uprising. The first post-war Social Democrat chancellor was making an official visit to Poland in December 1970 to seal a new era in relations. That year, Germany had declared that its border with Poland on the Oder–Neisse line was final and non-negotiable, renouncing any future claims. In 1945, Germany forfeited vast swathes of territory in Pomerania and Silesia, accounting for about a quarter of its pre-Weimar territory. In 1950, under pressure from the Soviets, the GDR had confirmed the border. Adenauer had refused, sticking to a line that these lands were under temporary Polish and Soviet administration. Some maps even in the 1960s continued to count them as German.

Brandt's dramatic act of atonement split public opinion. Conservatives hated it. He insisted that he made the decision there and then, suddenly deciding that laying a wreath was not enough. 'Under the burden of millions of victims of murder, I did what human beings do when speech fails them,'[22] he said. It is worth watching a clip of Brandt, a war exile and opponent of Hitler, doing what many Germans would until that point have never dreamt of doing: going onto his knees to beg forgiveness.

The second moment involved Meryl Streep. *Holocaust*, a four-part miniseries, was first aired on NBC in the US in April 1978. Focusing on two fictionalized families in Berlin, one Jewish, the other Christian, it brought the Shoah into the homes of millions around the world. It was dubbed into German and broadcast by the WDR network a year later, in spite of attempts by the far right to stop it. Two transmitter masts were bombed. Nearly half of all households with TVs, more than twenty million Germans, watched. Schmaltzy and sanitized it might have been, but it was a broadcasting and societal sensation. With extraordinary effect, it broadened the issue of culpability beyond the Nazi leadership and into every home. It dramatized the Wannsee Conference, when the Final Solution was planned, with cold detail. It showed the deportations and exterminations at the camps. It led to ruptures within families. Daddy, just what did you get up to in the war? Tens of thousands of viewers called WDR to express their shock and shame.

By the 1970s, the German school history curriculum had become more candid about the Nazi era, but the way it was taught was still largely dry and statistical. This one TV series had a transformative effect. Schools requested copies of the show; they bought projectors for classrooms. A new canon of trade and academic books on the Holocaust started to be researched and written. The Bundestag, having cautiously extended the time frame for retrospective punishments, immediately abolished the statute of limitations, paving the way for further prosecutions.

Enough is enough became enough is never enough. At the start of 2019, *Holocaust* was shown again on prime-time television to mark the fortieth anniversary of its original screening. The viewing figures were good, but not that good. Germany has come a long way in that time.

The third moment was the most august. In 1985, in a speech to parliament marking the fortieth anniversary of the Nazi surrender, President Richard von Weizsäcker (who had only been in office for a year) gave what has since been regarded as the definitive analysis of culpability by a German politician. The presidency is a ceremonial role, but the incumbent is held to be custodian of the country's moral compass. He spoke of the day the war ended by saying, 'May 8th was a day of liberation.' That single sentence was stunning. Germany had not been defeated, it had been freed. 'It liberated all of us from the inhumanity and tyranny of the National Socialist regime.' He then talked about the nature of guilt. Younger generations 'cannot profess a guilt of their own for crimes they did not commit', he told MPs. 'No discerning person can expect them to wear a penitential robe simply because they are Germans. But their forefathers have left them a grave legacy. All of us, whether guilty or not, whether young or old, must accept the past. We are all affected by the consequences and liable for it. The young and old generations must and can help each other to understand why it is vital to keep the memories alive.' He then paused for dramatic effect.

'It is not a case of coming to terms with the past. That is not possible. It cannot be subsequently modified or made undone. However, anyone who closes his eyes to the past is blind to the present. Whoever refuses to remember the inhumanity is prone to new risks of infection.'[23]

The Weizsäcker address was described by Israel's ambassador to Germany as 'a moment of glory'.[24] A quarter of a million copies of the speech were distributed to schools around Germany. It was important not just for what was said but who said it. The president's family had been steeped in the Third Reich. His father, Ernst, a career diplomat, became the secretary of state in the Nazi government's Foreign Ministry; in 1946, he was charged at Nuremberg with involvement in the deportation of French Jews to Auschwitz. He was found guilty and sentenced to seven years in prison. He died of a stroke two years into the sentence. After periods of study at Oxford and Grenoble, Richard was conscripted into the Wehrmacht and returned to Germany in 1938. His regiment, in which his brother Heinrich also fought, was among those that invaded Poland. His other brother, Carl Friedrich, a leading nuclear physicist, was attempting to construct atomic weapons for the Nazis. After the war, Richard returned to his studies, taking up law at the University of Göttingen. He was part of his father's defence. He joined the CDU in 1954, spending twelve years in the Bundestag before he was made head of state.

Weizsäcker was deliberately stepping into sensitive territory. This anniversary came at a time when the country was beginning to wonder how the passage of time might affect the overcoming of history. In Helmut Kohl, the country had its first leader who had not fought in the war. Yet even for him the memory was raw. He was nine when the conflict started. At the age of thirteen he was digging charred corpses of neighbours out of the rubble of his Rhineland home town of Ludwigshafen, which was a frequent target for Allied bombings. His older brother was killed in an air raid in Normandy.

Derided in the media for being a country bumpkin, with a strange accent and a penchant for *Saumagen*, a dish of meat and vegetables boiled inside a pig's stomach (which he enjoyed serving to queasy world leaders such as Boris Yeltsin and Margaret Thatcher), Kohl was one of the most important figures of the post-war years. 'I have made a very good living for more than 30 years by being underestimated,'[25] he once said. He may not have used the best choice of words. But he was adept at representing the Germany of his time – chastened but determined – to the outside world. On a state visit to Israel in 1984, after visiting Yad Vashem, the official memorial to the Holocaust, Kohl controversially told members of the Knesset that he was part of a generation of Germans lucky enough not to share responsibility. Invoking his down-to-earth Catholic stock, he declared: 'I speak as someone who could not be guilty in the Nazi time because he enjoyed the grace of a late birth and the good fortune to come from a particular family background.'[26]

That was as nothing compared with what came next. Kohl decided that, as part of his contributions to the fortieth anniversary, he would invite Ronald Reagan to visit a war cemetery with him. The one he chose, Bitburg on the Luxembourg border, contained alongside the graves of hundreds of ordinary German soldiers the remains of fifty members of the Waffen-SS. Relations with the US were particularly strong at the time. Reagan agreed to go. He wanted to show his gratitude to Kohl and to his predecessor, Helmut Schmidt, for agreeing to the deployment of Pershing II nuclear missiles in 1979 in the face of sustained protest. The consternation back home came from all quarters, from fifty senators appealing to him in a letter, to the Holocaust survivor Elie Wiesel urging him publicly to change his mind, to the Ramones and Frank Zappa writing songs to denounce him. One American Jewish group called it a 'callous offence'. In the end, Reagan spent all of eight minutes at the cemetery, combining that part of the trip with a homage to Bergen-Belsen. But he did lay a wreath. In so doing, he allowed some in Germany to conclude that their history had been 'normalized'.

Kohl may have been maladroit, as was his wont, but his motivations were more complex and considered. One of the most iconic photographs of that era was the German chancellor at Verdun holding hands with France's president Francois Mitterrand, marking the seventieth anniversary of the start of the First World War. That beautifully choreographed moment of reconciliation came in between his fractious trips to Israel and Bitburg. Kohl was doing what many Germans of his age were doing – they were trying painfully to navigate the past, refusing to brush it under the carpet, trying to define memory, while not being defined by it. At this time, I had just arrived in Bonn as a journalist. Forty years on from the war, it felt as if certain newspapers would not talk about anything else. This was the time of the *Historikerstreit*, the historians' dispute. It may have taken place among a small group of intellectuals in the feuilleton, the rarefied review pages of the *Frankfurter Allgemeine* and *Die Zeit*, but it marked the start of the battle for the soul of modern Germany.

At one level, this was a straight left–right fight. Three conservative historians began the dispute by asserting that Germany should not bear a special burden of guilt for the Final Solution. They were denounced by the liberal left, who saw their arguments as dangerous, revisionist and apologist. The hostilities commenced in June 1986 when Ernst Nolte, Professor Emeritus of Modern History at, of all places, the Free University of Berlin

(HQ for the radical protesters of the late sixties and seventies), published an opinion piece calling for a line to be drawn under the German past. The requirement to remember the Nazi era was 'suspended above the present like an executioner's sword.'[27] The article, entitled 'The Past That Will Not Go Away: A Speech That Could Be Written but Not Delivered' was, he insisted, in lieu of a speech he was hoping to give before a global gathering of academics before his invitation was withdrawn. One of the organizers, the British historian Richard Evans, who was one of Nolte's most vocal critics, retorted that Nolte had not been barred but had simply not bothered to show up in order to create a scandal. Nolte saw himself as an intellectual provocateur. Anything to rile the *bien pensants* of European academia. In a book published the following year, he began to flirt with Holocaust denial, hinting that some Jews were responsible for their own misfortune by sympathizing with communism. He was a frequent target for threats, which pushed him further away from the acceptable mainstream. In 2000, amid a public outcry, he was awarded the Konrad Adenauer prize, given to influential figures of the centre-right. The new CDU leader, Angela Merkel, declined an invitation to make the presentation, making clear that she had 'personal difficulties' with Nolte.

Lumped in the same group were two other historians, Michael Stürmer and Andreas Hillgruber. Stürmer, who was also an informal adviser to Kohl, wrote in April 1986 an essay entitled 'Land Without History' for the FAZ. He juxtaposed levels of patriotism in the US and other Western countries with the low levels of pride in Germany. He called for a campaign by the government, media and historians to create a 'positive view' of German history, focusing less on the twelve years of the Third Reich and more on the broader sweep. This 'loss of orientation', he wrote, was preventing West Germany from asserting itself, now that it was 'once more a focal point in the global civil war waged against democracy by the Soviet Union'.[28] At a subsequent international seminar, he went further, arguing that Germans 'cannot live by making our past . . . into a permanent source of endless guilt feelings'.[29] A derogatory term was coined: *Schuldkult*, the cult of guilt.

The third member of the troika, Hillgruber, was perhaps the most curious. Until this point, the historian from Cologne had enjoyed a global reputation for his work on the Nazi era. However, in his 1986 book, *Two Kinds of Ruin: The Shattering of the German Reich and the End of European Jewry*, he argued that, although terrible, the Holocaust was not a singular event. It was a response to and formed part of a historical continuum with other atrocities such as Stalin's reign of terror. He also insisted that there was no moral difference between the genocide and Allied carpet bombing.

The philosophical – and political – dividing line was set between those who saw the Shoah as an event unique in history, and unique to Germany, and those who did not. The theory of the *Sonderweg* (Germany's special path of ignominy) had been popular, particularly abroad, ever since the defeat of Hitler. One of its best-known proponents was an American journalist, William L. Shirer. His *Rise and Fall of the Third Reich*, first published in 1960, set out a path from Luther to Hitler. Germans were predisposed to blind obedience and servility. Shirer's work was panned by his many critics as being crude. By the 1980s, a more layered approach to the issue of war guilt had been developed; but it was no less impassioned.

The most renowned critic of the likes of Nolte and Stürmer was Jürgen Habermas, one of the giants of modern philosophy. Habermas took to the pages of *Die Zeit* newspaper to denounce the glorification of the Wehrmacht's last stand against the Red

Army on the Eastern front. The longer they held out, the longer the Holocaust could continue. In an article entitled 'A Kind of Damage Control: On Apologetic Tendencies in German History Writing', Habermas attacked the new nationalism of the right. He described Auschwitz as the great dividing line of German history. The future would have to be built on new foundations. The publisher of *Der Spiegel*, Rudolf Augstein, attacked Hillgruber as a 'constitutional Nazi', calling for him to be sacked from his academic post. The historian Hans Mommsen joined the fray, describing the Cold War as a convenient device enabling Germany's elite to escape punishment. The German argument went global. The Yad Vashem Institute in Jerusalem devoted an entire edition of its journal to the *Historikerstreit*. A conference was held in London on the issue, involving leading historians and public intellectuals including Ralf Dahrendorf, Isaiah Berlin, George Weidenfeld and Fritz Stern.

For the grand men of German public life (there were few such women at the time), it was often hard to disentangle the political from the personal. One of the most painful examples of memory and forgetting concerned the writer Günter Grass. A left-wing voice in the Social Democrats, he combined his literary writings with a prominent place in political and intellectual life. He was an ardent opponent of reunification, arguing that the concentration camps constituted a moral bar to unification, and peace in Europe depended on Germany's permanent division. When Grass won the Nobel Prize for Literature in 1999, the citation said publication of his novel *The Tin Drum* was 'as if German literature had been granted a new beginning after decades of linguistic and moral destruction'.[30] Seven years later, Grass admitted that he had served in the Waffen-SS. And he was one of those who had been most vehement in their criticism of the Kohl-Reagan Bitburg visit. His critics piled in. Joachim Fest, a biographer of Hitler, whose parents had stopped him from joining Hitler's elite forces, said: 'After 60 years, this confession comes a bit too late. I can't understand how someone who for decades set himself up as a moral authority, a rather smug one, could pull this off.'[31]

The passage of time, the distance that individuals could put on their families' role in the war, has not lessened the dilemmas. How could historians research, how could artists discuss the issue of Germans as victims of war without being accused of relativism?

In the first six months of 1945, more than 100,000 women in Berlin and over 1.5 million elsewhere in Germany between the ages of ten and eighty were raped by Soviet soldiers, in many cases on a multiple and continuing basis.[32] They did not talk about it. There was no counselling. They just carried on as best they could. Just dust yourself down and get on with the rebuilding of the country. Nobody, in any case, would be interested abroad. Spoils of war; the Germans were getting their just deserts, were they not?

In 1954, a book appeared in the United States in English describing the atrocities in gut-wrenching detail. *A Woman in Berlin* was written anonymously by a woman describing herself in the account as a thirty-two-year-old who worked in publishing. She chronicled her quest for survival over two months. She had the good fortune to speak Russian. She decided to 'adopt' a better educated officer, to become his courtesan, hoping that he would protect her from the gang rapes and other acts of violence that were occurring all around her. The book was translated into a number of languages, but not initially into German. When a German publisher was eventually found in 1959, *Eine Frau in Berlin* received a hostile reception. The author was accused of being calculating and unemotional. Most of all she had besmirched the dignity of German women. The author refused to have any further editions published in German.

Nearly half a century later, in 2003, a literary editor revealed that the author was a journalist called Marta Hillers, who had died in 2001. The book was immediately reissued and this time it received critical acclaim. It was on the bestseller list for months, republished in 2005 with an introduction from the British historian Antony Beevor. He described it as 'the most powerful personal account to come out of World War II'.[33]

In 2002, another book appeared, which also garnered huge publicity. *Der Brand* (published in English as *The Fire*) was an account of the Allied carpet bombing of German cities, focusing on the destruction of Dresden by the British. The author, Jörg Friedrich, was no stranger to controversy. A campaigner against Vietnam and against the Iraq War into which the Bush/Blair coalition was hurtling, Friedrich was seeking to reclaim the issue of German suffering away from right-wing nationalists. Yet his chosen destination for serializing his book, the mass-circulation tabloid *Bild*, was hardly an obvious location for an activist from the left. Still, it worked. The book rose to the top of the charts. His previous work on Nazi horrors insulated him to an extent. But his use of language such as *Vernichtung* (annihilation) about the firestorm, prompted accusations of moral equivalence.

Perhaps the book that most changed the mould was W. G. Sebald's *On the Natural History of Destruction*, published in German and English on either side of the millennium. The Bavarian-born author and historian, who had settled in Britain, wrote a series of essays about writers through which he discusses the vexed issue of *Vergangenheitsbewältigung*, coming to terms with history. His most outspoken chapter was about the Allied bombing which flattened scores of cities in the final year of the war. A few years earlier, the Queen Mother had unveiled a statue in central London of Arthur 'Bomber' Harris, who had directed the saturation bombing of German cities. Sebald reminded readers of the stats: up to 700,000 civilians, including about 75,000 children, burnt or choked to death, 1,000,000 tonnes of bombs on 131 cities and towns, 31 cubic metres of rubble for every inhabitant of Cologne, 6,865 corpses burnt on pyres by the SS in Dresden, flames leaping 2,000 metres into the sky over Hamburg. He interpreted the amnesia of the Adenauer years not as a refusal to engage but as delayed trauma. 'The sense of unparalleled national humiliation felt by millions [of Germans] in the last years of the war had never really found verbal expression, and those directly affected by the experience neither shared it with each other nor passed it on to the next generation.'[34] Reviewing the book, the Irish writer John Banville, described it as 'a quietly spoken but fierce protest at the mendacity and moral evasiveness of our time'.[35]

Germany could now talk openly about its own suffering, not as a means of exculpation, but because from the 1980s onwards, from reunification but even before, it was able to talk unencumbered about its own guilt. *Zivilcourage*, the courage to stand up for your own beliefs, was inculcated in schools. It is one thing to obey laws, but what if they take a country in the wrong direction? Pupils were encouraged to think for themselves, to say 'no', to resist, where they had to.

It is instructive to dwell on Germany's own perspective on the war. It demonstrates how, with each decade, the reckoning has become more detailed, more painful but also more nuanced, in schools, academia, media and politics. It shows a country coming to terms with its past – in a way that no other war perpetrator has done; not the Japanese, Austrians or Italians. Compare and contrast with Spain, and the decades of resistance to the idea of removing General Franco's body from the Valley of the Fallen. It finally took place in 2019, but only in the teeth of resistance, not from a tiny extreme but a sizeable group of the electorate, quite happy to display their adoration of the fascist dictator for all to see.

Museums and monuments to Germany's damaged history abound. In some places they overshadow. In others they are hidden away. In a quiet street in Leipzig, Doris Lehniger, a volunteer, is waiting for me at the gate. It is early on a Saturday morning and she has come specially to give me a private tour of the School Museum. They don't get that many visitors and when they do, it tends to be prearranged classes. This used to be a school itself, but when flooding from the nearby river damaged the building in 2003, it relocated, and a group of well-meaning historians decided to turn the classrooms into a series of exhibits of school life down the ages. Lehniger takes me first to the top floor, to the Kaiser's room, where the pupils learn about the Reich and war and obedience. On the next floor down is the class from the Weimar Republic. It highlights the radicalism of that era. Instead of learning by rote and being admonished by a teacher with a ruler or cane, boys and girls sat together in small groups. They were even invited to take part, to write on blackboards. It reminded me of the 1970s. Next we go to the GDR room, with its life-size models of a boy and a girl, young Free German Youth pioneers and pictures of the leader of the GDR Walter Ulbricht and his successor, Honecker, alongside slogans about peace and socialism. A cabinet contains letters sent to pen pals in the 'fraternal states' of Tanzania and Mozambique. Memorabilia is shown from civil defence camps, which children had to attend in the countryside once a year. Also obligatory was UTP, the Day of Production, Soviet-era work experience, when children were sent to factories once a month to learn about socialist production.

The only room that does not seek to create a lifelike reproduction of a class of the time is the Nazi room. Hitler memorabilia is banned across Germany. This space is more didactic, descriptive. The displays show that more than two hundred disabled people were taken to a nearby 'sanatorium' where they were systematically gassed over one month in 1940. It tells the story of the seven thousand Jewish families in the city, explaining how children were divided up according to blood lines. The Jewish ones were first separated within the school, then given their own school; then they disappeared. These accounts are told in writing. There is little of the colour or personal touch contained in the other rooms. 'This is still very sensitive territory,' Lehniger tells me. This mini-museum is not a visitor attraction. It is not designed to make a splash. I have the feeling that it is more about civic duty, the personal obligation to remember and to pass it on to others.

Reunification, and a sense of a fresh start, have given Germans the time and space better to work through the many traumas their country inflicted – and the traumas it underwent. They have had to process history twice, two dictatorships, both terrible but not comparable. It is still a work in progress. Perhaps it always will be. But there is no attempt ever to forget.

2

Mutti's Warm Embrace

Angela Merkel and the Eastern legacy

No matter how hard people try, it is not easy to demonize a country which has been led for a decade and a half by a sturdy scientist from a nondescript small town.

The rise of Angela Merkel and the role she has played in defining contemporary Germany is one of the more unlikely political stories of the early twenty-first century. She could not have appeared more ill-suited to the job – a woman, a Protestant, a physicist by training and a divorcee. On the night the Berlin Wall came down, thirty-five-year-old comrade Merkel didn't join her friends in their champagne-fuelled celebrations on the unfamiliar streets of the West. She had heard some rumours and so she phoned her mother, Herlind. 'Watch out mum, there's something up today,'[1] she said. It was a Thursday and she did what she always did on Thursdays – she went to the public sauna with a friend near her two-bedroom flat in Prenzlauer Berg. 'I didn't really understand what I was hearing,'[2]

Merkel later recalled. 'I figured that if the wall had opened, it was hardly going to close again, so I decided to wait.'[3]

After her sauna, seeing so many people on the streets, she decided to join them at the nearby crossing point Bornholmer Strasse. 'I'll never forget it, it was maybe 10.30 p.m., or 11.00, or even a little later. I was alone but I followed the crowds. Suddenly we found ourselves on the western side of Berlin.'[4] There she met some random strangers who invited her in. 'We cracked open some cans of beer – we were just so happy.'[5] Then, like many East Germans, she went back again. She had work to do the next morning. In those heady first days, all East Germans were given 'welcome money' by the West German government – 100 Deutschmarks. Instead of spending it on luxury food or drink, or a keepsake or something for a loved one, Merkel focused on the practical. 'You needed money to go to the toilet, or to get a cup of tea – it was November and it was cold.'[6]

She had long planned to go *nach drüben* (over there) but only once she had reached sixty, when pensioners were allowed to leave East Germany for the West (when they had outlived their economic utility). She had worked out her plan for that eventual day. She would go to a police station, exchange her GDR passport for a Western one, then travel to America where it was her dream to go coast to coast on a road trip. 'I wanted to see the Rocky Mountains, drive around in a car and listen to Bruce Springsteen. That was my dream,'[7] she later mused. On her way she would go to West Berlin's Kempinski Hotel and eat oysters with her mum. (She never got around to doing that before her mother died, aged ninety, in 2019.)

An entire generation of Germans has known only *Mutti*, Mummy, as chancellor. She has embodied Germany's profound longing for stability. In all that time, she has rarely spoken about herself. Even when *Time* magazine made her Person of the

Year in 2015, she declined to be interviewed. She doesn't like talking about her gender or her background. This reticence has become her brand. One former aide told me that Merkel rarely showed strong emotions close up – not, he insists, because of any coldness but because of her upbringing. 'She has been socialised by her life in the GDR system. She was fully aware that people betray their friends. She is rarely disappointed because she expects little from people.' Others who have worked with her say that her interest in culture kept her grounded. Ulrich Wilhelm, government spokesman from 2005 to 2010, recalls that on long plane journeys to and from global summits they would discuss not just political strategy but also literature and art.

In 1990, the year of the *Wende* (the turning point, as the unification process became known) and the year I first met her, she seemed to have risen from nowhere. The established Western parties were looking for Eastern politicians not sullied by the past and who could fit into the order. They alighted on this steady-as-she-goes adviser. In December, in the first elections to an enlarged Bundestag, Merkel stood for the ruling CDU in the East German region of Mecklenburg-Vorpommern. Helmut Kohl immediately took her under his wing. He made her a cabinet minister, giving her the junior post of minister of women and youth. He called her *Das Mädchen*, the girl. She didn't appreciate it but kept her counsel. She absorbed events and conversations. 'She had to be cautious,' Wilhelm remembers. 'She had no choice. People kept on wondering if she was too lightweight. She is very clever. She played the game.'

A mere year after the Wall came down, Merkel became a minister in a political system that was completely alien to her. To this day, she is one of very few East German politicians who have made it to the top in the West. Kohl trusted her. He sought her advice on the mindset of the *Ossis* (easterners). She was just as curious about *Wessis*.

She later recalled that she had expected West Germans to be more dynamic. She adjusted accordingly, playing safe with her decisions. One of her biographers, Mariam Lau of *Die Zeit*, says that Merkel quickly saw voters as risk-averse and anxious. These impressions stayed with her throughout.

In 1994, Kohl rewarded his protégé with the environment portfolio. The appointment was in the middle of Germany's presidency of the EU. Immediately, she had to chair gatherings of her European counterparts. One of them was Britain's John Gummer. 'She was entirely fresh to the chair,' he recalls. 'I was one of a triumvirate helping her. She was brilliant. I remember phoning my wife to tell her that this new minister is remarkable.' Gummer invited Merkel to visit his constituency in Suffolk. She brought her husband who was assessing a PhD student in Cambridge at the time. They stayed at the Gummer family home and spent most of the time chatting by the fireside. On the Friday evening, Gummer took her to his local Conservative association. She was taken aback by the anti-European sentiments, the incessant invocation of the war. 'I now know how difficult it is for you,' she told him afterwards. That lesson about the English, or a certain type of English, stayed with her.

Wherever she went, Merkel was diplomatic and discreet. Kohl invited her to accompany him on a number of official visits, well above her cabinet status. She was particularly excited to meet Ronald Reagan, her hero during the Cold War. She had loved his tough talk on the USSR. Her profile was growing, but still not dramatically so. By the mid-nineties, Germany was going through one of its cyclical bouts of self-doubt, as the economy stagnated and the excitement of unification ebbed. A younger generation of politicians was emerging across the Western world led by Bill Clinton and Tony Blair. In Germany, the CDU had suffered a series of reverses in regional elections and Kohl was seen as beyond his sell-by date. In the 1998 elections he was defeated by the charismatic new leader of the Social Democrats, Gerhard Schröder.

In the CDU, a number of people were lining up to take over from Kohl as party leader. They were uniformly grey-haired men who had made their way up the party ranks in the regions. Merkel turned on her mentor and those allied to him. It was a risk, but a calculated one. Kohl and his chosen successor, Wolf-gang Schäuble, had been caught in a party funding scandal. Some in the party's grassroots were advocating radical change. In December 1999, she penned an opinion piece in the *Frankfurter Allgemeine* newspaper declaring that it was time for a generational shift. The political world was aghast. A woman seen as caution personified had shown that she also had a ruthless streak. This was patricide. She swiftly engineered herself into the top party post. The men in suits were stunned. They assumed she wouldn't last long. She didn't, they reassured themselves, have the smell of the stable, a term used to show experience gained from years smoking cigars in party backrooms. They won a short-term victory by outmanoeuvring her and installing the Bavarian prime minister and head of the conservative Christian Social Union (CSU) sister party, Edmund Stoiber, as candidate for the 2002 elections. The move backfired horribly. Stoiber managed to turn a big poll lead into defeat. Schröder based his campaign on his opposition to the Iraq War. He was decisively re-elected.

Stoiber's defeat opened the door for Merkel. Kohl was cast aside. He was deemed such an embarrassment by Merkel and the new team in charge of the CDU that a seventieth birth-day gala for him was abruptly cancelled. He grew increasingly embittered. He never forgave Merkel. In 2014, *Der Spiegel* released tapes in which he told the ghost writer of his autobiography of his rage at her treachery. 'Mrs Merkel couldn't even eat properly with a knife and fork. She used to mope around at state dinners, and I often had to set her straight.'[8] She quietly endured his taunts, knowing that she had got the better of him. Yet it was a desperately sad end for a giant (in all respects) of a politician.

The Merkel era began in November 2005. Schröder's coalition struggled after he introduced a series of controversial economic reforms. In a last throw of the dice he called snap elections. Merkel's campaign seemed lacklustre and she made a number of mistakes on the stump. She was left exposed at having given her strong support to the Americans on Iraq – in defiance of public opinion. The CDU won, but only by a narrow margin. She became chancellor but was forced to give the SPD eight of the sixteen cabinet seats. This was the first of her four successive administrations, three of them so-called grand coalitions (*GroKo*), with the Social Democrats. In many countries, such a sharing of power would either be impossible or would not last long, but this first *GroKo* was a model of stability and is looked on by many as one of Germany's most successful governments. Merkel did deals, at home and abroad. Within a year or two she had emerged as the senior statesman in Europe. She achieved such stability and recognition, at home and abroad, by an absence of grand gestures.

Merkel is the opposite of ostentatious. She has kept her small cottage near her home town of Templin, goes to her customary hairdresser in Berlin and from time to time is seen grocery shopping. She devours art. She sometimes phones her one or two favourite museum directors directly to ask them if they wouldn't mind staying open a little longer so that she can see a particular exhibition without any fuss.

On the international stage, she respects interlocutors who

do their preparation and don't spring surprises. She loves holidaying in the United States but has struggled with its two most recent presidents. Her relations with Trump are terrible. She disdains his visceral vulgarity. He reciprocates by insulting her in public. More surprisingly, she didn't get on with Barack Obama, at least not at first. She was suspicious of his rhetoric. In 2008, when he was vying for the Democratic candidacy, his campaign asked the German authorities if he could give a speech in Berlin. They asked if he could use the Brandenburg Gate as a backdrop. Fearing a repeat of John F. Kennedy's 'Ich bin ein Berliner' and Reagan's 'Mr Gorbachev, tear down this wall,' she let it be known that she was against the idea. 'You can't solve the tasks [of government] with charisma,'[9] she has told a biographer.

The longer she remained in office, the more convinced she was of the merits of caution, of doing everything in small steps, cross-checking against all eventualities: 'For me, it is always important that I go through all the possible options for a decision.'[10] She is an inveterate texter to friends and advisers, even when sitting in the parliamentary chamber, consulting them in real time. This has given her the nickname of the *Handy-Kanzler*, the mobile phone chancellor. The Langenscheidt dictionary's word of the year for 2015 was *merkeln*, meaning to sit on the fence or dither.

For the first two decades of this century, reliability and prudence, as personified through Merkel, have been two of the dominant characteristics of contemporary German life. For good and for ill, German political culture is set up as a shock absorber. When Merkel took over, the country had been crying out for stability. Schröder's liberalization reforms had kickstarted the economy but divided the country. Iraq had shattered Germany's foreign-policy allegiances. Fifteen years after the fall of the Wall, the euphoria had worn off.

The key to understanding this yearning for stability is to understand its opposite. I still blink when I cast my mind back to the heady days of 1989. Anything and everything could have gone wrong. It is a testament to those involved that it didn't.

In early summer 1989, I was settled full time in East Berlin – I still have my GDR press accreditation with the compass symbol on the front. I was living in a block of monotone concrete high-rise flats in what was then, and still is now, the ugliest street in Berlin, Leipziger Strasse. Anyone who has watched the film *The Lives of Others* can picture the scene: men in desaturated grey suits and beige shoes sharing the lift, heads down, as they make their way to the top floor – the one that ordinary residents cannot access – to listen in on conversations. I was one of very few foreigners in that building. The nearby streets were dark and almost completely silent. This was the border area, a stone's throw from Checkpoint Charlie. On the other side of the Wall, the high-rise block of the Axel Springer building – the staunchly conservative, anti-communist newspaper house – dominated the view.

As an occupying ally, I could cross from East to West at will. Within a few months I had to change my passport as I had run out of stamps (I had got to know some of the border officers at the checkpoint). I tried not to mention this to the East Germans I had become friends with. It was painful for them to hear. Nobody had an inkling that within a few months their cage would be opened. Even as the dam began to break – with the Hungarian authorities opening the border to Austria – nobody, not even the smartest intelligence officer, could have predicted the events of that November. Although reunification was always on the statute, and the constitution of the divided country was supposed to be provisional, few thought it would actually happen. Even at the end of 1987, at the height of Gorbachev's reforms, fewer than a tenth of West Germans believed that the two Germanies would be one by the end of the century.

The first concerted protests began in May after elections had conjured 98.85 per cent support for the ruling Socialist Unity Party (SED). Even by the standards of the Soviet bloc, this was absurd. On Alexanderplatz, a concrete architectural monstrosity that had become the central square of East Berlin, and in Leipzig, groups of activists connected with churches and environmental groups began to demonstrate. They had heard that round-table talks were taking place in neighbouring Poland involving the Solidarity trade union and others, so why not in East Germany?

A month later, on 7 June, in front of the international media, the reformist Hungarian government opened its border with Austria. That was the first physical break in the Iron Curtain. Hungary was a popular holiday destination for citizens of 'fraternal' states like East Germany, particularly the beaches at Lake Balaton. For East Germans that required a long journey, in their sputtering *Trabis* or by train, through Czechoslovakia. On 19 August, inhabitants of the Hungarian town of Sopron requested permission to have a 'friendship' picnic with Austrians just over the border. Even though the government agreed, it took some time for East German holidaymakers to understand what this really meant. On the first day, only nine hundred went over – and stayed over. That small stream would turn into a flood. Back in Berlin, many of the activists were frustrated when they realized how many of their compatriots were getting out. Quaint though it now feels to recall, these idealists wanted to change the GDR, not abolish it.

Two churches were the main venues for the peaceful revolution – the Nikolaikirche in Leipzig and Gethsemanekirche in East Berlin. The impending visit on 7 October by Mikhail Gorbachev, ironically to celebrate the GDR's fortieth birthday, galvanized the opposition. I remember standing with the crowds greeting him on the main thoroughfare, Unter den Linden. The SED was petrified by the popularity of the general secretary of the Soviet Communist Party, a man who should have been its protector. The torchlit march-past by assembled members of the Free German Youth was supposed to be regimented and sombre. Yet all around me on the street people were shouting 'Gorby, Gorby' to the consternation of plain-clothed Stasi officers swarming around. That visit produced two of the most famous phrases of the end-of-communism era. Gorbachev recalls in his memoirs saying to Honecker: 'Life punishes those who arrive late.' Honecker was defiant throughout: 'Those who are declared dead usually live a long time.' He also remarked: 'Everything will collapse if we give an inch.'[11] He was wrong on the first, but right on the second.

Crowds gathered again on Alexanderplatz before marching up the road to the Gethsemane Church. A vigil had begun there a few days earlier. At the church I met a man I have stayed friends with ever since. Uwe Fechner was an engineer in his twenties working at a state television plant. He lived next door to the church. Prenzlauer Berg was nothing like it is today. It was close to the Wall, dark and quiet. Many of the houses were empty. Fechner, like several of his friends, was squatting in a flat. He didn't consider himself particularly political, although he used to hang around the Environmental Library, a dissident meeting place nearby. When the vigil began, he asked if he could help. First, he went to the doctor's to get a sick note. He said he had the flu; he was given a month off, no questions asked. He went straight back to the church where the priest suggested he might try his hand at being press spokesman. Fechner had no idea what that entailed but he gave it a go. The Gethsemane Church had something many buildings didn't – a telephone that actually worked. It became one of the key contact points for the opposition. Western journalists began to learn of the vigil and started to report what was going on. It was easier for them to get there than to Leipzig – foreigners needed a special permit to visit places outside the capital.

That weekend was the turning point. Inside the church, people linked arms, sang hymns and said prayers. By Sunday, hundreds were camped inside. The authorities served notice that they would clear the area. Those inside, and by this stage I was one of them, could see the searchlights through the windows and hear the yelping of police dogs. 'My God, the Chinese solution is finally here,' cried a woman near me. Only a few weeks earlier, a high-level delegation of the SED had visited Beijing. Honecker's heir-apparent, Egon Krenz, had thanked the Chinese government for cracking down on the student movement at Tiananmen Square that June. Krenz's speech was widely disseminated by the East German state media as a warning to protesters back home. The service drew to a close; the priest, an unsung hero by the name of Bernd Albani, invited us to leave in silence. We had no idea what we would encounter. I counted about fifty army trucks. A loudhailer told us to put our hands on our heads. Many people were badly beaten that night. Hundreds were taken away, chanting 'no violence' as they were grabbed by the head or hit with truncheons while being bundled into vans. Yet crucially, nobody was killed. Given what had happened in the past, the communist state appeared to be losing its nerve in front of our very eyes.

The next night in Leipzig was even more dramatic. Truckloads of riot police, the People's Militia, were waiting for the protesters, primed and ready to shoot. Testimony produced later by police officers, however, confirmed that they disobeyed orders and did not open fire. Now, the Nikolaikirche is a popular tourist spot where guides explain the story. 'Saxons don't fire on Saxons,' they declare. I'm not sure their regional affiliation has much to do with it, but the locals insist that it does. Anything could have happened had the authorities in either of the cities responded with live ammunition. The GDR was one of the most efficiently surveilled societies and one of the most militarized spaces on Earth, and given the desperation of the authorities at the time it is remarkable that events didn't escalate into violence. An ailing Honecker was replaced by Krenz in the middle of October. He installed a moderate from Dresden, Hans Modrow, as prime minister, but Krenz was the unlikeliest of reformers. Several years later he was jailed. To this day he regrets the Wall coming down.

And yet, a month later, the hapless Central Committee spokesman Günter Schabowski declared that travel restrictions for East Germans were being lifted *sofort, unverzüglich*, immediately, without delay. Did the authorities really think that people would calmly line up at checkpoints, get their passports stamped, go shopping in the West, be home for dinner and continue to serve the GDR as they had always done?

With hindsight, one can conclude that by then the East German state had ceased to be viable. Just as the exodus of two million people in the late 1940s and 1950s led to the Wall being built in 1961, so as soon as it came down, the system had no chance. One might argue that on its own terms it worked. The 'Anti-Fascist Protection Rampart' comprised two walls interspersed by a death strip containing booby traps, guard dogs, trenches, watch towers and mobile patrols. It stretched 97 miles around the city. The 866-mile border separating the two Germanies was patrolled by 50,000 armed guards. Over the half-century of the GDR's life, 75,000 people were caught and 140 killed while trying to flee. Only 5,000 managed to get out without permission.

In Germany, 9 November is called *Schicksaltag*, the day of fate, as it coincides with a number of momentous events in the country's history – the crushing of the 1848 revolution, the declaration of a communist state by Karl Liebknecht in 1918 and Hitler's failed Beer Hall Putsch in Munich in 1923. More happily, Albert Einstein was awarded the Nobel Prize in 1922. It is most synonymous with *Kristallnacht*, when in 1938 the Nazis unleashed attacks on synagogues and Jewish homes and property while most Germans went about their business. For that dark reason, 3 October instead has been declared the Day of German Unity and is now a national holiday. Nevertheless, since 1989 the major anniversaries of the fall of the Wall have been extensively commemorated. Each occasion has given rise to reflection on the nature of democracy, freedom and reunification. The thirtieth, in 2019, was pored over more than most, reflecting an increase in anxiety about the state of German society.

Whenever I'm in Berlin, I trace the Wall in my head. Whether I'm on the U-Bahn or S-Bahn, or on foot or in a car, I know when I'm going 'over'. In most places it is still comparatively easy to identify where it stood. My friend Fechner is now a social worker for the disabled. His teenage son and daughter say they try to understand what the old life was like. They understand a little about the GDR, vicariously through him, they say.

On the last anniversary, I arranged to meet Fechner outside the Gethsemane Church. For thirty years he has lived in the same flat. It has been spruced up; it didn't have central heating and hot water in the old days. Now the block is one of the most desirable in the whole city. He has a secured rent, ensuring that someone working in the care industry on a small salary is not thrown out. Where else in the world would that happen, I wonder?

A video of those momentous days was being displayed on the church's brick façade. Inside we watched an earnest debate about #Mauer30 (the Wall at 30); the altar was then vacated for an ageing East German folk band called Engerling. We walked past the designer clothes shops and cocktail bars towards the Bösebrücke bridge on Bornholmer Strasse. This is the spot where the border was first opened. This is where Fechner and his friends rushed to that night. The chaos is brilliantly captured in a popular 2014 film, also called *Bornholmer Strasse*. The guards were initially disturbed by a dog running across the eerily silent checkpoint. When they saw crowds beginning to gather, they had no idea what was going on. They had watched Schabowski's press conference; but they were none the wiser. Nobody in power had taken responsibility or given them clear orders. At 11.30 p.m., and against the views of his political commander (who was dealing with the stress by glugging a bottle of schnapps in his office), the officer in charge ordered that the barrier be raised.

The first of the East Germans marched past the French border guards on the other side, only to be met by more darkness and gloom. This wasn't how the West was supposed to be. This area, like almost everywhere close to the wall on the other side, was devoid of people. The road contained some scruffy allotments. It took the *Ossis* a while to find a petrol station, by which time news had begun to reach the West that something dramatic was afoot. The scenes of all-night revelling on West Berlin's main shopping street, the Kurfürstendamm, where people were feted with champagne, beer, handshakes and hugs, took a little while to materialize. As for Fechner, like many of his compatriots he spent all night celebrating, but (like Merkel) he too went back over the border in the early hours to go back to work. And he was a dissident. At work, many of his comrades on the shop floor had no idea that anything had happened. He recounted all this to me as we stood on the exact spot on Bornholmer Strasse where pedestrians or car drivers would have been taken to have their papers checked. That spot is now a Lidl supermarket. After the revolution, normality of sorts.

Even before the Wall came down, the dynamic had started to change. As the protests extended from activists and students to ordinary workers, anti-communism turned into pro-unification. The original chant for freedom, *Wir sind das Volk*, we are the people, turned into a slogan for reunification, *Wir sind ein Volk*, we are one people. In the last months of 1989, more than half the GDR population went over to the West to see life there first-hand. Many decided to stay there, particularly the young, more ambitious, more employable and female, in search of decent job prospects.

The day after the Wall came down, Willy Brandt, the former chancellor who led the country through the most fraught years of the Cold War, declared: '*Jetzt wächst zusammen, was zusammen gehört*.'[12] (What belongs together, grows together.) The grand old man of the left, of detente, was signalling that it was no longer dangerous for Germans to think of themselves as one. Nobody knew what the new normal would look like. Kohl declared in front of ecstatic crowds outside Berlin's Schöneberg town hall that it was important 'to find our way carefully into the future, step by step. For it is our common future that is at stake.'[13] A fortnight later he presented a ten-point convergence plan for a confederation. He thought it might take a decade.

The period to reunification was punctuated by more dramatic moments: the first democratic elections in March 1990, currency union in July, and the decisions that led to the formal dissolution of the GDR. From early on it became clear that this was not the coming together of two states, but the incorporation of one into the other. The Federal Republic became larger, taking in five reconstituted states of the East. Nothing of the GDR was retained.

The politicians of the East relished their new democracy. In its seven-month life as a proper parliament, in the thirty-eight sessions it held between the March elections and reunification, the Volkskammer meticulously passed a staggering 261 laws – including the one that abolished the country. The cabinet was composed of politicians who hadn't been tainted by the past (a small group) and civic activists. They vowed to do politics differently, not just differently from the old regime but also from the Western mainstream. The newly appointed disarmament and defence minister (he had stipulated the title) was a former conscientious objector and dissident priest called Rainer Eppelman.

The momentum, however, was elsewhere. Lothar de Maizière may have taken over as the GDR's leader, but it was Helmut Kohl in the West who was in charge of the process. Many East Germans were quite happy for Kohl just to get on with it. A bearded and bespectacled former lawyer (defending dissidents) and one-time professional viola player, de Maizière came from a well-connected Huguenot family which had fled France. He and Kohl were polar opposites in physique and demeanour. They did not get on. Kohl was frustrated by his pessimism. The historian Fritz Stern, a key figure in the historiography of contemporary Germany, recalls a conversation in June 1990: 'I remarked to de Maizière that I thought that the economic problems of unification, though huge, would turn out to be manageable, but that the moral-psychological problems would be far greater, and their resolution take much longer. He agreed, saying, "I don't want to bring seventeen million psychological cripples into the new Germany."[14] In October, on reunification, de Maizière was one of five East Germans co-opted onto Kohl's cabinet, awarded the non-job of minister for special affairs. Two months later he was dumped over allegations that he had been an informer for the Stasi. These were eventually disproven, but the damage was done.

On 1 July, East and West were tied economically when the Ostmark, the currency of the GDR, was abolished. Kohl and his ministers opted for a 1:1 conversion, a rate that bore no relation to its actual worth. It was a boon for East German savers and a psychological statement of confidence. For East German indus-try, though, it would prove disastrous, rendering it overvalued and even more uncompetitive than it already was. The occasion was another excuse for East German partying, but this time the mood was as ironic as it was euphoric. I was at one such gather-ing at a warehouse in Adlershof, a research centre and old Stasi regimental HQ that would later become a tech start-up centre. We were spending our last Ostmark, drinking Ost-cocktails, eating Ost-Wurst and listening to Ost-Music. *Ostalgie* was, for some, already setting in.

In a televised address to both nations (or rather the soon-to-be one nation), Kohl promised a better life for all. 'This is a crucial step on the road to the unity of our Fatherland, a great day in the history of the German nation.' Urging citizens of the East to look confidently to the future and of the West to make sacrifices for the common good, he declared, with no caveats: 'Through our joint efforts, we will soon succeed in transforming Mecklenburg-Vorpommern and Saxony-Anhalt, Brandenburg, Saxony, and Thuringia into blooming landscapes, in which it will be great to live and work.'[15] That phrase, blooming land-scapes, would be relentlessly mocked.

Kohl was determined to get the job done, casting aside

doubters along the way. The Unification Treaty of 1990 allowed the newly created five Bundesländer of the East, plus a single Berlin as a city-state (a status afforded also to Hamburg and Bremen), to use Article 23 of the Basic Law and simply accede to the Federal Republic. This was not what was envisaged by the founding fathers. They had imagined that, if reunification ever took place, the Basic Law would be abolished using another of its articles, and something permanent would be put in its place. Instead, what had been regarded as temporary was simply allowed to become permanent. The Basic Law had become so popular and sturdy, why not simply apply it to the enlarged area?

The following year, the Bundestag approved by a narrow margin to move the seat of government back to Berlin. There were several reasons for wanting to stay in Bonn. One was personal comfort – Berlin was seen as grubby. The others were less frivolous. Bonn's location, close to the Dutch and Belgian borders, signified a Western orientation. It had none of Berlin's associations with Germany's – and Prussia's – history. But the advocates for Berlin prevailed. Germany was mature enough to confront its past.

A massive building programme was approved to construct a new seat of government. Much of it took place in the area surrounding the Wall, some of that no man's land that had been the domain of rabbits, foxes and the guard dogs of GDR border troops. The glass cupola of Norman Foster's redesigned Reichstag, a masterstroke, gave physical form to the ethos of the new Germany. The public could walk around, looking down from on high on their elected representatives. Like most modern parliaments, the parliamentary chamber is arranged in a hemicycle. It is designed for consensus, not confrontation. Reputations are made in committees and constituency work, rather than by rhetorical flourishes. The old imperial parliament, with all its negative connotations, where Hitler would hold forth, was given a stunning modern twist – by a Briton. Since it reopened in 1999, the building has proved extremely popular among MPs and public alike.

Buildings help to define behaviours. Parliaments define nations' reputations. Reunification was taken as an opportunity to improve the country, with a new political architecture striving for stability and transparency. This aspiration was embodied in Merkel, the reliable woman from the East making it in the West. In an interview with the main tabloid, *Bild*, in November 2004, shortly before becoming chancellor, she was asked what emotions Germany aroused in her. She replied, 'I am thinking of airtight windows. No other country can build such airtight and beautiful windows.'[16] This was about more than buildings. It is a metaphor for constructing a country, a society, where reliability is the most prized asset.

I was told this story by Stefanie Bolzen, UK correspondent for *Die Welt*, married to a Brit and a keen observer of both countries' politics. We laughed about the anecdote, only for Bolzen to say that she agreed with Merkel. She had wanted to replace the draughty windows of their London home with proper German *Kippfenster*, ones that can swing open horizontally or vertically, depending on how you turn the handle. She couldn't find British workers who could do it to the quality that she wanted, so she imported some. As with politics, as with homes, they are baffled by Britain's make-do-and-mend gentlemen-amateur political culture. They liken Britain to a stately home. Overgrown gardens, creaking floorboards, crooked beams and sash windows that never quite close properly; beautiful in places, but quirky. The weekly newspaper *Die Zeit* even used the subject to have a rare swipe at a Brit they all seem to adore: 'Even the Queen could do with a cheaper energy bill. It costs €3.6 million a year to keep Buckingham Palace warm, making it the least energy-efficient building in London. Her Majesty is no different from the majority of English homeowners in this respect: they don't have money for repairs, their houses are in bad shape, and the heat that the boilers pump into them escapes through old masonry and simply glazed sash windows.'[17]

Britain's Houses of Parliament building, with its leaky pipes, Victorian toilets, fire hazards and rat-infested floorboards, darkens the soul. Billions of pounds have been spent trying to restore it, with much more to come. With its absurd quirks, its flunkies in ridiculous outfits, it removes parliamentarians from the lived experience of voters and elevates tradition over pragmatism. Sadly, it is more synonymous with the pantomime leering and jeering of set-piece interactions in the chamber, rather than the earnest and more collaborative work that most MPs would like to be associated with.

German governments look as much as possible for buy-in to all major policies. Anything contentious is often put out to a special commission, which is asked to come back whenever it's ready with recommendations acceptable to all. As the share of the votes received by the mainstream parties dwindles, the broader the coalitions have had to become, just to be viable. Bizarrely, they are named after the flags of other nations. Jamaica (black, yellow and green) denotes the CDU working with the Free Democratic Party (FDP) and Greens; Kenya (black, red and green) is CDU, SPD and Greens. Now, in some regions, there is talk of Zimbabwe (black, red, yellow and green). These combinations are tried out in regional governments, serving as prototypes, giving all parties the opportunity to work with each other in different combinations before embarking on a national level. This mosaic of coalitions is an extraordinary strength and source of stability.

Co-opted into a series of grand coalitions, the SPD has supplied Merkel with the votes she has needed to govern from the centre, while having little notion of what it is there to do. The SPD is potentially facing extinction, or at least being relegated to the margins. As *Der Spiegel* put it, the last time the SPD was cool was back when everyone had Nokia mobile phones. Its demise is consistent with broader European trends, but it is among the most pronounced and significant. During its heyday of Willy Brandt and Helmut Schmidt, it could count on a broad and dependable voter base. But since then it has struggled to keep pace with demographic change. According to the Institute for Economic Research, between 2000 and 2016 the percentage of voters who identified as working class dropped from 37 to 19 per cent. It struggles to know how to represent those fearful of the pace of change, or the emerging digital class, whether to focus on the urban or semi-rural voter. Its constituency is old and dying out. Such is its status as a national institution and such is Germany's commitment to the fabric of its post-war democratic parties that Chancellor Merkel attended the SPD's 150th anniversary celebrations in 2013, even though the party is her political competitor. That would be barely thinkable elsewhere.

The third party, the liberal FDP, used to garner between 5 and 10 per cent, making it the pivot in most post-war coalitions. Now it is in a mess, not knowing what it stands for, and struggling to get over the threshold for representation at all.

Germany's political system has an uncanny ability to absorb insurgents. The most remarkable transformation has come from the Greens. The party that emerged from the peace movement and the 1968 protests was riven by division in its early years. Its *Fundi* wing wanted nothing to do with conventional politics. Its *Realos* argued that they could only engineer change by working through existing structures. The latter group won the day and in 1983 the first Greens were elected to the Bundestag. They immediately made waves inside and outside the chamber, including taking part in a joint protest with dissidents in the centre of East Berlin. Their parliamentary team contained some of the most colourful figures in politics. Petra Kelly, a long-time anti-nuclear activist, was the biggest household name. As a lawyer, Otto Schily had defended the Red Army Faction terrorist group. Schily quit the Greens for the Social Democrats, becoming a hard-line interior minister in Schröder's government and then taking on corporate lobbying jobs.

The most famous Green was Joschka Fischer. A student activist in 1968, he became involved with fringe terrorist groups. He was a leader of a gang called the Proletarian Union for Terror and Destruction, which went around beating up police in the seventies. He was a mercurial figure in parliament, once addressing the deputy speaker: 'If I may say so, Mr President, you are an arsehole.'[18] In 1985, he became the first Green minister in the world, taking on the environment portfolio in the state of Hesse. The white trainers which he wore when he took his oath of office are preserved in the Museum of German History in Bonn. In 1998, the Greens joined the federal government for the first time, with the SPD. Fischer became vice chancellor and foreign minister, an extraordinary turnaround. By the time the coalition was defeated in 2005, he had been the second-longest serving foreign minister in post-war Germany. Opinion polls consistently rated him the most popular member of the cabinet.

The Greens have been a major player ever since they entered the political mainstream. In the 2000s, they vied with the FDP for third spot nationally, while playing an increasing role in state governments. In the past couple of years, they have grown further in stature – partly as cause and effect of the demise of the SPD, partly because of the climate emergency, and partly as a response to the nationalist-populist threat across Europe. In the manner of the original post-war establishment parties, the Greens have become a broad church, vested in the constitution. What is remarkable is that they have broadened their appeal beyond hippie/hipster urban pockets and into the small towns and villages across Germany. Green candidates in conservative Bavaria and Baden-Württemberg can be found wearing the traditional *Lederhosen* and *Dirndl* while out campaigning. This message of *Heimat*, homeland, emphasizes the need to preserve the natural beauty of the countryside, embedded in sentimental poetry such as 'The Blue Flower', written two centuries ago by Joseph von Eichendorff. In some ways, the Greens too have become staid. In this time of doubt across the democratic world, the success of Germany's Greens provides a considerable amount of hope. It also points to the depth of the problems facing the original parties.

In the 1970s, the top two parties used to hoover up 90 per cent of the vote. Now they have sunk below 50 per cent. Now, for the first time, all the three people's parties are under serious threat from insurgent forces. According to two seasoned observers, Jens Fischer (once an aide to Helmut Schmidt) and Heinz Schulte (a long-time pundit), there are now three types of German voter. These are the 'urban elite', most likely to be Green, the 'angry voter', who opts for either the AfD or the left-wing Die Linke (the party formed from the offshoot of the East German ruling communists), and the 'valley of the romantics', mainly older urban and suburban voters in the West who still cleave towards the established parties.

Mainstream politicians struggle with mavericks. In May 2019, at the height of the campaign for the European parliamentary elections, a video on YouTube (by far the most popular online platform in Germany) went viral. Twenty-six-year-old Rezo, a musician, vlogger and son of a Lutheran pastor in Aachen, delivered an hour-long lecture about the state of politics. Mixing expletives with 250 citations or data sets, and delivered from his mixing desk, Rezo accused the CDU and SPD of 'destroying our lives and our futures'. He went through, in detail, policies on climate change, wealth distribution and foreign policy. He described EU politics as 'fucking boring', but still encouraged young people to vote. Concluding his self-styled 'personal rant', he warned the country's leaders: 'You always say that young people should be political, in which case you have to get to grips with it when they think your politics are shit.'[19] Rezo has become symbolic of a younger generation (Eastern and Western) trying to find new ways of making itself heard. In less than a fortnight, this political lecture had received fifteen million hits, a record for a non-music post in Germany.

The Rezo moment should have been nothing special. Why shouldn't a young blogger vent his fury at the establishment? The response from a number of senior politicians and talk-show hosts bordered almost on panic. What on earth, they wondered, has gone wrong? Self-denigration is the media and political default. It can be tiresome, but it is infinitely preferable to the self-grandeur of decades of post-war British governments, spurred on by newspaper magnates in their shared delusions.

The run-up to the thirtieth anniversary of the fall of the Wall in November 2019 led to another fevered bout of self-criticism. The big decisions were deconstructed and reconstructed. Could more have been done to salvage parts of the East German economy that could have been reconfigured and made to work? The answer was indubitably yes. Industrial production halved in the East between July 1990 and April 1991. Tens of thousands of people were made unemployed each week. Within a year, a third of the workforce was out of work or on short time. In any assessment of this era, one organization is invariably blamed for such failures, the Treuhandanstalt, the Trust Agency. Established by the East German parliament in June 1990 (under pressure from Bonn), its job was to take in hand the more than eight thousand state enterprises employing four million workers. Its remit was to decide between privatization and liquidation. It didn't take long to ascertain that very few firms were remotely competitive in a German market, let alone a global one. The woman who led the organization for four of its five years, Birgit Breuel, used the thirtieth anniversary of the fall of the Wall to give a series of interviews about those times. Breuel had, over the years since, become a hate figure. The *Treuhand* was denounced as over-zealous, heartless and bureaucratic. Now in her eighties, she admitted that the organization had failed to see communities in the round, to do enough to help enterprises with potential to bridge from one system to another. 'We demanded too much of people,'[20] she said.

One evening in August 2019, I was watching one of Germany's many good political programmes, hosted by Markus Lanz. Panel discussions such as these remain the main platform for public engagement. The group included two important figures, who began the programme with strongly divergent views. Bernhard Vogel is a well-heeled man from the university cities of Göttingen and Heidelberg, now in his mid-eighties, and is the only person to have run states in West and East – Rhineland-Palatinate in the West from the mid-1970s to mid-1980s, and then Thuringia in the East. Up against him was Jana Hensel, a journalist and author in her mid-forties who lived through the fall of the Wall as a teenager, and whose 2004 book *After the Wall* brilliantly captures the trials and tribulations of a generation of former GDR citizens. Initially, they both played to type. He complained of the perpetual *Jammerei* (whinging) of the *Ossis*; she dwelt on the arrogance of the *Wessis*. They eventually conceded that both were right. 'For those in the West [reunification] was the end of the story,' Hensel noted. 'For us it was just the start.'

For older generations, for those who spent most of their life in the GDR, there is a catch-all phrase to describe such sentiments: the wall in the mind.

Someone with first-hand experience of this is Reiner Kneifel-Haverkamp, a civil servant and one of the first from the West to work in the East. Originally from near Dortmund, he had a solid job in the legal department at the Foreign Ministry in Bonn. In August 1991, he accepted the call to go East, to help the newly established government of Brandenburg to set up a Justice Ministry. He recalls that when he arrived in Potsdam, the historic city that was to be its HQ, it was an entirely new world. The first justice minister of the state, Hans Otto Bräutigam, had a big telephone on his desk. For the first few weeks that was the only direct line to West Germany. He and other civil servants would have to ask him to use it. Kneifel-Haverkamp's basic income was considerably more than that of his Eastern counterpart; Westerners were also given a bonus as an incentive to up sticks and help. This was dubbed the *Buschzulage*, jungle money. It was a term from Germany's colonial past given to officials working in inhospitable faraway lands under the Kaiser.

He describes two sources of tension – between East Germans, wondering who had informed on whom, and between *Ossis* and *Wessis*: 'Many of my colleagues were offhand with me to begin with, something I could understand. Then as things gradually warmed, some people divulged more to me than they would have done to others. Once I had crossed a certain threshold I would be told things by colleagues which in a West German workplace would never occur, unless you were talking to a really close friend.'

Western 'implants' in the East are often derided as *Di-Mi-Dos*, Tuesday to Thursday commuters who go back for long weekends to their families in, say, Hamburg or Munich. Kneifel-Haverkamp tried to buck the trend, to assimilate, to become an adopted *Ossi* – even though he made no secret of continuing to live in West Berlin. He tried, he says, to understand an identity that is part regional and part derived from history (although by no means sympathetic to that history). Most of all, it is about pride. At social events in the West he gets annoyed with people mocking their 'poorer cousins' and with journalists and politicians resorting to stereotypes.

What exactly is an East German now? In its cover story in October 2019, *Der Spiegel* wondered out loud: '*So is' er, der Ossi*' (So that's what the Ossi is like). Its subtitle added: 'How the East ticks and why it votes differently'. Everyone was reflecting on such matters that autumn. Berlin's Volkbühne theatre devoted a series of evenings to considering matters of East-West identity. The *Tagesspiegel* newspaper brought out a forty-eight-page special supplement on the same topic.

Bettina Leetz has been a judge in the Potsdam family court since 1982. After reunification, she told me over ice cream in one of the city's spruced up central squares, about half the judges had been removed; the higher the court, the more likely you were to lose your job, as you would have been closely involved in the political system. In the High Court, only one judge was retained. Some retrained as lawyers, legal advisers to companies, or worked for security firms. Others retired. There wasn't a whole lot to do in the old days. If the state wanted to punish you, it didn't take long. Divorces weren't complicated as few people had assets to haggle over and children were looked after much more by the state. Now that people have money, litigation is booming, and the law profession is thriving. There used to be six hundred judges for the whole of the GDR. Now, she notes, there are at least that number for Brandenburg alone. Leetz is one of those who has adapted, who appreciates her better life. Then she says something that initially shocked me – until I heard it from so many people that it became a recurrent theme. Initially, everyone worked hard at resolving differences, but in the past few years, she says, they have become accentuated again. Her daughter, in her mid-twenties, now feels less compatible with friends originally from the West than when she was younger.

How do you tell people apart? It's no longer the clothes or cars. Easterners note the way people walk (more assertively in the West) and the way they talk. ('I'm a bit tired of the Maldives, perhaps I need to trade in my Audi.') Certain conversations are giveaways – foreign travel, investments, inheritance. And the desire to argue. In the East you kept your head down. Then there were the social mores. As a judge, Leetz was married to a plumber. Shortly after the *Wende* they divorced. I gently ask her if that was a purely personal decision or if the political upheavals had had anything to do with it. She said she couldn't disentangle one from the other but noted that in the East such a pairing would not have seemed out of place. When she started mixing with Westerners, they couldn't quite understand such a mismatch in status. 'You have to concede that the takeover was efficient, but many issues were papered over.'

Helmut Haas runs a company in Leipzig that makes prosthetics, employing 100 people. He married a local woman and has lived there for twenty-five years. He has also worked in the US and in Austria. Like Kneifel-Haverkamp he has tried to assimilate but is acutely aware of the differences. Does he feel at home? 'We are all searching for our identity,' he replies, before adding wistfully: 'Things have definitely got worse in the past few years. I'm hoping it's short lived.' The transition from excessive expectation to resentment has ended up somewhere in between.

Dirk Burghardt is the managing director of the Dresden State Art Collections, which oversees fifteen museums across the city. Sitting in his office in Dresden Castle, with a view onto the Zwinger Palace, we talk about art and politics. Dresden's modern art museum, the Albertinum, has been at the eye of a storm, with local politicians complaining that it has shunned works from the GDR. Burghardt, a native of West Germany, says low-level hostility has emerged, but only recently. He told me that a few months earlier he had been at a rock concert. A man standing next to him nudged him and shouted: 'Hey you, where you from then?' It is all still raw, for him too. At the start of his tenure, Burghardt was one of those cultural leaders charged with checking the Stasi links of ministry employees. He was an outsider and barely thirty years old. 'I was expected to sort through eight to ten people a day. Some would burst into tears. Others would stare back at me with ice-cold eyes.'

'The West Germans were the first foreigners to disappoint us.' Antje Hermenau is a political iconoclast. During the *Wende* she was one of the GDR's first Green politicians, sitting on Leipzig's round-table negotiations (she was the only woman of seventeen participants). She was a prominent member of Saxony's regional parliament between 1990 and 1994 and of the Bundestag between 1994 and 2004. Fiercely independent and outspoken, married briefly to an American (something that was very rare in the GDR), she would tick the box of classic centre-left dissident. As we walk through Leipzig's old town, she points out her old flat overlooking the Nikolaikirche. She had a front-row seat at the peaceful revolution.

Now it all feels different. She quit the Greens in 2014 after twenty-five years, believing that the conventional parties (she lumps the Greens in the same category as the others) failed the people, particularly *her* people – East Germans and her beloved Saxons. Her region, she points out, propped up the GDR, providing half of its industrial production, even though it accounted for only 20 per cent of its population. She recently published a book entitled *The View from Middle Europe*. Her argument is that *Mitteleuropa*, broadly embracing Saxony, Thuringia and neighbouring pockets of Germany are culturally aligned to Poland, Hungary, the Czech Republic and Austria. They embrace older traditions. In short, they do not belong to the West. She points out that even as a Green she was saying as much. In a speech in 2005, she argued: 'We'll go our own way.'

She did go her own way in Saxony's regional elections of 2019, bringing together a group of candidates under the name Free Voters. She takes me to the small town of Zwenkau, about 15 kilometres south of Leipzig, where, one might think at first glance, things are looking up. A former opencast lignite mine that blighted the area is being turned into a reservoir and recreational lake. Otherwise, there's not a whole lot going on, but the houses are neat and tidy. We've come to meet the local candidate, Heike Oehlert. Recently widowed, Oehlert is a popular figure involved in community politics and a self-employed physiotherapist who does home visits for the elderly. I listen to the two of them speak, my response alternating between sympathy and consternation. The aim of the Free Voters is to give a voice to people who otherwise would opt for the far right AfD. A word commonly used in these parts is *abgehängt*, Germany's equivalent of 'the left behind'. 'They like to portray the people of Saxony and the GDR as wild beasts; they say we are hillbillies, even though we are more cultured than they are. We stayed here while others left. We had to build everything from scratch but weren't valued,' Hermenau says. She spends hours with me, helpful to a fault, trying to get me to understand. 'We feel doubly insulted. We feel threatened and then when we complain, we get called racists,' Oehlert adds. I ask about her children. Her son teaches politics in the city. 'He's as multicultural as you like,' she admits. 'He doesn't understand the concerns of our generation.'

I try to understand why they feel the way they do, but when they move on to the subject of immigration, I struggle. They tell me how outrageous it is to walk into shops in some parts of Berlin only to find that the people working there can't speak German. As for the media, they are controlled by the two main parties and their friends with deep pockets. They have not let go of the past: 'We are all trained to read between the lines and not to believe what is written.' A sense of grievance is embedded across the East. Terms such as *Anschluss*, previously referring to Hitler's 1938 takeover of Austria, but now to the 'takeover', as they see it, of the East by the West, and *Besserwessi* (the know-it-all Westerner) became common parlance early on.

Perhaps the single biggest error of reunification was the failure to identify more people from the East to serve in senior positions and as broader role models. It would, for sure, have been unthinkable not to remove the Communist Party top brass and senior figures in industry, law and other professions. But even now, not just across Germany but in the six Eastern states, almost all the top jobs are occupied by *Wessis*. Thirty years on, just 1.7 per cent of East Germans hold top posts in politics, the courts, military and business, even though the East accounts for 17 per cent of the population. Not a single university in the whole of Germany is run by an *Ossi*. As for business, just 7 per cent of Germany's top five hundred companies are headquartered in the East, and not one in the DAX 30 index.

The writer Frank Richter has coined the phrase 'embitter-ment disorder',[21] a delayed response by East Germans to the shocks. The *Wende* was not just the end of a state; it was the dismantling of mindsets. The resentment has little to do with economic factors.

According to one recent poll, 75 per cent of citizens in Sax-ony described their financial situation as either good or very good. Yet an almost equal number said they were treated as second-class citizens.

The six Eastern states now have a per capita GDP much higher than elsewhere in the former communist bloc and higher than many southern European countries. Yet the development hasn't been uniform. Leipzig is so fashionable and popular for investors that it is dubbed *Hypezig*. Many young people now see it as more attractive than Berlin – cheaper beer, better music, more affordable flats. The place that I find uncomfortable, even though financially it is doing reasonably, is Dresden. History weighs on it. Much of the remains of the bombed-out centre was torn down by the GDR government and rebuilt with its charac-teristic flat, concrete *Plattenbau* buildings. After reunification, the historic centre was restored to its former glory, but the place feels artificial. The most striking building could be said to be the Palace of Culture, a concrete box built in 1962 and adorned with a giant socialist realist mural called the 'The Way of the Red Flag'. The *Kulti*, as it was known back then, was supposed to be the centrepiece of a 'socialist town centre'. Unlike the Palast der Republik in Berlin, plans to demolish it were shelved. Instead it was gutted on the inside and turned into the home of the Dresden Philharmonic.

The more remote the location in the East, the smaller the population base, the bigger the problem. A number of villages and small towns have been stripped bare. The shop, doctor's surgery, pub have gone. The proportion of older people, who depend more on public services, has increased. At railway stations, at stop after stop, the once-grand ticket office is boarded up, an automatic machine on the platform serving as the only customer interface.

Expectations were not managed in the euphoria that followed the fall of the Wall. Experts in the early 1990s who identified the task as a long haul, predicting that it would take decades for the economies of East and West to align, were criticized for their pessimism. Now, as the Institute for Economic Research in Dresden points out, a convergence target of 2030 looks about right. Currently, living standards in the East are just below 80 per cent of the West. With transfers, other subsidies and lower prices for certain goods, it is heading towards parity, but will still take a few more years. Compared with the poorest parts of western Germany, it is already doing better. Unemployment rates across the former GDR are lower than in the post-industrial regions of the Ruhr or Saarland, bordering France. Western companies may not have put many locals in leadership positions, but at least they are investing. Large and medium-sized companies have been encouraged, and incentivized, to open plants in the East. The former Trabant works in Zwickau were quickly acquired and reconfigured by VW. Opel moved into Eisenach. Porsche and BMW have a presence in Leipzig. Railway lines and rolling stock have been modernized. A new network of *Autobahnen* has been built – all at a time when infrastructure in Western regions has deteriorated due to a lack of spending.

The amount that has been spent overall in the past thirty years is staggering. Aufbau Ost, Rebuilding the East, has seen an injection of €2 trillion into infrastructure projects. No country has seen such a long-term shift of funds and resources – a modern-day equivalent of the Marshall Plan. That is only right and proper, given that their Western counterparts benefited from American largesse straight after the war. Roughly a fifth of the total has gone on cleaning up the East's environment, closing unsafe nuclear plants and reducing reliance on brown coal. Anyone who lived in the East remembers their towns disfigured by above-ground pipes and shrouded in black smog. Residents would use damp cloths to wipe the soot off window sills. Now, the air is vastly cleaner. Life expectancy, a reliable guide to economic differentials, has narrowed. It has all had to be paid for. Which other country would have introduced a Solidarity Tax, the *Soli*, in which taxpayers are levied an additional 5.5 per cent on top of income tax to pay for rebuilding the East – and with so little grumbling? It is still being charged, although it will be abolished for all but the top 10 per cent of earners by 2021.

This scoresheet is extraordinarily impressive – although if any West German presumed to say this, they would be denounced by their compatriots as conceited and complacent. The air is cleaner than it was. Much of the infrastructure has been transformed. The big cities have been renovated. The economy is on track to converge with the West. For all its mistakes, for all the resentments – real or imagined – Germany did what others would not have been able to. It did so on its own, while also being a net contributor to the EU. It weathered one recession and one financial crash.

What therefore lies behind the embitterment disorder? It is not helped by the fact that people in the East have not been required to come to terms with their past – either in the Nazi or communist times. Nor have people in the West been asked to consider what they would have done had they found themselves on the wrong side of the inner German border. *Täter oder Opfer*, perpetrators or victims: these binary terms ignore the complexities, terrible immediate choices and grey areas of ordinary lives.

On reunification, a small number of Communist Party and *Stasi* leaders were tried for specific offences. Many who had enjoyed senior positions in other parts of the system were kicked out of their jobs. For the most part, questions of culpability and degrees of culpability were argued out within families and communities. Everyone knew someone. The *Stasi* had 85,000 full-time agents, half a million informers and files on six million people (pretty much the entire adult portion of the eighteen million population). With so many people having worked on the dark side, it would have required a huge bureaucratic operation to decide on levels of complicity. Judgementalism from the outside was rife. But one question that was rarely asked by West Germans, or foreigners for that matter, was: how would you have behaved if you had been forced to live under such a system? It has become a common refrain to say that the people of the East suffered twice, from two successive dictatorships. Yet this formulation is problematic, as it relies on the concepts of innocence and passivity and suggests moral equivalence between the Third Reich and the GDR. It has given rise to a fascinating discussion about how to place GDR dictatorship in the wider context of German twentieth-century history.

And what of denazification? East Germany did not accept culpability for the Third Reich. As an anti-fascist state under the dictatorship of the proletariat, it was supposed to mark a fresh start. Fascism was the natural corollary to rampant capitalism, and capitalism was continuing in the West, albeit in different form. The standard interpretation among West Germans is that, although their state struggled with the process, particularly in the first two decades, they did at least try to go after the worst offenders; the GDR did not. Where was its Nuremberg process?

A Berlin-based American moral philosopher, Susan Neiman, has challenged this thesis. Neiman is director of the Einstein

Forum in Potsdam, a foundation of ideas established by the Brandenburg regional government. A central tenet of her recent book, *Learning from the Germans: Race and the Memory of Evil*, is to compare favourably German attempts at atonement for the Holocaust with America's at best partial expiation on slavery. Her most contentious passages relate to the differences between how the East and West German parts of the country dealt with the memory of the war. She argues that 'East Germany's ways of working off the past have been largely forgotten. The very nicest thing a West German will say about them is that East Germany had "anti-fascism by decree". Such remarks bring East Germans to laughter on good days and angry incomprehension on others.'[22] She quotes the writer Ingo Schulze as saying: 'Anti-fascism was state policy and rightly so.'[23]

Neiman is a fascinating thinker on ethics and an engaging interlocutor, but I cannot help thinking that she lets the GDR too easily off the hook. Nevertheless, she, like some other contemporary authors, is developing an important school of thought that goes beyond easy good–bad, freedom–oppression comparisons. Another with a somewhat benign but also interesting take is Uwe-Karsten Heye. A former government spokesman under Gerhard Schröder, Heye published a book in 2014 about the life and family of Walter Benjamin, a German-Jewish philosopher and committed anti-fascist. Benjamin's politics endured after his death, famously, or rather infamously, through his sister-in-law. Hilde Benjamin became known as Red Guillotine and Bloody Hilde for the number of show trials she presided over and the death sentences she handed down while vice president of the GDR Supreme Court. She became minister for justice in 1953, but in 1967 she was pushed out by East Germany's leader Walter Ulbricht. Her political fanaticism, her voracious communism, had become too much, even for that regime.

Perhaps one individual personifies the traumas and con-
tradictions of the GDR more than any other. Christa Wolf's
history could be a history of post-war Germany. A member of
the female counterpart of the Hitler Youth as a young child,
she was ten when she watched the SS march through her town
on their way to Poland. At the end of the war, she was expelled
with her family from Poland into the Eastern part of Germany.
She quickly joined the Communist Party, eventually becoming
a junior member of the Central Committee. Her novels, such
as *Divided Heaven* and *The Quest for Christa T*, describe relationships between lovers and between individuals and the state.
Wolf, like many East Germans, believed ardently in the communist project until disillusion set in. The 1953 uprising, when
Soviet tanks crushed protests by around a million people in
a number of cities, marked that point for many. Support gradually turned into toeing the line, a sceptical and pragmatic life
in the shadows in which private friendships assumed enormous
importance.

Wolf went from being tolerated by the regime, even occasionally praised, to distrusted. She became disillusioned with
the state but, even so, she always opposed unification. Her
books were devoured, attracting nervous audiences to churches
to hear her read. In 1993, it was revealed that she had been an
informer for the *Stasi*. Although it was only for three years, the
fact that she had snitched on other authors led to a torrent of
denunciation. When the revelations were made, she expressed
shock and claimed that she must have repressed her memory. A
public debate, similar to the historians' debate decades before,
developed around the Wolf affair. She had already been criticized for delaying publication of one of her later books, *What
Remains*. The book, written in the first person and describing
a day in the life of an author (presumably herself) living under

Stasi oppression, came out within months of the communist system collapsing. The character was portrayed as having suffered at the hands of the state. Had she, really? A number of literary figures rallied around Wolf, not least a bruised Günter Grass. 'It was like a public execution,'[24] he wrote. What would others have done in that situation?

Post-reunification, a new cohort of writers, artists and filmmakers has been looking afresh at the fascist and communist legacy they have been bequeathed. Some dare to do so with humour. In the 2003 film *Good Bye, Lenin!*, a mother falls into a coma on the eve of the Wall coming down. When she wakes, her son tries to protect her from the shock that her life's architecture has collapsed.

In her book *After the Wall*, Jana Hensel, who was thirteen when the Wall fell, describes her peers as being the lost generation, caught between those too young to remember and those too old to make a new life. Another moving book of that genre is *Red Love*, by Maxim Leo. He recalls the conflicting politics of his parents and grandparents in the GDR – those who worked in the system and those who tried to rebel. As the regime began to disintegrate in 1988 and 1989, with people fleeing through Hungary and elsewhere, he writes: 'The ones who stay behind feel like failures. The stupid leftovers, is what the GDR was called at the time.'[25] His mother, who had defied the system in the hope of reforming it, couldn't handle the sight 'of all those happy faces. She sensed that something was coming to an end even though it hadn't yet really got going.'[26] The film that most people associate with that era is *The Lives of Others*, an award-winning work of docudrama telling the stories of bored *Stasi* officers who would listen in to people's conversations for hours on end. 'I suddenly had this image in my mind of a person sitting in a depressing room with earphones on his head and listening in to what he supposes is the enemy of the state and the enemy of his ideas,' said the director Florian Henckel von Donnersmarck. 'What he really hears is beautiful music that touches him.'[27]

In a quiet leafy street in the neighbourhood of Karlshorst, in the eastern part of Berlin, stands a hidden gem. The German–Russian Museum, previously known as the Central Museum of the Armed Forces, is the place where the Nazi capitulation was signed. On the ground floor, they have preserved the grand but sparse hall that had been the officers' mess of an engineering corps. The four victorious Allies chose this inconspicuous spot in what was the Soviet Zone to sign the documents marking the Nazis' unconditional surrender. An austere, long, dark brown wooden table, covered in green baize, with the four flags behind, provided the backdrop for the event. The ceremony, filmed in black and white, is replayed on a loop on a small TV set. In 1967, the building was turned into a museum to celebrate the heroism of Soviet forces and the evils of fascism. When the Russians left in 1994, it was handed to the city of Berlin. Curator Margot Blank takes me around. I spend hours, far longer than planned, transfixed by the displays – from the day-to-day routines of the soldiers, to Nazi propaganda leaflets dropped from the air as they advanced through Belarus and western Russia, to the murder of Soviet Jews and the blockades of Stalingrad and Leningrad. The stories of these terrible events are candidly told.

I go straight from Karlshorst up the road to the Friedrichsfelde Central Cemetery. By the main gates is an area which is separated from the other graves, a pantheon to past heroes. These are heroes to the communist cause. The monument was originally designed by Mies van der Rohe, one of the architectural greats of the first half of the twentieth century and the last director of the Bauhaus school. His Monument to the Revolution lasted only nine years before it was pulled down by the

Nazis in 1935. In 1951, the GDR government built a new one, the Memorial to the Socialists. In its central site lie ten graves. I take pictures on my phone of the graves of Rosa Luxemburg and Karl Liebknecht. Next to them lies Ulbricht. My stomach begins to churn. At least the cemetery authorities had the good sense to bury the head of the *Stasi*, Erich Mielke, in a more out-of-the-way part of the grounds. The monument's central obelisk bears the inscription: '*Die Toten mahnen uns.*' The dead remind us. Indeed, they do.

These people and their regime are no more. When East Germans complain about their lot, it is worth reminding them of the life they previously lived, caged in, their cities filthy with soot, their every move monitored by informers. Why not celebrate that a little more? The chancellor, too, seems only to see the glass as half empty. 'We must all learn to understand why for many people in east German states, German unity is not solely a positive experience,'[28] Merkel said in her address to mark 2019's national day. Yet there is another way of looking at it. Instead of asking whether mistakes were made, a different question should be posed: Could any other nation have dealt with a situation such as that with so little upheaval? The task would have bankrupted other states and caused far greater societal trauma. For all the problems past and future, that is an extraordinary legacy for Merkel and her country. She beats her breast from time to time. But she does not boast. Yet she has outlasted all her European and Western peers. And her place in history will be far more distinguished than most.

3

Multikulti

Immigration and identity

In August 2015, in Heidenau, a small town just outside Dresden, a mob of around six hundred skinheads attacked a group of migrants as they were being bussed into a temporary shelter in a closed-down factory. When police were called late that Friday night, they were attacked with bottles and stones. Thirty officers were injured, one seriously. The police responded by firing teargas and pepper spray to secure the entrance road to the shelter. A few days after the violence had subsided, Angela Merkel went to visit. 'There can be no tolerance for people who question the dignity of others; there can be no tolerance for those who are not willing to help where legal and human help is required,' she said with her characteristic gravity. One person in the crowd responded: '*Die schaut uns nicht mal mit dem Arsch an.*' She doesn't look at us even with her arse.

In Berlin, another story that year: a middle-aged couple wanted to put another disused building to a similar use. Hardy Schmitz and Barbara Burckhardt were told that the Senate (the city government) had taken over a former psychiatric clinic close to their house to turn it into a dormitory for four hundred Syrians and other refugees. Instead of complaining, Schmitz and Burckhardt and a group of active neighbours founded an association, organized the funding and got permission to take over the first floor of a beautiful villa that had been empty for fifteen years. The idea was to turn it into a workshop, library and meeting place for the new arrivals. Their business plan was well thought through. Their credentials – he a successful entrepreneur, she a well-known theatre critic – were impeccable. Other members of the association brought in the experience of one of the most active refugee support networks in the city. The only problem was the neighbours, or at least some of them. The fine burghers of this affluent part of Charlottenburg sent out a flyer complaining about the project. Just think of the reputation of your street. Think of your daughters' safety. You wouldn't be able to walk home at night.

They threatened a lawsuit, something not to be dismissed lightly. Complainants in a wealthy part of Hamburg had won a similar case a few months earlier. Burckhardt started a group to try to see them off. 'We posted opposing flyers in which we wrote, "If we all can't do it, then who can?",' she tells me as we drink tea in the villa's drawing room. They held meetings to discuss the feasibility of the project. They also wanted it to feel exciting. Burckhardt called in favours from some prominent figures in Berlin's cultural scene, asking actors, impresarios and writers to give talks or introduce films or music soirees. She invited those very same neighbours to these evening events, together with the refugees. The chance to rub shoulders with cultural celebrity was too good to miss; the resistance folded. The association grew fast. Members offered language cafes, job services, legal support. Many of the volunteers were elderly ladies, working alongside mostly Arab men in their twenties. There were some intercultural teething problems. Should they serve alcohol in the evenings? They did. Embarrassment was caused early on when some films contained sex scenes. Burckhardt chose more judiciously after that. As the space became livelier, as trust grew, the more experienced volunteers curated sessions where Syrian and German artists met. In the daytime, Schmitz and other volunteers now organize job application training on and off site. They try to get the migrants apprenticeships or internships. They visit job centres to talk to officials who struggle to relate to these new applicants. They fundraise relentlessly, seeking donations, from high net worth individuals and corporations to a collection box in the building.

The acceptance from the neighbourhood is not universal, but some people are doing their bit. Individual refugees are taken in as lodgers. Burckhardt and Schmitz have had a young man called Mohammed staying with them. He has been working part-time for Oxfam while also studying. Whenever he encounters racism or hostility (not a daily occurrence but frequent enough to be part of his life), he tries to make light of it. '*Alles unter Kontrolle*,' Everything is under control, he tells them. In December 2016, a failed Tunisian asylum seeker drove a truck into one of Berlin's most popular Christmas markets, killing twelve people and injuring more than fifty. Mohammed and his friends were petrified, fearing retribution. 'He came and said: "What can we do?",' Schmitz recalls. 'They organized via Facebook, deciding to queue at the Charité hospital to give blood as a gesture of solidarity.'

I met Burckhardt and Schmitz through their daughter, Tine, who works on tech start-ups. They are extraordinary people. I ask them whether they feel things are getting better or worse. Both, Burckhardt says. 'We go through big mood swings.'

As a thought exercise, I compare and contrast the hostility of the people of Heidenau with those of Charlottenburg. One group is raw, angry, downtrodden, violent. The only viable industry in that town in Saxony, close to the Czech border, is a tyre factory. It is a typical case of far right meets economic dislocation meets resentment meets foreigners of a different hue. In the second case, in Berlin's leafy West End, the arrival of asylum seekers momentarily disturbed the comfort of a well-heeled neighbourhood. They responded with passive-aggressive legalese. Which is worse? I would suggest they deserve each other.

One of many inspiring examples of social entrepreneurship is a restaurant called Lawrence. It is located in my favourite part of Berlin, the Scheunenviertel, the Barn Quarter, a collection of galleries, cafes and cooperatives. The restaurant is situated on a corner opposite the main synagogue, one of the most painfully evocative (and heavily guarded) buildings in the city. The restaurant was started by Frank Alva Buecheler, a theatre director who has worked with some of the top names in theatre around the world over a forty-year career. In 2015, he had a mid-life moment. He was invited by a relief organization to visit a refugee camp in northern Lebanon. 'It was a life-changing trip. I was close to the Syrian border. I heard all the bombings and machine-gun fire. I was aged fifty-eight. It was my first sight of war.' His parents and grandparents did not lead such cosseted lives.

The Berlin authorities had opened another refugee shelter, in a disused hospital near the synagogue. Just after he came back from the trip, Buecheler found that the hospital was being refurbished and reassigned. The refugees would be dispersed around the city. They needed a meeting place. He found the building where we were sitting, an old pharmacy cum barber's shop. 'There were forty organizations bidding for this space, including Starbucks.' The council gave it to Buecheler, impressed with his idea of opening a gallery and cultural forum upstairs, which would be cross-subsidized by a restaurant downstairs. I immediately thought: what councils in other global capitals would hand over a highly prized piece of rental property to a not-for-profit organization such as this? Readings and lectures on subjects involving the Middle East and Arabic culture take place most days. The art space has put on more than a dozen exhibitions. Buecheler says roughly a third of his visitors to both the restaurant and culture forum are from the Middle East, a third from other parts of the world and a third are Germans. Most of his staff are war refugees. His organization, called Freeartus, has become super-fashionable. People like to be seen there. A former economics minister is on the board. The wife of President Steinmeier comes to eat. She sometimes asks for a doggy bag to take any of her group's uneaten food home for her husband when he is working late. Buecheler says they plan to do a swap, and to open a restaurant serving German food in Beirut.

In 2015, the UN's refugee agency, UNHCR, put the world's displaced population at a post-1945 record of sixty million. By the following year, the war in Syria had displaced an estimated thirteen million citizens.[1] Half of them fled across its borders; most ended up in Lebanon, a country already weighed down by years of violence, instability and poverty. Jordan also took well over a million. A similar number ended up in Europe. Germany has become home for many of them.

'*Wir schaffen das*,'[2] declared Angela Merkel after visiting a refugee camp inside her own country. She would say it again and again in the subsequent weeks. We can handle it. She could – and she couldn't. In September 2015, Germany welcomed the world's destitute. The numbers were far in excess of anything anyone else was doing. She did it to help the Greeks and

Italians, who were suffering as the first ports of call. She did it out of compassion, and to show the world a new Germany. She also did it as a European leader, not just a German one. Hundreds of local people gathered at Munich's central station over the next few days to applaud incoming refugees. Locals opened their doors for 'welcome dinners'. Sports halls and community centres were turned into emergency relief centres. Health clinics absorbed the sick. Schools took in children.

This was Germany at its best. So what went wrong? Did it actually go wrong? For Merkel, it certainly did. Her standing didn't recover. She was forced to bring forward the date of her retirement. Many questioned her motives, and if not her motives then her competence. I don't see it that way. I see it as one of the most extraordinary moments in Germany's postwar rehabilitation.

The chancellor and her civil service were certainly caught napping. That period, 2014–15, when huge waves of destitute people were piling into southern Europe – those who had not perished on the high seas along the way – was a time when Europe's leaders were dealing with another crisis. The saga of Greece's debt and bailout had been all-consuming and fractious. Under a treaty signed in Dublin in 1997, the EU decided that asylum seekers must register and remain in the first EU country they entered. In other words, it was the duty of the state where a migrant first landed to deal with their case, even if they had no intention of staying there. A simple solution this might have been; it was also unfair and impractical. The EU's fledgling border protection agency, Frontex, had been set up in 2004 to help control the external border. It was mainly an advisory body and it was hugely ineffective. Greece and Italy, on the southern flank with the Middle East and North Africa, were in no position to cope.

Germany's post-war record on immigration was patchy. It was also based on a traditional definition of citizenship through bloodlines. From the 1950s to the 1990s, the country became increasingly reliant on hundreds of thousands of *Gastarbeiter*, guest workers, mainly from Turkey and Italy. They ran shops and cafes. They did menial jobs in factories. They also worked in heavy industries such as coal and steel. They had few rights. There was little integration, èven less representation. The government had no intention of changing their status. If they didn't like it, they could always go home. One can contrast that with the open-door policy shown towards the Volga Germans. In the eighteenth century, when the 'German Princess' Catherine the Great took the imperial Russian throne, tens of thousands of Germans moved east, setting up communities mainly along the Volga river. They kept their language and customs. In Soviet times they were given their own 'autonomous republic', with a capital (appropriately enough) called Engels. When Hitler invaded in 1941, the Volga Germans were persecuted; many were sent to labour camps. A third of that total didn't survive the privations. During the *perestroika* era of Mikhail Gorbachev, they were told they could leave if they wished to. As a result, Germany is now home to more than two million of these *Aussiedler*, emigrants who because of their ethnicity were immediately admitted into the country, no questions asked. *Jus sanguinis*, blood rights, is a determiner of citizenship applications in many countries around the world. Given Germany's history, it was striking that this principle continued to be applied, with characteristic rigour, for so long.

The policy changed in 2000. Legislation passed by the Schröder government gave some groups of children of foreign parents, but born and raised in the country, the right to a German passport. In 2014, that right was extended to all German-born children. Now every fourth person living in Germany, nearly twenty million people, has a 'migrant background', with at least one non-German parent. There are over four million people of Turkish origin, making up 5 per cent of the population. According to the Organisation for Economic Co-operation and Development (OECD), Germany is now the second most popular destination for immigration (after the US, which keeps the top spot in spite of Donald Trump's best efforts).[3] Germany is ahead of Australia, which raised the drawbridge years ago, even of Canada, which has long prided itself on its welcoming culture.

The reasons behind Germany's change of direction on immigration were numerous and complex. It was driven in part by the desire of a new crop of politicians, particularly from the centre and the left, to see their country as more heterogeneous and open. It was driven in part by necessity, by a fall in the working-age population and a rise in old-age pensioners. Germany was simply running out of workers. The manpower shortage was particularly acute in the health service, social care and the construction industry. Demographic experts say that because of the sustained low birth rate and ageing population, Germany even now needs to bring in around 500,000 people every year. A new labour immigration law, with the wonderful title *Fachkräftezuwanderungsgesetz*, allows skilled workers such as IT technicians to enter the country for six months to job-hunt, provided they can support themselves financially throughout that time. The law offers the prospect of permanent residency to asylum seekers who find employment and speak adequate German. Since 2015, a third of the migrants who came in the great wave have found work. Does that mark success or failure? Not a bad record, I would say.

Two images have come to represent an extraordinary forty-eight hours at the start of September 2015. Everyone can recall the photographs of the lifeless body of a three-year-old Syrian boy, called Alan Kurdi, lying face down in the surf on a tourist beach near the Turkish resort of Bodrum. He and his family had tried to make it to the Greek island of Kos. Many people paid extortionate sums to people traffickers only to drown on ramshackle boats like theirs. They continue to do so now. The only difference is that many Europeans seem more inured to their suffering.

On the next day, 3 September, nearly 2,000 miles away at Munich's central station, something quite different was happening. Hundreds of locals lined up, holding banners saying: 'Welcome to Germany' (in English). They brought flowers, gifts and food for the first trainloads of refugees who had finally been allowed to leave Hungary via Austria on their epic journey to safety. This outpouring of compassion was covered live on TV. Images were flashed instantly around the world on social media. The refugees had finally found someone to take them in. Their ordeal, it seemed was over.

As the numbers of refugees flooding through Lampedusa, Kos and other islands and ports in the south of Europe grew out of control, this caravan of misery made its way through the Balkans. From Serbia, they tried to cross into Hungary, only to be confronted by hastily erected fences made of razor wire, guarded by dogs. Those that tried were met with tear gas, pepper spray and water cannon. The nationalist right-wing government of Viktor Orbán was unapologetic, saying the refugees looked like an invading horde. This former anti-communist dissident was the first European leader to harness (or foment) an increasing disquiet among the indigenous population. He would later be showered with praise by President Trump.

Merkel had seen what was going on and immediately decided to act. She had ordered that Germany's doors be opened and up to twenty thousand people arrived in that first weekend wave alone, most of them from Syria. So many donations had been received from shop owners and households at special collecting points for food, clothing, toiletries and children's toys, the police had to issue an appeal for people to stop. A new word was born, *Willkommenskultur*, welcome culture. According to the Allensbach Institute, a polling firm, in the first few months just over half the German population over the age of sixteen got involved in one way or another to help refugees. Some gave donations, while others gave more practical help, such as with language or dealing with bureaucracy. Over the next few weeks, hundreds of thousands of people flocked to the country. They came by train, bus and on foot. Most were penniless; many were ill. Many were unaccompanied minors, traumatized by civil wars and long, gruelling journeys. In inimitable German style, the authorities set in place measures to deal with the problem. Tent cities were built, empty buildings taken over. Volunteer doctors, nurses, psychiatrists, helped by interpreters, were put into place. In the second phase of the operation, each state was assigned a certain number of migrants, in a formula based on population and tax revenues.

No other country came close in its generosity. Central Europe wanted to shut up shop. France and Britain reluctantly said they would consider taking more, but only if staggered over a long period. None of that was of any immediate help. The contrast was telling. A columnist in Britain's *Mirror* newspaper summed it up: 'I can imagine lots of things, but I can't picture hundreds of Britons writing *Wilkommen zu Britannien* on their bedsheets and waving them from atop the White Cliffs.'[4] She noted that the UN had, even prior to the influx, listed Germany as having the third-largest migrant population in the world. The UK was ninth. 'Yet we're the ones who panic most about migrants. They learned their lessons, discovered humility, and tried hard to be nice. We just mocked them and told the world we were morally superior. And now we're in serious danger of forfeiting the right to do either.'[5]

It should be a matter of shame to its neighbours that they have not shown such generosity. From 2014 to July 2019, more than 1.4 million people applied for asylum in Germany, which is nearly half of all applications to the EU, and six times the number made to France. Britain has taken in virtually none of the migrants, building ever higher fences at French and Belgian ports. When a few dinghies of Iranians arrived on the beaches of Kent in December 2018, the then home secretary, Sajid Javid, let it be known that he was 'rushing back from his family holiday' on a safari in South Africa to declare it a 'major incident'. He redeployed two Border Force ships from the Mediterranean to protect the British shoreline. The British media portrayed it as decisive and tough, rather than the embarrassing piece of gesture politics that it was.

Prior to the 2015 crisis, the general approach of Merkel's government to immigration had fluctuated. The CDU had previously tried to stop asylum seekers from Albania, Montenegro and Kosovo coming in, arguing that these were now safe states of origin. These plans were blocked by her SPD coalition partners. Two months before the scenes in Munich, Merkel had done a car crash interview on television. The show was called *Living Well in Germany* and involved a studio audience of teenagers. The chancellor had done such a thing before and it started fine, then it all went wrong. One member of the panel was fourteen-year-old Reem Sahwil. A Palestinian, she and her family had fled her refugee camp in Baalbek, in Lebanon's Bekaa Valley, four years earlier. Speaking in a shaky voice and ever so politely in what commentators afterwards pointed out was her *perfektes Deutsch*, she said everyone in Germany had been very friendly to her. She wanted to go to university to fulfil her goals, but she was scared that they would end up being deported. 'It's not nice seeing how others can enjoy life, and I can't,' she said. 'I want to study like them.' Instead of empathizing with her, *Mutti* Merkel delivered a lecture. If Germany allowed her to stay, then thousands of Palestinian refugees, thousands of people from Africa would flood into Germany, she admonished her. 'We can't cope with that.'[6]

Reem dissolved into sobs. It went from bad to worse. 'Oh my God! But you were really first rate,' a shocked Merkel sought to console her. 'I don't think it's about being first rate,' the moderator responded, 'it's about her being in a stressful situation.' Merkel shot back: 'I know it's a stressful situation. That's why I want to give her a little pat.' She proceeded to go up to the girl and rub her arm. The word she used, *streicheln*, is usually used in German to refer to stroking a kitten or other small pet. The footage went viral, prompting a hugely popular Twitter hashtag #merkelstreichelt. The next day, reporters went to Sahwil's school in Rostock in northeast Germany. They found out that not only was she a refugee, but she had come on a medical visa. Born two months premature, she had not received enough oxygen at birth and had ended up with a severe walking impediment. That had worsened when she was involved in a car crash at the age of five. The daughter of a welder, she had arrived in Germany with little formal education and no knowledge of the language. She was now top of her class.

Merkel was denounced as both tactless and heartless. It seemed her attention had been elsewhere. She had just come back from a fractious EU summit on the European debt crisis. A bailout had been agreed for Greece, but, from its prime minister down, the country had felt humiliated by Merkel and by Germany. Her stock around the world had plunged.

Did this affect her next steps? One can only assume so. Another criticism was also gnawing away at her. The consensus among the German commentariat was that her leadership style was dull and risk-averse. So perhaps that is one reason why – a month later, when she saw the TV pictures of the barbed wire at the Hungarian border and images of the desperate refugees – she put caution aside and went with her heart. She didn't bother to coordinate her decision with her European partners or to seek parliamentary approval at home. She just allowed them in. And she took the moral high ground. 'If we have to apologize for showing a friendly face in an emergency, this is not my country anymore,'[7] she declared.

Did she do it mainly or completely out of compassion? Or were the motivations purely political – to keep the EU together (in the midst of the Greek ruptures), to get herself out of a scrape and/or to fill job vacancies for German companies? Was it, as some commentators were eccentrically suggesting, a new manifestation of German nationalism – the humanitarian superpower?

Two books published at the time about the crisis became bestsellers. *Die Getriebenen*, The Driven Ones, by Robin Alexander, a journalist for *Die Welt*, reads like a political whodunnit. It suggests that Merkel was toying with the idea of taking a hard line until she saw the opinion polls. At the height of the wave of global compassion, before other interests came back into play, 93 per cent of Germans were advocating a more liberal immigration policy. Konstantin Richter's book *The Chancellor, A Fiction* is more a psycho-drama looking at her character, which he sees as more complex than both detractors and supporters appreciate. Richter links the saga back to the Third Reich and to *Vergangenheitsaufarbeitung*. 'Germans have now embraced their role as moral leaders. In the post-war years, other nations envied us for our economic success. But we were not exactly considered warm-hearted or lovable. Now millions of people in the world dream of coming here, and we feel flattered.'[8] He is less than generous about Merkel. She had piggybacked off the Greens who had organized the welcome in Munich and in other cities. She loved being mobbed by the refugees, having selfies taken of her and them. 'This was collective narcissism. The refugees made us feel good about ourselves.'[9]

I was taken aback by the vehemence with which he summarizes it all. I hear a similar refrain from others now. A boss of a small company in Leipzig described the whole affair as Germany's *Schuldschein*, its debt certificate. 'We must save the world, shut energy plants, take people in.' At the University of Mainz, I hear a similar message from Andreas Roedder, professor of Modern History and author of a new book called *Wer hat Angst vor Deutschland?* (Who is Afraid of Germany?): 'This was the great moral reparation for Germany's war guilt.'

In a way it doesn't matter why Merkel did what she did – whether she was influenced by ethics, narrow political gain or the grand sweep of history. She did it, and it changed Germany.

It didn't take long for the mood to turn sour though, on both sides. The refugees had high hopes. Smugglers had told them they would prosper and find jobs quickly. Months after arriving, they found themselves languishing in temporary dormitories, homesick and struggling to acclimatize. Locals had assumed the refugees would express an enduring gratitude for the welcome they had received. It became fashionable in some circles to dismiss volunteering as liberal privilege. Volunteers were disparaged as *Gutmenschen* (do-gooders).

The more she was criticized, the more passionate Merkel became. She appeared on Germany's most watched Sunday-night talk show, Anne Will, to explain why she did what she did. 'I am fighting for this,' she said. She had no Plan B. 'It is my damned responsibility and duty to do everything I can to find a common European route out of this.' She could see public support and European cohesion disintegrating before her eyes. She could not afford to let that happen.

Even at this point, animosity towards migrants was still largely hidden. One incident brought the brewing resentment to the fore. The mass sexual assault of women by gangs in Cologne on New Year's Eve 2015 changed everything. In the first few days after, only sporadic reports appeared on the chaos that had taken place. In fact, according to a police press release on New Year's Day, the mood had been 'exuberant' and the festivities 'largely peaceful'.[10] That same day, however, posts about sexual assaults in and around the central railway station started appearing on Facebook groups. On 4 January, the chief of police changed tack. Crimes of 'a completely new dimension'[11] had taken place, announced Wolfgang Albers. The suspected perpetrators appeared to be Arab or North African. This became front page news around the world. *Bild* warned of 'sex mobs across Germany'.[12] Meanwhile, the number of reported crimes from that one evening kept rising. On the first day police received thirty complaints. In the end, a total of 492 women reported incidents of sexual assault, a category including sexual harassment, assault and rape.[13] Cologne had an immediate effect. The talk was of 'our women' and the need to defend them.

Why did the news come out only piecemeal? At a closed journalistic seminar in Berlin a few years later, one senior reporter admitted: 'We were too slow, too cautious, in the way we reported problems with refugees. Certainly, at first. That exacerbated the problem of mistrust.'[14] It did. This liberal cringe, as one of those present put it, was not unique to that incident or to Germany. It wasn't just the media. The police and the city authorities were also reluctant to make much of it. There were other examples around Europe at the time. One was in the UK in the northern town of Rotherham. It transpired that for years (from the late 1980s to early 2000s) groups of mainly Muslim men had been grooming for sex vulnerable girls who were predominantly white. Even when it was reported by *The Times*, the authorities failed to act. The official report was shocking, revealing that a mix of opacity, incompetence, sexism and reluctance to offend an ethnic minority had led to the problem being ignored for many years.

In the 1970s and 1980s, Germany had thought it had found the solution to any possible resurgence of the far right. Give the right a voice but make sure it stays on the respectable side of the line. The most important politician of that era and of that type was Franz Josef Strauss. As defence minister under Adenauer, he was a staunch supporter of NATO; he was also an advocate of detente with the USSR. As finance minister and later prime minister of Bavaria he championed the growth of German industry. He became such a powerful figure he was seen by Chancellor Kohl as a perennial threat. Strauss was right-wing, proudly so. He was a self-confessed patriot, praised the military's role in the Second World War (differentiating it from the Nazis and their specific units), and had no time for soul-searching about the past. At his funeral in 1988, one of the many statesmen attending was President P. W. Botha of apartheid South Africa. The Greens refused to pay tribute, and the SPD did so mutedly. Strauss and his CSU party played a vital function in representing a strong body of public opinion. It was not to everyone's tastes. But it was within the bounds of acceptability and it did not challenge the constitution. Beyond that lay danger. 'No legitimate party can be to the right of the CSU,'[15] Strauss warned.

For a good while he was right. Until the AfD came along.

The origins of the *Alternative für Deutschland* belonged to the rarefied world of academe. In September 2012, a group of economists, ex-politicians and other assorted hangers-on founded the Electoral Alternative, a group opposed to the Greek bailout. The Eurozone, they believed, was inherently unstable, requiring weak and workshy countries in the south to conform to structures to which they were ill-suited, while Germany and other 'responsible' and 'hardworking' nations were forced to pick up the pieces. Some of the early members toyed with the idea of restoring the beloved Deutschmark. Its first public figure was Bernd Lucke, an economist at the University of Hamburg. Their discussions barely made it into the political mainstream. They were dismissed as eccentric, cranks.

Six months later they changed their name and set up as a fully fledged party. Lucke was joined by Frauke Petry, a businesswoman from Dresden and chemist by training. Their Eurosceptic pitch began to garner publicity and popularity, at least among a niche. Its first breakthrough came in the 2014 European elections, the same elections that saw Nigel Farage's UK Independence Party take the highest share of votes in Britain, shocking the establishment. Other right-wing groups did well in other countries. Within months, the AfD had easily crossed the 5 per cent threshold, entering parliaments in the three Eastern states of Saxony, Thuringia and Brandenburg. No sooner had they arrived, however, than they became wracked with division, with the various leaders forming splinter groups.

The refugee crisis saved the party from oblivion and made it what it is today. It curated a narrative that the concerns of 'hard-working white folk' were not being listened to, that the left-liberal establishment was involved in a giant cover-up, and the mainstream media was not to be trusted. It was not operating in isolation. Such views were being legitimized by Donald Trump; they were being harnessed by advocates of Brexit. While in other European countries populist parties such as the Front National in France and Geert Wilders's PVV in the Netherlands gained strength in the 2000s and early 2010s, Germany believed that, because of everything that had been learnt from the war, its people were immune from the simplistic narratives of the extremes.

However, within months of the migrants arriving, the AfD broke through in regional elections, gaining a 15 per cent share in wealthy Baden-Württemberg and 12 per cent in Rhineland-Palatinate – both states in the West. In Saxony-Anhalt in the East, it secured a staggering quarter of the total vote, coming second. It suddenly became part of the political furniture.

That was just the start. The September 2017 general election produced a political earthquake. Merkel's CDU won, just. Her fourth successive victory should have dominated the headlines. It didn't. Everything was overshadowed by the stunning success of the AfD. It garnered 12 per cent of the vote nationally, giving it ninety-four members of parliament, more than the Greens or FDP. When Merkel was forced to form another *GroKo*, Grand Coalition, with the reluctant SPD, the AfD became the biggest party of opposition. This was an extraordinary moment, one that most Germans thought would not, could not, ever happen. It presented an immediate threat to the political system and to the country's sense of self-belief.

The AfD's popularity has not waned. People have projected whatever they wanted onto this party of protest. It became a *Sammelbecken*, or collecting bowl, for a range of grievances, part economic but much more about identity. It is one thing to be popular in the East, but how to explain its strong performance in the West too? The AfD has hoovered voters from all parties

– from the CDU, SPD, Die Linke, even the Greens. It became the natural port of call for those who had given up going to the ballot box. The generalized picture of the AfD voter – the elderly, left-behinds in small towns in eastern Germany – tells only part of the story. Some of its most striking recent successes have come in the twenty-five to thirty-five age bracket. Many of these younger generation supporters in the East have comparatively well-paid jobs in industry or secure positions as university lecturers. It is as if they are extracting delayed revenge, living through the traumas of their parents during the upheavals of the early 1990s (although they were not around to experience them). Their parents may have lost their jobs or sense of place during the upheavals of the 1990s. They are nostalgic for the GDR even if they have little memory of it. They are conservative and risk-averse, seeing globalization as adding to their pressures.

The AfD has found itself in a virtuous circle. The more seats it wins in parliament, the more state funding it is entitled to, the more TV airtime it gets, the more votes it acquires. In October 2017, viewers were welcomed to the world of Alexander Gauland and Alice Weidel, an odd couple who had just taken over as joint leaders of the party. She was an unlikely choice by a party that abhors 'alternative lifestyles'. A devotee of Hayek, she has worked around the world for the Bank of China and speaks fluent Mandarin. She shares the mantle with Steve Bannon, Donald Trump's one-time chief strategist, for being possibly the most right-wing ex-Goldman Sachs banker on the planet. More intriguingly, she lives in Switzerland, where she raises two boys with her lesbian partner, a thirty-six-year-old Sri Lankan-born Swiss film-maker. What binds her to a party of older white males who defend traditional family values is their shared dislike of foreigners – except for her partner and the Syrian refugee who, according to a report in *Die Zeit*, they employed illegally as a housekeeper. Gauland, a seventy-something former journalist, is an avowed Anglophile who believes Margaret Thatcher, of all people, destroyed good old-fashioned British values by ushering in multiculturalism and globalization. In summer 2018, in a speech to his party's youth wing, he played down the importance of Hitler's crimes. 'We have a glorious history and that, dear friends, lasted longer than those damn 12 years,' he declared, before describing Nazi rule as 'mere bird shit in 1000 years of successful German history'.[16]

Despite the AfD's far right views, successive attempts to have the party banned or its activities restricted have failed in the courts. In February 2019, a regional court rejected an attempt by the domestic intelligence agency, the BfV, to classify the party as a 'case to investigate'. The AfD has sought to ensure that it stays just on the correct side of the line, in terms of a precise interpretation of the law. It is close to but claims not to be formally associated with right-wing street organizations. The most important of these is Pegida (Patriotic Europeans Against the Islamisation of the Occident). This was formed by Lutz Bachmann, a PR executive who invited residents of Dresden to join him on an 'evening stroll'. Each Monday they gathered at the city's landmarks, outside the restored Frauenkirche or the nearby Altmarkt. Within weeks they were starting to attract crowds of tens of thousands. By late 2015, Pegida was attracting crowds of 25,000 in Leipzig and Dresden. 'Islam doesn't belong in Germany,'[17] was one of their favourite chants. Or 'Down with asylum tourists'.[18] Sometimes they shouted: 'Refugees should be left to drown.'[19] Counterdemonstrations took place, with the two groups needing to be separated by police, leading to skirmishes. Some citizens showed their disapproval more quietly. The head of Dresden's opera house and concert hall, the Semperoper, switched off the opera house's lights in protest whenever the Pegida marchers passed by. Street clashes across Eastern towns (and sometimes in the West too) became more frequent. Far right groups encouraged citizens to report the whereabouts of new migrant centres in their towns, under their 'no refugee camps in my backyard' campaign. Google was forced to delete from its My Maps service a map, put together by one of these groups, which used red flags to identify the precise locations of asylum centres. This was seen as an open invitation to attack them.

Local police forces, particularly in the East, initially seemed reluctant to deal with the intimidation. Newspapers speculated whether the AfD had infiltrated police ranks. In some cases, commanders were brought in from other regions to shake things up. The most recent domestic intelligence report identifies 24,000 people in Germany as being right-wing extremists, half of whom are believed to be willing to use force. A TV documentary carried out a poll, finding that 50 per cent of city government officials get hate mail or other threats. Some 8 per cent of municipalities have reported assaults on local officials.[20]

The threats and violence began within a month of the migrant influx. Henriette Reker was out campaigning in Cologne in the city's mayoral elections when she was stabbed in the neck. She was deputy mayor, aligned to the SPD but independent. Within her portfolio, she was in charge of refugee housing in the city. She had very publicly taken a strong pro-immigration stance. The assailant was an unemployed house painter with right-wing connections, who shouted about an 'influx of refugees' as he attacked her. In a moving show of solidarity, Reker was elected mayor the following day, with support from all the mainstream parties – even though she had been put in an induced coma.

She recovered to take over a month later. The assailant was given fourteen years in prison. Reker testified at the trial that she was still having nightmares.

The attacks were not confined to targets on the centre-left. Two years later, Andreas Hollstein, the mayor of Altena from the conservative CDU party, was stabbed in the neck in a kebab shop. His town in North Rhine-Westphalia was well known for having accepted more than its assigned quota of migrants. Hollstein survived thanks to the quick reactions of the two employees. He has since gone back to work and refused police protection. 'There is no point in a local politician who is no longer accessible to the citizens he or she represents,'[21] he said. Politicians in small towns and rural areas are seen as particularly vulnerable. A terrible new line was crossed in June 2019. Walter Lübcke, a civil servant in the state of Hesse, was shot in the head and killed on the front porch of his home in a village near Kassel. He too had been vocal in defending immigration, at one point telling an audience that people were free to leave Germany if they didn't want to help integrate refugees. The killing shocked the nation. A rally was held in Kassel under the banner 'together we are strong'. Parliament held a special session to discuss right-wing violence, noting that it was now at least as much of a threat as militant Islamic terrorism. Thomas Haldenwang, head of domestic intelligence, apportioned much of the blame to online speech. 'A person who defends the building of refugee camps is massively attacked in social media, covered in hate posts and finally executed in his garden,'[22] he said.

The authorities' increased vigilance against hate crimes from right-wing extremists did not stop the threats and attacks. Reker, Cologne's mayor, let it be known that, even after Lübcke's murder, she was getting more death threats than ever. The AfD was careful to distance itself, accusing mainstream politics and the media of exploiting such incidents to denigrate it – and of causing the problems in the first place. 'If there had been no illegal opening of borders through Chancellor Angela Merkel,' a party press release noted, 'then Walter Lübcke would still be alive.'[23] The killing focused minds on the right of the CDU. Some senior politicians, including those vying for the chancellor's mantle, had in previous months been flirting with populist language to describe the refugee problem. They quickly swung back. One of those was Annegret Kramp-Karrenbauer, who in an effort to distance herself from Merkel had projected herself as the tough-talking, anti-political-correctness candidate. She now made clear that any talk of electoral deals in the regions with the AfD was impossible and that any politician who might even consider going into a coalition with that party 'should close his eyes and think about Walter Lübcke'.[24]

The AfD has been adept at using inflammatory language, wrapped in the cloak of victimhood. When police in North Rhine-Westphalia tweeted New Year's greetings in Arabic (a year after the Cologne assaults), one of its senior figures, Beatrix von Storch, responded: 'What the hell is wrong with this country? Are we trying to appease the barbaric Muslim rapist hordes of men?'[25] The AfD dominates YouTube (where they have more subscribers than all the other parties combined) and Facebook. 'From the beginning we concentrated on Facebook,' a party spokesman, Christian Lüth, was quoted as saying in an analysis conducted by the Technical University of Munich. 'It provides quicker, more direct and more cost-effective access to voters.'[26] They operate mainly in their own curated world. They claim to have opened an 'opinion corridor' in which issues around identity, culture and immigration can be discussed without ritual denunciation from the 'woke brigade'. They speak of opinion dictatorship. Their mantra is that 'real people' are not represented in mainstream media. Broadcasters and news-papers are controlled by dark forces in hock to the liberal elite.

One quiet Sunday evening in Leipzig I was walking past the headquarters of MDR, Central German Broadcasting, the regional broadcaster for the states of Saxony, Saxony-Anhalt and Thuringia. I was with a local politician, one who didn't directly identify with the AfD, but shared some of their views. '*Lügen-presse*', she shouted as we passed. The term 'lying press' was coined in 1914 to dismiss enemy propaganda. The Nazis used it to accuse Jews, communists and other cosmopolitan foreign forces of spreading false information. It was revived by Pegida in 2016. I asked her what her problem was with MDR. They never told the truth about 'our women' being raped and assaulted, she asserted. They put out 'fake news' all the time (the Germans don't have their own term for it so use the English one). Which specific stories had been hushed up and not reported? Surely it was hard in the age of citizen journalism to keep a crime com-pletely under wraps? She simply shrugged her shoulders at each of my gentle prods and said, without elaboration, 'It happens all the time.'

The Trump effect has boosted the self-belief of Germany's alt-right. They can see that, if views such as his can prevail in 'the land of the free', then why not at home? He has legitimized speech among some Germans that only a few years earlier would have been seen as entirely unacceptable. At the same time his success (and the success of people like Viktor Orbán in Hungary and Matteo Salvini in Italy) has focused the minds of mainstream politicians and media bosses. One of the most shocking of many incidents that really resonated in Germany was Trump's response to the violence in Charlottesville in 2017. When Trump declined in a press conference to distance himself from white supremacists who had been chanting 'Jews will not

replace us', the officially impartial German public media struggled to conceal its shock. 'There is a new reason to be worried
about the condition of the US', declared Claus Kleber, one of the
presenters of ZDF's main news bulletin *Heute Journal*, somewhat portentously. Eight years after the election of the first black
president, 'we thought America had overcome its original sin
of slavery and racism. Is this a relapse?'[27]

As in other countries, business leaders like to keep their
heads down. One of a small number prepared to speak out is
Joe Kaeser, CEO of Siemens. When the AfD's Weidel spoke
derogatorily of German Muslim women as 'headscarf girls',
he responded: 'We'd rather have headscarf girls than a League
of German Girls'[28] – a reference to the Nazis' youth group for
young women. 'With her nationalism, Frau Weidel is damaging
the reputation of our country in the world, which is the main
source of German prosperity.' He added: 'Maybe it's time to
once again nip things in the bud.' Kaeser – whose uncle refused
to join the Hitler Youth, was sent to Dachau and later killed in
Mauthusen concentration camp in Austria – has encouraged the
heads of other big companies listed on the DAX stock exchange
to push harder against right-wing populism, but has so far found
few supporters. In his Berlin office I asked him why he so often
stuck his neck above the parapet. He was disarmingly frank and
pragmatic. 'For all companies, there is often a conflict between
values and interests. In this case, this was a unique situation in
which both correlated. Before you had to consider customers,
employees and shareholders. Now there is a fourth consideration: society.'

One of the largest industrial companies in the world, one of
Germany's flag carriers, with a market capitalization of €100 billion and a presence in every continent, Siemens might think of
playing it safe. They don't. Kaeser and his UK country manager

Jürgen Maier (half Austrian, half Yorkshire) were initially outspoken in their criticism of Brexit. It might be easier for them, as they are mainly a business to business operation. They are less exposed than car makers, for example, to losing customers who disagree with them. Siemens is no angel, as I note later when looking at its environmental record. No multinational is. But, having had a front-row seat in watching the cowardice of most British firms and their response to Brexit, I find it welcoming that, on some issues at least, Siemens has a corporate culture that isn't scared to say what it thinks. Kaeser likes to tweet. In July 2019, he responded to Trump's 'send them home' missive about 'the Squad', the group of outspoken left-wing congresswomen who had taken Washington by storm. 'I find it depressing that the most important political office in the world is turning into the face of racism and exclusion,'[29] Kaeser wrote. His message was hugely popular.

Most of Germany's immigration travails are common across the West – the murder or attempted murder of politicians (think Jo Cox in Yorkshire, Gabby Giffords in Arizona), the schism within the populace between two self-affirming opinion bubbles, corporate cowardice in failing to speak out, and the role of social media in stoking extremism. It is particularly sensitive, though, for Germans in this highly volatile environment to navigate the boundaries between what is illegal and what is distasteful and unpleasant, but legal. Germans acknowledge the vital right of freedom of expression, and do their best to encourage it, even when holding their nose.

Roland Tichy is a right-wing talk show host who makes fun of the liberal elites, and why they can't understand how anyone can be proud of Germany. His high-profile career included a stint as editor of the weekly finance magazine *Wirtschaftswoche* and advising governments and companies such as Daimler.

He is a favourite of think tanks such as the Hayek Foundation and Mont Pelerin, and his weekly *Tichy Talk* TV programme online features like-minded commentators. Since its launch in 2004, the weekly magazine *Cicero* has gained a circulation of just under 100,000 attracted by its iconoclastic, mainly conservative commentaries. One of its favourite interviewees is Thilo Sarrazin. Everyone has a view about Sarrazin. Think of a German cross between Steve Bannon and Jordan Peterson. His emergence as conservative polemicist-in-chief is an unlikely progression for a stalwart of the establishment. Sarrazin was a civil servant in a number of ministries and German railways, before becoming Berlin's finance senator for seven years. He had to resign over allegations of fraud involving a payment to a golf club. He became briefly an executive at the Bundesbank. He was a member of the Social Democrats. His first big book, *Germany Abolished Itself*, became a sensation, ferociously dividing opinion. It gave a now-familiar denunciation of Islam and multiculturalism, but it was published in 2010, well before the rise of the AfD, or the emergence of Trump and the global alt-right. The book included a discussion about intelligence in which he wrote: 'All Jews have a particular gene.' He was thrown out of the Bundesbank. An embarrassed SPD tried repeatedly to expel him but hasn't managed to, apparently because of its arcane rules. His second book, *Hostile Takeover: How Islam Impairs Progress and Threatens Society*, followed a similar argument on genetics.

Sarrazin is part of a European and indeed global movement that predated the refugee crisis. One of the most influential books of its type was published in 2012. *The Great Replacement*, by the French author Renaud Camus, argues that globalization and the free flow of people has imperilled white indigenous Europeans. Camus accuses governments of 'genocide by substitution'.

This nativist conspiracy theory has since become mainstream in right-wing circles. In September 2019, Hungary's Viktor Orbán hosted a 'demography summit' in Budapest, attended by among others the Czech prime minister, Serbian president and the former prime minister of Australia Tony Abbott.

Unlike other leaders, Merkel has been desperate to establish a cordon sanitaire between the political mainstream and the fringe. Two episodes in early 2020, one in her own country and one in the UK, illustrate how vital but also how difficult her stance is.

In the UK, Boris Johnson's adviser-in-chief, Dominic Cummings, wrote in one of his many colourful blog posts which regularly denounce the establishment 'blob' – civil servants, the BBC and others – that he was looking for 'weirdos and misfits' to join the government, preferably if they were clever data scientists. One such person was Andrew Sabisky. In one post from 2014, Sabisky had suggested that politicians should pay attention to 'very real racial differences in intelligence'[30] when designing the immigration system. Another from that year suggested black people on average have lower IQs than white people. In another piece of writing, he argued that welfare claimants should be encouraged to have fewer children than people in work with more 'pro-social personalities'. Downing Street doggedly defended the appointment. He was forced to step down, but this was seen by those around Johnson, and many in the media, as just another political spat. Imagine in Germany if anyone close to views such as those had been allowed anywhere near power? There would have been a furore, at home and around the world, not least among Brits who love to demonize the country.

Around the same time, a row in the Eastern state of Thuringia led to an extraordinary national controversy and anxious discussion about the health of German politics. The details are complex and somewhat arcane, so to summarize: the AfD had a few months earlier secured electoral success in three regional elections. Thuringia had been run by Die Linke, the left-wing party, in a coalition with the SPD and Greens. The electoral upshot made such a repeat impossible. The AfD there was in the hands of a particularly extreme figure, Björn Höcke, who famously walked out of a television interview when invited to compare his views with those of the Nazis. Höcke and his colleagues in parliament came up with a ruse, pushing through the appointment of a centrist liberal candidate, even though he had only 5 per cent of the vote and would be dependent on them. This would give them power via a proxy. The local branch of Merkel's CDU went along with the AfD in approving this puppet candidate, to the chancellor's fury. Her party chief, Kramp-Karrenbauer, had rushed to Thuringia to urge the local party chief to change his mind. He sent her packing, undermining her in public. Protests took place around the country, as voters feared that the goings-on in Thuringia were the thin end of the wedge.

Merkel, who was on an official visit to South Africa, appeared before the cameras with a statement that was piercing in its simplicity. The decision in Thuringia, she said, was 'unforgivable'. Another way of translating the word is unconscionable. She was appealing to Germans' conscience. The hapless Kramp-Karrenbauer was forced to announce that she would quit, throwing Merkel's succession as chancellor back into the open. Various local party chiefs also stood down. With one simple word Merkel pulled the emergency brake. In doing so, she made clear that she would do anything to try to preserve the moderate political consensus. She caused short-term mayhem, but she concluded she had no other choice.

*

Merkel's decision to open the borders has changed Germany forever. On that everyone can agree.

Even though she has consistently defended her policy, she did eventually change tack, striking a deal with Turkey in March 2016 which, although complicated and fragile, allowed Turkey to take back any illegal immigrant from Greece who did not claim asylum or whose asylum claim was rejected. In return, the EU would accept a number of Syrian refugees, equivalent to the number returned. Turks would be granted visa-free travel to the Schengen area and a speeding-up of accession negotiations, plus a €6 billion grant to help with the refugees. That arrangement has been repeatedly rolled over. Turkey's authoritarian leader Recep Tayyip Erdoğan knows that he has the whip hand. Germany and Europe would struggle to cope again if they hadn't transferred their problems offshore. Meanwhile, the previously hapless Frontex border guard has been beefed up, from a mere 1,300 officers seconded from member countries to a standing corps of 10,000. For the first time the EU will be able to dispatch armed guards in EU uniforms to patrol its fringes. One area that appears not to have been tackled is the pace and efficiency of removing those who have failed their final leave to stay in the country.

When one considers multi-ethnic societies, one immediately thinks of the United States. Other countries with a long history of empire, such as France (West Africa and the Maghreb) and Britain (the Indian subcontinent, East Africa and the Caribbean), have also developed a strong multi-ethnic identity. Germany doesn't have that image. But the facts tell a different story, and it was happening well before the 2015 crisis. Now, some twenty million Germans, or a quarter of the population, have a migrant background of one sort or another. Only 15 per cent of them came as asylum seekers, the rest as regular migrants. Roughly two thirds of migration into Germany comes from within the EU. Unlike Brexit Britain, Germany's population has not had a particular problem with Eastern Europeans – as long as they paid their way. The relationship with ethnic Turks has been the most difficult. But who has the right to judge? Think France and Algeria; think of Britain's Windrush scandal.

I am sitting with Cihan Sugur in the canteen of Porsche's headquarters in Zuffenhausen, an affluent suburb in the north of Stuttgart. He is on the company's fast track, a poster boy for assimilation, success and harmony. He is a corporate influencer, working in the central IT team. He has already worked for IBM, Deutsche Bahn and Olympus – and he is only twenty-nine. His grandfather was a coal miner from Turkey, one of the original *Gastarbeiter* in the 1950s. Part of his family hails from Georgia. Sugur became politically active at a young age. As a student he wrote an open letter to politicians and TV talk shows to complain about the government's refusal to give Turkish-Germans (unlike nationals of some other countries) dual citizenship. He was invited onto a youth programme on ZDF. He did what few young people from ethnic minorities do and joined the party of the centre-right. He was invited by the CDU's think tank, the Konrad Adenauer Foundation, on a delegation to Israel. So far, so uplifting. It was when he founded the Muslim council of the CDU that he detected a change of mood. Some thirty of the party's approximately one thousand Muslim members joined. He invited his local party group to celebrate Iftar, the feast that marks the end of the fasting season of Ramadan. People started muttering, 'They are taking over the party.' We all know who they meant by 'they'.

Undeterred, Sugur is amassing accolades. He is a global shaper for the World Economic Forum, setting up a Stuttgart hub. He is on the artificial intelligence working group of the

Baden-Württemberg state Economics Council. He also works for a foundation that mentors local migrants. Sugur is a classic third-generation immigrant, who is fully integrated and fully at home in Stuttgart (he couldn't imagine another place to live). Yet he, like others, is questioning just how much he is really wanted. 'The better the integration, the more the conflict,' he notes drily to me. 'When you get to the core of power structures, then you are a threat.' He believes he will never be *biodeutsch*, biologically German – the term increasingly used by AfD adherents to signify true Germans. Instead, like the football star Mesut Özil and more than a million others, he will always be a 'plastic German', another right-wing term that denotes something manufactured, fake. In 2018, a row developed involving Özil, the Germany and Arsenal midfielder. Özil, German-born of Turkish heritage, was lambasted in the media for appearing in photographs alongside President Erdoğan. This was at a time when his form for club and country was poor. 'I am a German when we win, but I am an immigrant when we lose,'[31] he tweeted as he announced his retirement from the national team. In a deliberate act of defiance to his detractors, Özil then asked Erdoğan to be best man at his wedding a year later in a luxury hotel on the shores of the Bosphorus.

Immigration policy in Germany is based on an assumption, even requirement, to integrate. Language is seen as a crucial prerequisite for assimilation. Lessons are offered as a matter of course. High school teachers give up their Saturday mornings to teach and to test. Germans pride themselves on their mastery of English and other languages, but that talent (and dogged determination) masks the importance they attach to their mother tongue, as confirmation of identity. A gentle backlash (if that isn't an oxymoron) is taking place against what is seen as an encroachment of English. Recently a cross-party group of MEPs wrote to Merkel asking her to insist that German be granted parity of status with English and French in the various EU institutions. One of those vying for the chancellor's throne, the health minister, Jens Spahn, railed against the almost ubiquitous use of English in Berlin's restaurants: 'It drives me up the wall the way waiters in Berlin restaurants only speak English. Co-existence can only work in Germany if we all speak German.'[32]

Politicians such as these are trying, if somewhat clunkily at times, to reconcile a more confident sense of national pride with atonement for the past and vigilance about the future. They derive certain facets from earlier periods of German history. The first is *Kulturnation*, a theory that goes back to the seventeenth-century rational philosopher Gottfried Leibniz, who argued that a people defines itself through culture rather than borders or other trappings of state. Language, he stated, 'unifies people in a strong but invisible way'.[33] Writers and philosophers such as Friedrich Schiller developed the theme, defining a concept of Germanness – still then a collection of city states and princedoms – as united in language and culture. In 2015, a former speaker of parliament and prominent East German SPD politician, Wolfgang Thierse, described *Kulturnation* as 'a beautiful great word'[34] that had been besmirched by the Nazis.

More problematic is the concept of *Leitkultur*. The idea of a 'leading culture' is that anyone who wants to live in Germany should accept that German values and culture take precedence. This does not preclude multiple identities, but one comes first. In a way, it is not dissimilar to swearing allegiance in the US. In 2017, the then interior minister Thomas de Maizière presented a controversial ten-point plan on *Leitkultur*. This included accepting without caveat Germany's historical culpability, its special relationship to Israel and the importance of European unity, alongside cultural diversity, human rights and tolerance. So far, so virtuous. It becomes more complicated when it is wrapped in what conservatives have called a Christian-Occidental system of values. Some Germans and Austrians have cited that value system as reason enough to hold back on Turkish membership of the EU – the 'they are not like us' argument.

When I was working for the first time as a reporter in Germany in the mid-1980s, on the rare occasions when the news was quiet, I had an easy fallback. I would scour the local press for anything on neo-Nazis. You could always find something; a gang of hoodlums in Bochum or Bielefeld chanting Hitler songs or getting into a scrap with anti-Nazis. My paper would love it. If it was a slow news day back home, it might even appear on the front page. If English or Dutch or Italian football gangs got up to the same thing, the story might be noted somewhere, in brief, but it would not gain the same traction. From time to time a splinter far right party, such as the Republikaner or National Democratic Party (NPD), would get someone elected to a town council. At their peak, these groups might even get over the 5 per cent hurdle and gain representation in a regional parliament. But they disappeared as quickly as they arrived.

This crowing from afar against the Germans has not gone away. In late 2019, the Chinese dissident artist Ai Weiwei announced that he was leaving Berlin for Cambridge. He cited a variety of reasons. One of them was rudeness. Taxi drivers were particularly abrupt. In that, he is not wrong. Berliners pride themselves on their abruptness, often comparing themselves to New Yorkers. It isn't pleasant being barked at by waiters, shop assistants or police officers. But if it is any consolation to him or anyone else, they do it to everyone. But Ai Weiwei's criticisms were deeper than that. Germany, he said, did not criticize China for its actions in Hong Kong for fear of jeopardizing trade. Well, actually it did, at least as much as other Western countries. Then he went for the they-are-all-fascists-at-heart trope. 'Germany is a very precise society. Its people love the comfort of being oppressed. In China, too, you see that. Once you're used to it, it can be very enjoyable. And you can see the efficiency, the show, the sense of their power being extended through the connected-mind condition.' He added: 'They have a different kind of suit: it doesn't look like what they wore in the 1930s, but it still has the same kind of function. They identify with the cult of that authoritarian mindset.' Asked specifically if he was comparing today's Germany with the Nazi era, he said: 'Fascism is to think one ideology is higher than others and to try to purify that ideology by dismissing other types of thinking. That's Nazism. And that Nazism perfectly exists in German daily life today.'[35]

That interview, published in the *Guardian* newspaper, led to a renewed bout of anxiety. But it was also tinged with hurt. Germany had rolled out the red carpet for the artist. He was perfectly within his rights to move somewhere else, but why did he feel impelled to make these sweeping denunciations? It is not as if the Germans don't ask themselves these questions, almost on a daily basis. They know all too well that the threat of extremism is real. The turbulence of the last five years has come as a shock to many in Germany, forcing them to realize that a country they had hoped desperately was immune from a resurgence in racial, religious and ethnic hatred was just as susceptible as anywhere else. What has the unremitting soul-searching of the past twenty to thirty years achieved? Germans ask themselves incessantly: has it all been a waste of effort?

The biggest of all these anxieties revolves around the country's relationship to its Jewish population. In October 2019, a gunman tried to force his way into a synagogue in Halle, a city near Leipzig. He was hoping to open fire on as many Jews as he could find. The congregation had been celebrating Yom Kippur, the Day of Atonement, the holiest day in the Jewish calendar. He was unable to get through the reinforced door. Out of frustration he then killed a bystander walking past and a man in a kebab shop. Several more were injured. The terrorist, a far right sympathizer, filmed his rampage and uploaded the live feed to a video-game streaming platform.

Many Germans were proud of the fact that their country was beginning to be embraced again by the world's Jewry. For several decades theirs was the fastest-growing Jewish population in Western Europe, with Berlin back as an important centre. The recent influx has come mainly from Israel, the republics of the former USSR and other countries where Jews have felt under threat. The numbers are still small, at just over 100,000. In the past few years, since the rise of nationalist-populism in the US and Europe, incidents of anti-Semitic harassment, verbal abuse and even physical attacks have increased across Germany. Interior Ministry figures report that such crimes rose by 20 per cent in 2018, blaming nine out of ten cases on the extreme right. That the figures are not as high as, say, in France, provides cold comfort.

In 2018, the government created a new position of commissioner on anti-Semitism. It was a good move but also sad that it was necessary. In May the following year, in one of his first major public statements, Commissioner Felix Klein said: 'I cannot advise Jews to wear the *kippah* everywhere all the time in Germany.'[36] He explained that he had changed his mind on the level of danger, because of a 'mounting disinhibition and spreading of views which poses a fatal breeding ground for anti-Semitism'.[37] He called on law enforcement to be more alert. Klein thought he was being responsible. Instead, he was accused of pandering to the extremes and victim-shaming, neither of which he was intending to do. His remarks produced shock at home and abroad. Marches were called to protest against anti-Semitism. The tabloid *Bild* issued cut-out-and-keep skull caps to wear for the occasion. Along with other publications, the *New York Times* went into overdrive. Germany was back to its worst, it declared. Jews were not safe.

In December 2019, Merkel visited Auschwitz on the eve of the seventy-fifth anniversary of its liberation. Accompanied by the president of Germany's Central Council of Jews, she walked through the gates with the insignia *Arbeit macht frei* (work sets you free) before standing for a minute's silence. Remembering the crimes 'is a responsibility which never ends. It belongs inseparably to our country,' she said. 'To be aware of this responsibility is part of our national identity, our self-understanding as an enlightened and free society.'[38]

Two months later, one of the worst attacks yet took place, with migrants, particularly Muslims, the target. Nine people were killed when a forty-three-year-old man opened fire in two shisha bars in the town of Hanau, just outside Frankfurt. The man was found to have had a long-standing past of posting 'deeply racist' content online. The response to the terrorist outrage in Hanau has been one of grief coupled with exasperation. The *Frankfurter Allgemeine* reflected a widely held view when it said: 'The organs of the state . . . must now . . . arm themselves to the teeth because migrants and other foreigners living in the country are surrounded by mortal enemies.'[39] He may have been a lone wolf, but politicians and media pointed to an atmosphere of intolerance and urged the police and security forces to recalibrate their priorities more towards right-wing extremism. Merkel, even in her twilight months in charge, still had an ability to capture the mood. After the Hanau atrocity, she declared: racism is a poison. She knew that words would not suffice. The security forces were instructed to overhaul their methods. 'The security threat from right-wing extremism, anti-Semitism and racism is very high,' Interior Minister Horst Seehofer declared, after agreeing with regional leaders to increase security in a bid to prevent copycat attacks. Right-wing extremism, he said, posed 'the biggest security threat facing Germany'.[40]

The surge of populist-nationalists around the world, and the AfD on their own doorstep, has made Germans question the durability of democracy, particularly their own. Panel shows discuss whether the 1930s might be on the way back. One strain of intellectual thought has become increasingly common again: the *Sonderweg*, the special path. German friends ask whether their country has a particular predisposition to an ugly and dangerous politics they had hoped had been banished for good. That vigilance is vital, but there is no evidence to support any claim that these trends are any more pronounced in Germany. The surge of bigotry of the past few years is global. Even the supposed paragons of liberal democracy, the Nordic countries, have had their own versions. The historical context is what sets Germany apart. And that very context is what gives rise to hope that, unlike other liberal democracies that have chased a populist agenda, it will withstand the era of intolerance.

4

No Longer a Child

Foreign policy in an age of populism

The Berlin political bubble is a home for wonks. They all know each other and their friends inside Washington's Beltway or in the Westminster Village, and in foreign policy, they all discuss the same thing – when will Germany start to behave like a major power? Political scientists have called Germany a 'reluctant hegemon' and a 'new civilian power'.[1] Or as Henry Kissinger put it: 'Germany is too large for Europe and too small for the world.'[2]

Since the end of the war, Germans have always had someone else to fall back on. They subcontracted defence and security to others – the Americans, NATO and latterly the EU. They played a loyal backup part, passing on intelligence, assisting in humanitarian missions and siding with allies at crucial votes. But they have not had to get their hands dirty. Germany was the protected child.

Reunification changed expectations. Allied forces in the West began slowly to withdraw (the last British contingent left only in

2019); the Russians left almost immediately. The enlarged Germany acquired a new status, and along with that came increased demands. The first military intervention of the post-Cold War era was Operation Desert Storm, the American-led 'coalition of the willing' that drove Saddam Hussein out of Kuwait in 1990. Some thirty-five countries clubbed together – a display of unity that his son George W. Bush failed to achieve a decade later. The German chancellor at the time, Helmut Kohl, needed no persuading. He committed hardware and billions of dollars of financial support. The constitution (or politicians' interpretation of it) had not changed. Germany was precluded from direct military action.

In 1992, months after the dissolution of the Soviet Union and the final collapse of European communism, a book that encapsulated the era – and Germany's dilemma – Francis Fukuyama's *The End of History and the Last Man*, proclaimed the ascendancy of liberal democracy. Borrowing from Hegel and Marx, he argued that mankind had achieved a new level of progress. Or to put it another way: the West had won. Bill Clinton and Tony Blair developed the notion into a more assertive foreign policy: liberal interventionism. The West had a duty to stop oppression wherever it found it, by force if necessary, and to implant the values of human rights and democracy.

Kosovo could not have come at a more difficult time for Germany. After sixteen years at the helm, Kohl had been forced out. The SPD had regained power with a fresh face in charge. Gerhard Schröder had been in the Bundestag for only a few years and had no foreign-policy background. In October 1998, within weeks of taking office, he was presented with a desperately difficult challenge. Public opinion had been horrified by the Serbs' ethnic cleansing across the Balkans. The refusal to act during Serbia's invasion of Bosnia, including the massacre at Srebrenica, and also the genocide in Rwanda – even though French and Belgian troops were stationed in large numbers on the ground – had shamed public opinion.

The pressure from Clinton and Blair was strong. To their surprise, Schröder and his ministers agreed readily. Germany sent forces into combat for the first time since the Second World War – and without a UN resolution. NATO launched 38,000 combat missions (including the supposedly mistaken bombing of the Chinese Embassy in Belgrade). Taking part were fourteen German Tornado fighter jets. In his memoirs, published in 2006, Schröder wrote: 'Perhaps it was a trick of history that of all things a Red-Green coalition had to take over political power in order for Germany to live up to its responsibilities.'[3] Perhaps it was another case of 'Nixon in China'? If it took a Republican in America to normalize relations with Chairman Mao, perhaps it needed the two parties synonymous with anti-militarism in Germany to commit forces into front-line action. In 1994, the principle of armed intervention had been tested by the Constitutional Court. It decreed that Germany was able to take part in multilateral missions, but only on securing parliamentary support. The key figure in delivering that approval was the coalition's foreign minister. Joschka Fischer had to make the highest possible moral argument: 'No more Auschwitz. No more genocide. No more fascism. All that goes together for me,'[4] he declared in an emotional statement to the Bundestag. And this was the Greens, the political wing of the peace movement. Once Slobodan Milošević withdrew his troops in June 1999, a German general was chosen to lead NATO's peacekeeping troops, KFOR. Germany's involvement in the campaign was praised by its allies. This was, they concluded, the start of a new phase in its foreign and security policy.

Two years later Schröder was faced with an equally acute

dilemma. He expressed his 'unlimited solidarity'[5] with George W. Bush after the terrorist attacks of 9/11. The US had invoked Article 5 of NATO's founding treaty – an attack on one is an attack on all. The chancellor was determined that Germany should be demonstrative in its support, but he knew the parliamentary arithmetic was difficult. In October 2001, he decided to link the decision to back the American-led invasion of Afghanistan with a vote of confidence in his government. It was a risky strategy, but he got it through. In the two decades of conflict in Afghanistan, German troops have been present throughout. More than fifty soldiers have been killed. This was a small fraction of the American and British totals; German forces were operating in the quieter north of the country, but it was still a harsh reality for a generation hardwired against war. 'I am often asked whether I believe that the deployment of German soldiers in Afghanistan is justified and successful,' Schröder wrote in 2009. He recalled visiting a newly opened school in Kabul in 2002. 'I was greeted by young, unveiled girls. The students were doing something that we take for granted: attending school and learning. Many of us have forgotten that this was precisely what the Taliban denied these girls and young women for many years. It confirmed my belief that Germany had to make a contribution to bringing down the Taliban.' He added: 'The Bundestag's decision put an end to the chapter of Germany's limited sovereignty after World War II. It made us an equal partner in the international community of nations, one that had obligations to meet, such as those that have arisen from the NATO alliance in the case of Afghanistan. However, we Germans also acquired rights, such as to say "no" in the case of the Iraq war, because we were not convinced of the merits of a military intervention.'[6]

Schröder not only opposed the Iraq War; he defined the second half of his leadership by it. With Bush denouncing

French and German reluctance to go to war, Old Europe versus New Europe, the issue dominated the German elections of September 2002. Schröder's approach was spectacularly successful, turning around opinion polls that had been pointing to a CDU/CSU victory. The White House was furious, denouncing the Germans and French for their 'cowardice'.

Then came Libya in 2011. David Cameron and Nicolas Sarkozy were eager to intervene, to save Benghazi from being overrun and to force out Colonel Gaddafi. This time it was Angela Merkel who was ranged against them. Germany, only three months into a two-year membership of the UN Security Council, abstained on a resolution imposing a no-fly zone. It did so alongside Russia and China and against all its Western allies. Unlike the dispute over Iraq, it didn't have France as cover. 'It was not an easy choice,' noted the foreign minister, Guido Westerwelle, with studied understatement.

In Iraq and Libya, the German position was thoroughly vindicated. The Bush/Blair adventure in Iraq turned a fractured country into a breeding ground for international terrorism. While Gaddafi was removed, Libya has become a failed state, its citizens joining the ranks from other countries willing to risk their lives for a fresh start in Europe. Joschka Fischer's emotional Kosovo speech seemed to belong to a different era. Iraq, Libya and Afghanistan (a more complicated case) reawakened in German public opinion a revulsion for military action.

At the start of each year, diplomats and politicians from around the world gather for the Munich Security Conference – a Davos for defence. It has been the scene of many moments of drama. One was the address given by the German president in 2014. An ordained pastor from the rural north of the GDR, Joachim Gauck had been a prominent member of the protest movement, before being elected to the short-lived parliament of East Germany's final months. After reunification he became head of the organization overseeing the Stasi archive. In 2012, he became president of Germany, a popular choice. For a few years, the country had two Easterners in the top positions – a first.

'This is a good Germany, the best we've ever known,' Gauck told the audience in Munich. Germany was a reliable partner. He listed the contributions: international development, environment, multilateralism, pro-Europeanism. He then addressed the intervention complex head-on. Germany, he said, was accused of being a 'shirker', a country 'all too ready to duck difficult issues'. He didn't disagree. It should not let its past serve as a reason for looking away. It should be willing to take on more responsibility for promoting security in the world. 'Are we willing to bear our fair share of the risks?' he asked, before answering the question himself. 'He who fails to act bears responsibility too. We would be deceiving ourselves if we were to believe that Germany was an island and thus protected from the vicissitudes of our age.'[7] He was supported by Foreign Minister Frank-Walter Steinmeier (who succeeded him as president) and Defence Minister Ursula von der Leyen (who became president of the European Commission). Steinmeier set out a series of carefully calibrated principles: 'The use of military force is an instrument of last resort. It should rightly be used with restraint. Yet a culture of restraint for Germany must not become a culture of standing aloof. Germany is too big merely to comment on world affairs from the sidelines.'[8] This came to be known as the Munich Consensus.

A people bound to America has also felt a close affinity to its Cold War adversary, Russia. This has been driven by geography, culture, history – and war guilt. Before 1989, the dilemma was easier to navigate. Soviet communism's diktat over Eastern

Europe; its suppression of uprisings in East Berlin in 1953, Hungary in 1956 and Prague in 1968; and the building of the Berlin Wall in 1961 propelled all but the most diehard left-wing Germans into the orbit of the West. Konrad Adenauer declared that the integration of Germany into the Western fold was more important than unification. A rearmed West Germany joined NATO in 1955. Under a doctrine developed by the Foreign Ministry's top civil servant, Walter Hallstein, the Federal Republic would not have relations with any country that recognized the GDR. By the time of the Vietnam War, though, loyalties to America were already fraying. Social Democrats coined terms differentiating between positive Westernization and negative Westernification – selling out to a warmongering Uncle Sam. This was just at the time when Chancellor Willy Brandt was developing his eastern policy, *Ostpolitik*, seeking an accommodation with the GDR and the broader Warsaw Pact. *Ostpolitik* came in two parts. The first was soft power. West Germany promoted people-to-people exchanges, tourism and academic and cultural collaborations. The second part was double-edged. In seeking better relations with the USSR and its satellites, Brandt and his successors ended up legitimizing and strengthening the regimes themselves. Dissidents felt let down. For instance, when Lech Walesa and his Solidarity trade union mounted the first successful opposition movement in Poland in the mid-1980s, the West German establishment seemed more interested in maintaining the status quo in the region.

Helmut Kohl was, like Adenauer, seen as a trusted partner by the US – if not by the UK and Thatcher, at least as far as reunification was concerned. The Americans' relationship with Schröder was much more difficult, not just because of his opposition to the invasion of Iraq, but also his close friendship with Vladimir Putin. Throughout the Cold War, German and Russian trade links were strong. The Soviet Union had gas but needed technological and financial support to develop the industry. The 'gas for pipelines' arrangement suited both well. The Nord Stream project involved the construction of a pipeline from Vyborg, northwest of St Petersburg, across the Baltic Sea to Germany's border with Poland. The majority shareholder in the project was Gazprom, Russia's utilities giant, inextricably linked with Putin and his political-security chums. The agreement to build the pipeline was hastily signed ten days before the 2005 elections, which Schröder narrowly lost to the new CDU leader, Merkel. A few weeks later, as Schröder was preparing to step down, the German government came to an extraordinary deal with the Russians. It guaranteed to cover €1 billion of the Nord Stream project cost, should Gazprom default on a loan. A few weeks after that, Schröder was appointed to run the shareholders' committee of Nord Stream AG.

Many muttered about a conflict of interest, but nothing was done about it. The personal and the political appeared interwoven. Even though he was sixty, Schröder and his wife (his fourth of five), Doris Schröder-Köpf, were allowed to adopt two young children from St Petersburg (Putin's home town). Russian procedures for Westerners to adopt Russian children had by this point become arduous, but for the Schröders, the way was smoothed. Schröder made no secret of his admiration for the Russian president. On three separate occasions, in 2004, 2006 and 2012, Schröder used the same formulation, *lupenreiner Demokrat*, crystal clear democrat, to describe Putin. On the second instance, while presenting his memoirs, he went further: 'President Vladimir Putin's historical achievement is to have restored the [Russian] state's foundations for democracy.'[9]

Schröder kept up the sycophancy towards Russia seemingly no matter how bad its actions, from the invasion of

Georgia to the state-sponsored poisoning in London of Alexander Litvinenko. He defended the Kremlin during its dispute with Estonia in May 2007, when the removal of a Soviet-era war memorial from the centre of Tallinn led to a cyberattack – on a NATO member state. Instead of doing what everyone else in the West was doing and condemning Russia, Schröder said that Estonia had contradicted 'every form of civilised behaviour'.[10] In March 2014, Schröder said Putin had developed justifiable 'fears about being encircled'. He described Crimea as 'old Russian territory'[11] and that its invasion was legal, because it was supported by locals. In 2014, as the West was considering sanctions against Russia, Schröder was toasted by Putin as he celebrated his seventieth birthday at a party in St Petersburg's Yusupov Palace. Germany's supposed ally Ukraine was furious. 'Gerhard Schröder is the most important lobbyist for Putin worldwide,'[12] its foreign minister said. In 2016, Schröder become head of a second Nord Stream project, an even more controversial expansion. This time Gazprom was the sole shareholder. A year later he was nominated to become a non-executive of the Russian state's biggest oil producer, Rosneft. The term used by intelligence agencies is elite capture. More colloquially, a Twitter hashtag was created to describe the corruption of the political elite: #Schroederization. 'Imagine Barack Obama now being, I don't know, the lobbyist for Chinese government in the United States,'[13] the Greens' foreign affairs spokesman Omid Nouripour said.

Some in the Berlin bubble resorted to snobbery, noting that Salesman Schröder (as he was dubbed for his acquisitive image) had left school early to become an unskilled construction worker. What more could you expect? Others scoffed, suggesting that he needed to make money in order to pay maintenance to his ex-wives. He seemed to quite enjoy the lothario image. On his fourth marriage, he was called Audi Man, for the four rings in the car's symbol, but on his fifth, he himself announced that he had achieved Olympic status.

Merkel's instincts towards Russia could not have been more different from her predecessor's. She was the first child of communism to run Germany. Like all school pupils in the GDR, she learnt to speak Russian. Not one to shirk her studies, she won third place for the best student Russian speaker in the whole country. The award included a trip to Moscow – where she bought her first Beatles record. She has always been fascinated by Russia. On the wall of her office in the Chancellery she has a portrait of Catherine the Great, the Pomeranian princess who became empress of Russia.

Putin was the first Russian leader who had served in Germany, a mid-ranking KGB agent stationed in Dresden. In December 2018, his Stasi identity card was discovered in German archives. Issued in 1986 with the serial number B217590, the card bears Putin's signature next to the black-and-white photograph of a tie-clad young man. On the reverse side, quarterly stamps show it remained in use until the final quarter of 1989. By the time the Wall fell, he had been promoted to major. Biographical accounts, which he has not disputed, say that he brandished a pistol to stop an angry crowd from ransacking the KGB's offices in Dresden and taking away files. He and other comrades burnt reams of files.

They might have been on opposing sides of history, but one might have thought that Merkel and Putin had enough shared reference points to get along. After his love-in with Schröder, Putin was appalled to be confronted by a woman – a woman, the temerity of it – who had his measure. After meeting him for the first time, in 2002 in the Kremlin while she was still leader of the opposition, Merkel remarked to her aides that she had passed 'the KGB test'[14] for holding his gaze. (I can attest, having once spent four and a half hours with him at a small late-night gathering at his residence on the outskirts of Moscow in late 2004, that Putin's stare is chilling, and it takes quite some strength to return it.) The most bizarre encounter took place at his Black Sea palace in 2007. Seemingly aware of the fact that his guest had a fear of large dogs stemming from a childhood incident in which she was bitten, Putin had his large black labrador run into the room where they were holding talks. The dog, called Konnie, stayed beside him while he and Merkel sat across from each other. Photos of the encounter show Merkel looking anxious as the hefty dog sniffs her then settles near her feet. She does not flinch. Putin looks her way and flashes a mischievous grin. 'The dog doesn't bother you, does she? She's a friendly dog and I'm sure she will behave herself.'[15] To which Merkel responded with a dig of her own, in perfect Russian: 'It doesn't eat journalists, after all.'[16]

Merkel has, according to one biographer, total impulse control. She rarely shows any emotion at the time, but lets her displeasure be known afterwards. Putin subsequently apologized, claiming he was not aware of her phobia. German officials suggest he was almost certainly briefed. The dog incident is not the kind of thing that would influence Merkel unduly; however, it formed a pattern of distrust. She owed Putin no favours and in 2014, to the quiet satisfaction of the Americans and others in Europe, she made clear she was prepared to take him on. Within weeks of the Crimea and Ukraine crises, the Russians were suspected of being involved in the shooting down of Malaysian Airlines Flight 17, killing all 283 passengers and 15 crew. In response, Merkel ensured that the EU imposed the most wide-ranging sanctions since the fall of the USSR. She was hawk-in-chief, pushing them through in the face of resistance at the heart of her coalition. The sanctions were hardened in successive rounds. In November 2014, she declared: 'Who would have thought it possible that 25 years after the fall of the Berlin Wall something like this could happen in the middle of Europe? Old thinking about spheres of influence, whereby international law is trampled underfoot, must not be allowed to prevail.'[17]

Alongside her decision on migrants, Merkel's hard line on Russia was one of the big and uncharacteristic risks that define her tenure. An obsessive follower of opinion polls and focus groups, Merkel was fully aware of widespread public sympathy towards Russia and was constantly lobbied by corporations to go easy. Some of her boldness was born out of her own personal background: she had a visceral distaste, from her time in the GDR, for cold bullies like Putin. But I also think that it was a question of principle. When she felt it was the moment to dispense with caution, she did.

The one area she felt unable to touch was Nord Stream. As the first project was nearing completion, parliament approved a second pipeline alongside. The official German line was that the enlarged project posed no threat. Instead it would create a mutual interdependence, pushing Russia further into the West's orbit. Putin's behaviour suggested otherwise. Business leaders urged Merkel to ignore America's security concerns, and she did. Germany's big corporations were not the only lobby to apply pressure. All the leaders of the Eastern Länder, irrespective of party affiliation, urged her to improve relations with Russia. Michael Kretschmer, Saxony's prime minister and a member of her own CDU, said during his re-election campaign in September 2019: 'As a German politician, I think of the many businesses, especially in the former East German states that have been especially affected by the consequences of the sanctions policy.'[18] He claimed that, according to the Dresden Chamber of

Commerce, Saxon companies, which had enjoyed long-standing ties to Russia, exported around 60 per cent less to that country in 2018 than 2013. Brandenburg's Dietmar Woidke, ahead of his state's elections taking place on the same day, said: 'Many people in eastern Germany have a personal relationship to Russia, cultivate friendships and speak the language. The result is that there is an emotional connection for many people.'[19]

Repeated polls show that a large majority of voters, particularly in the East, want closer relations with Russia. This might seem incongruous given how desperate so many were to flee the GDR for the West, but this affinity has its deep roots in culture, geography and history. Yet much of the credulousness towards Russia is contemporary and pernicious. What Putin and his sophisticated propaganda machine have managed to do is to decouple his Russia from the record of Soviet communism in East Germany. Russia is suspected of funnelling money to both the AfD and Die Linke, although so far investigators haven't landed the knockout punch (unlike its links to Marine Le Pen's Rassemblement National, previously Front National, in France, where the financial link is not denied). The Kremlin is catholic in its tastes, embracing parties of the far right and far left, campaigns for independence and, of course, Brexit – anything to undermine liberal democracy and European cohesion. It has developed an information loop. The AfD toes the Kremlin's line. Its leaders have supported the annexation of Crimea and invasion of eastern Ukraine, even sending what it laughably called election observers. They have also met members of the nationalist youth group Nashi. RT, Russia's global television network, generally adopts the AfD's line. It transmits live the toxic marches of the Pegida group. Its German-language service has strong penetration in the Eastern states, capitalizing on the hostility felt by some towards mainstream *Wessi* media. One of its most viewed programmes is *The Missing Part*, which provides a regular diet of alarmist coverage about immigration and job security. Many of the three million or so ethnic German immigrants from Russia, known as late resettlers, retain pro-Kremlin sympathies. Seemingly, they expected to find a more ethnically homogenous and traditional country, a country as described to them by their grandparents. Instead they found a cosmopolitan country and were horrified. These resettlers were directly targeted by the AfD. Given their automatic right to vote, they are an important constituency.

Germany's annual Defence White Paper in 2016 first talked of Russia using techniques of hybrid warfare. 'By increasingly using hybrid instruments to purposefully blur the borders between war and peace, Russia is creating uncertainty about the nature of its intentions.'[20] The Russians, it said, were blurring them in a number of ways. The GRU, military intelligence, coordinated a series of cyberattacks through one of its units, APT28, known in the hacking world as 'Fancy Bear'. The most dangerous was an infiltration of the Bundestag's email system in 2016. A huge amount of data was stolen, ready to be leaked to undermine particular politicians and institutions. *Die Zeit*, in an investigation called 'Merkel and the Fancy Bear', revealed the extent of Russian hacking but also the woeful lack of preparedness by parliament's cybersecurity team. It quoted the head of cyber policy at the Foreign Ministry as calling for countermeasures. The term being used was 'hack back'. Merkel's Security Council decided against launching a retaliatory strike, instead drafting a law providing a framework for digital counter-attacks in the event of future incidents.

In the run-up to the 2017 election, German politicians and security officials were on the alert for more sabotage and more leaks. In the final days of the campaign, a blizzard of support for the AfD emerged from bots. By this point, its effect was probably limited. The most effective disinformation work had been carried out long before. A number of fake news stories have been published and spread in recent years, all with an anti-immigration bent. The 'Lisa' case was the most notorious. A thirteen-year-old girl of ethnic Russian origin from the East Berlin district of Marzahn was abducted and raped by a gang of men of Middle Eastern and African appearance. So angry were the locals that they mounted a demonstration against immigrants. They were joined by concerned citizens from further afield. Except it was all made up. It turned out that she had been with a friend and had played truant. She finally admitted this to her parents and school, but by then it had become an international sensation. It was started and stirred up by a German-language Russian website. Russian TV covered the story live. Donald Trump's favourite website Breitbart peddled it too. Another story had it that Germany's oldest church was burnt down by a man shouting '*Allahu Akbar*'. It was all untrue. What actually happened was a small fire at a church in Dortmund, by no means the oldest, caused by an electrical short circuit. It burnt some netting covering scaffolding and was put out after about twelve minutes.

Merkel has been targeted far more than any other major politician in Europe, according to EU and German cybersecurity experts, with a daily drip-drip of fake news designed to undermine her and particularly her tough line on Russia. Some of it is effective; some of it is fantastical. Apparently, she knew that a terrorist would attack Berlin's Christmas market and kept shtum. Apparently, she was the daughter of Adolf Hitler – and they had a (photoshopped) picture to prove it. Either he didn't die in the bunker and sired a child afterwards, or his sperm was frozen. They had not got around to working that one out.

Meanwhile, Russian hacking of parliament's communications has continued unabated. In December 2018, a fake Twitter account, designed to release stories over a series of days like an advent calendar, uploaded personal documents and data of a number of politicians that the Kremlin didn't like – senior MPs of most of the parties, with the notable exception of the AfD. The Greens were particularly targeted. Unlike the SPD, they have been strongly sceptical about Russia.

Merkel has ploughed on with her usual resilience and refusal to be dislodged by others. Just when the Americans and others think she has gone soft, she surprises. In August 2019, a Chechen exile who had commanded separatist forces in the war against Russia in the 1990s was murdered in a Berlin park while on his way to the mosque. The assassin, disguised in a wig, approached him on a bicycle from behind before shooting him with a Glock pistol fitted with a silencer. A man was arrested shortly after but for months, Berlin city police got no information out of him. The suspicion at foreign embassies was that the government was trying to sweep this under the carpet, to minimize diplomatic damage. Suddenly, in December, the decision was taken to bring in the federal prosecutor – something that should have been done at the start. Within twenty-four hours it was announced that two Russian diplomats would be expelled. This might not sound like a major retaliation, but it was the most serious step taken against Russia by a European power since more than a hundred Russian diplomats were expelled by twenty Western countries in 2018 in protest at the nerve agent attacks against Sergei Skripal and his daughter in the English city of Salisbury. Merkel was crucial in helping to coordinate that action across the EU – not that the Brits expressed particular gratitude.

In 2020 an even more sensitive incident took place, this time from afar. In August of that year Russia's most prominent opposition leader, Alexei Navalny, was poisoned. As he lay close to death at a hospital in the Siberian city of Omsk, Merkel persuaded Putin to allow German doctors to airlift him to the Charité hospital in Berlin. They finally acquiesced; eventually Navalny began to recover, was discharged and given a safe house. German, French and Swedish doctors confirmed the method used – Novichok, the same substance used against Skripal. Using the blunt language that had become her recent trademark, Merkel called it 'a crime against the basic values that we stand for'. She openly denounced the Russian state for the attempted assassination. In January 2021, Navalny returned to Moscow, knowing that a long spell in prison was a near certainty and another attempt by the state to kill him was a probability. As demonstrations took place across the country, Putin knew he faced a more potent threat this time. His default response was violence and intimidation. Would the world finally deal with him with greater vigour? Many eyes were on Germany.

Merkel has never been cowed by Putin. By contrast, Schröder's record on Russia was appalling, and the propensity of many voters to give the Kremlin the benefit of the doubt is worrying.

But – and it is a big but – before others condemn Germany, they should look closer to home. Under successive governments in the 1990s and 2000s, London became the money laundering capital of the world, dubbed Londongrad. Russian oligarchs were feted by ministers, royalty, members of Parliament and the House of Lords, celebrities, chief executives, private school heads, libel lawyers and of course wealth managers. As it rolled out the red carpet, the British establishment deliberately ignored the source of the wealth of their new best friends. I remember around 2005 berating a cabinet minister in Tony Blair's government. 'Just get with it,' he told me. 'All money is good money, particularly if it helps to build our schools and hospitals.' A number of spectacular murders forced the UK to toughen up in terms of security, but financially the links are at least as invidious as anything Germany has done. Britain's ruling Conservative Party has taken repeated gifts from oligarchs, totalling £3.5 million over the past decade[21] – including the absurd idea of paying tens of thousands of pounds to play tennis with either David Cameron or Boris Johnson. When Parliament's Intelligence and Security Committee raised concerns about these sordid dealings, Johnson spent months refusing to publish it. Other countries have allowed themselves to be bought, such as Italy. And then, of course, there are the continued questions around Donald Trump and his Kremlin connections.

From the outset, Trump loathed Merkel. She couldn't be accused of not trying. During the transition at the end of 2016, the outgoing Obama came to see her. They spent the evening running through the world's problems. She knew she was going to miss him. During his election campaign, Trump routinely insulted Merkel more than any other foreigner. 'They picked the person who is ruining Germany,' he said of *Time*'s choice of her as Person of the Year. What particularly upset him was the magazine calling her chancellor of the free world. 'What Merkel did to Germany, it's a sad, sad shame.'[22]

And yet the woman who adored Reagan and wanted to drive across the American plains is, by instinct, a staunch Atlanticist. She wanted the US to continue to see Germany as its most trusted partner. As Henry Kissinger famously asked: 'If I want to talk to Europe, who do I call?'[23] From George Bush senior to Obama, the answer was not what the Brits wanted to hear. It was invariably Germany. The so-called 'special relationship' with the UK, vital in the first decades after the war, had become a rhetorical construct of American diplomats to keep the Brits sweet. Prime ministers from Blair to Johnson saw subservience as the best way to curry favour.

Merkel did it her own way. But she also found setbacks hard to take. And there were several, dating back well before Trump. Some of the most damaging revelations uncovered in the tens of thousands of highly classified cables leaked by the whistle-blower Edward Snowden related to Germany. The worst of them was that the US National Security Agency (NSA) had been bugging Merkel's personal mobile phone for a number of years. In 2013, through research carried out on the Snowden files by *Der Spiegel*, it was revealed that the US Embassy in Berlin had been operating as an intelligence centre for the NSA. For years it had intercepted and stored communications between top-level German politicians, including the obsessive smartphone user Merkel herself. All the data gathered by Operation Einstein, as it was known, was relayed back to the NSA's headquarters where it was stored in a 'Target Knowledge Database'. A document from 2009, and published in 2014, showed that Merkel was one of 122 world leaders in the database system – also known as Nimrod. Listed in alphabetical order by first names, she was on the first page, below the Malian president and just above the murderous President Bashar al-Assad of Syria. This was the Obama regime. Germany was supposed to be one of America's staunchest allies. Merkel was incandescent when she was told, for once losing her famous impulse control. In an angry phone exchange with Obama, deliberately shared later with *Der Spiegel*, she told him: 'This is like the *Stasi*.'[24]

Relations worsened further with two cases of direct spying – a junior member of Germany's foreign intelligence service based in Munich and a serviceman based at the Ministry of Defence were caught handing over material to the Americans. In one of the cases, confidential evidence given to the very parliamentary committee investigating the eavesdropping of the chancellor's phone found its way back to the Americans. Merkel ordered the CIA's station chief to leave, an unprecedented step involving two allied countries. Intelligence cooperation was briefly suspended. Merkel invited Obama to agree to a non-spying pact, something that the Americans do not have even with their closest security allies. The row demonstrated the extent of the suspicion between the US and Germany. The security relationship is a far cry from the Five Eyes group, in which Australia, Canada, New Zealand, the UK and US share intelligence more readily. Obama refused Merkel's request. At the height of the argument, opinion polls showed that 60 per cent of Germans regarded Snowden as a hero. According to a survey by ARD television, support for Obama, which had been 88 per cent at inauguration, fell to 43 per cent. Only 35 per cent of Germans viewed America as a good partner, a figure only marginally higher than their view of Russia.[25]

And all that before Trump came onto the scene.

In March 2017, Merkel flew to Washington for her first meeting with the new president. She prepped assiduously. She studied a 1990 *Playboy* interview which had become a set text on Trumpism – or the nearest thing anybody could find – for policymakers. She read his 1987 book, *The Art of the Deal*. She even watched episodes of his TV show, *The Apprentice*.

It started badly. She offered him a handshake in the Oval Office in front of the cameras. He didn't take it. Her studied lack of emotion, her deeply analytical mind, were anathema to him. Her aides say she learnt to explain complicated problems to him by reducing them to bite-sized chunks. He read all of this as high-handedness. Trump certainly had a track record as a misogynist, and some cited this as the reason for his dislike. Others put it down to a narcissistic resentment that someone else was regarded around the world as the keeper of democracy. He loathed praise given to anyone else.

Eighteen months into the Trump presidency, Merkel concluded with regret that it would be impossible to develop any kind of meaningful relations with him. The best she could hope for was to manage the problem. In advance of a G7 summit in Canada in 2018, Trump slapped tariffs on EU and Canadian steel and aluminium. A month before that he had announced that America was withdrawing from the international deal with Iran, the JCPOA, which committed the Iranians to eliminating their stockpile of nuclear-enriched uranium in return for the gradual lifting of sanctions. Trump not only refused to be part of it, but he restored sanctions on Iran immediately and imposed further US sanctions against any international company trading with Iran. This hit German firms hard.

The run-up to the G7 was bad; the atmosphere at the talks themselves was terrible. At one point, with Merkel in the lead, all the others confronted a sedentary and pouting Trump. The picture, taken by the German government's official photographer, went viral around the world. By the end of the talks, they had managed to cobble together an anodyne communique in which all the leaders pledged 'free, fair and mutually beneficial trade'.[26] Trump left early for a meeting in Singapore with Kim Jong-un, North Korea's dictator and a man for whom he seemed to have a closer personal affinity than those he had just seen. On her overnight flight home, Merkel was woken up by an official to be told that the US president had torn up the G7 agreement. He had, she was told, taken issue with something that Justin Trudeau had said at his closing press conference, and launched a tirade against Canada's prime minister.

The relationship deteriorated further. The following year Trump withdrew the US from the Paris Agreement on climate change. In spite of that, France's Emmanuel Macron decided to adopt a different approach from Merkel. Instead of staring coldly, he poured on the bromance. He invited Trump to inspect the troops at the Bastille Day parade. Trump was mesmerized, bemoaning the fact that the US had no such military march-past for him to preside over. Within a year, Macron's approach had proved no more successful. Still, there was something about Merkel that wound up Trump more perhaps than any other leader. He used every opportunity to attack her, by his favourite medium, Twitter. 'The people of Germany are turning against their leadership as migration is rocking the already tenuous Berlin coalition. Crime in Germany is way up,' Trump tweeted, incorrectly. 'Big mistake made all over Europe in allowing millions of people in who have so strongly and violently changed their culture!'[27]

He dispatched a long-time hawk, turned shock-jock commentator for Fox News, Richard Grenell, to Berlin as US ambassador. Grenell went immediately on the warpath, denouncing the government on a regular basis. He vowed to 'empower conservatives'[28] across Europe. By that he did not mean Merkel, but the increasing number of nationalist authoritarians surrounding her. A number of German MPs urged the foreign minister to declare Grenell *persona non grata*. Merkel resisted, but the affair spoke volumes for the collapse in ties.

Trump's manner was not designed to endear. But that did not mean that all his criticisms were invalid. His misgivings about Russia and Nord Stream were legitimate. The most visible dispute was over defence spending, and that predated him. In 2014, at a NATO summit in Cardiff, member countries agreed to 'move towards' meeting the target of 2 per cent of GDP for defence by 2024. That was slow progress, but progress of sorts. At the time, only three countries met the target. Germany was not the only laggard. But, given its size and its economic strength, it was the most obvious one. Five years later, eight countries had more or less passed the 2 per cent threshold. Several had fallen woefully short, including Canada, Italy and Spain. Germany was spending just 1.24 per cent, promising that its share would rise to 1.5 per cent by 2025. Even that may be optimistic.

Before 1990, Germany had been meeting the NATO target. In the mid-1980s, the defence budget was roughly the same size as the social budget. Reunification changed many Germans' priorities. As Soviet troops began to withdraw from the GDR, voters sought a peace dividend. With so much money needing to be spent on reviving the moribund economy and infrastructure of the East, why not divert it from spending on a superfluous military? Politicians point to opinion polls whenever they are berated about low defence spending.

The most recent Pew Research Center Global Attitudes survey in 2019[29] sets out the ambivalence many Germans feel towards the Atlantic alliance and a desire for rapprochement with Russia. The number of Germans who have a positive opinion about NATO has fallen from 73 per cent to 57 per cent in the past five years. (The fall is even greater in France, from 71 per cent to 49 per cent. The only countries where NATO's popularity has increased are those that feel directly threatened by Russia, such as Lithuania and Poland.) Asked whether their country should honour Article 5, NATO's mutual defence obligation, only 34 per cent of Germans said it should, well below the European median. When asked whether it is more important to have a strong relationship with the US or Russia, 39 per cent of Germans said the former, against 25 per cent the latter. Only Bulgarians were better disposed towards Russia, and then only marginally.

In 1990, the German armed forces, the Bundeswehr, numbered 500,000 people. In 2018, recruitment fell to an all-time low. Just 20,000 joined that year. A similar number of officer rank and non-commissioned officer (NCO) positions were left vacant. The total in the armed forces now is around 200,000. The Bundeswehr has gone out recruiting, experimenting with YouTube videos to attract more young people. With near full employment, many young Germans would not contemplate the idea of a career in the armed forces. They are rarely visible. Germany does not have public shows of admiration for the military, unlike France, Russia, the UK and others. When they leave their barracks, soldiers almost always change into civilian clothes. The decision in 2011 to end conscription was an unlikely one by a government of the centre-right. National service had been compulsory for all young men, although they could opt for civilian service if they raised a conscientious objection. The biggest exclusion had been citizens of pre-unification West Berlin, still notionally under Allied control, a quirk that helped give the island city its unique character. Since the ending of conscription and closure of bases, large swathes of the country now have no connection to the armed forces. Some politicians in the CDU have tried to lobby Merkel to reintroduce civilian service for all, but she has continued to resist. The army has also lost specialists. A number of engineers have left for higher paid jobs in the private sector. The most significant problem is the deterioration of military hardware. At one point less than half of the fleet of military transport aircraft, Tornados and Eurofighter jet aircraft were combat-ready. All six submarines were out of action.[30]

Russia's actions in Crimea and eastern Ukraine forced a re-think. Since 2014, the defence budget has increased by 40 per cent, but still from a low base. Such a rise in spending, Merkel said, is 'a huge step from Germany's perspective'.[31] In other words, cut us some slack. In spite of the criticisms, Germany participates in a more extensive network of collaborative military relationships than any other European country. It has joint military units with six of its nine neighbouring countries. In an effort to bolster NATO partners on the front line with Russia, under what is called Enhanced Forward Presence, Germany was given responsibility for sending forces to Lithuania, alongside the British in Estonia, Canadians in Latvia and the US in Poland. The German air force is also operating in Estonia, helping its air force to ward off Russian planes infringing its air space. Germany has a joint corps with Poland and Denmark, and one with the Dutch. Germany has trained and supplied weapons to the Peshmerga, the forces of the Kurds in Iraq, as part of the multilateral campaign against Islamic State. German Tornados have flown aerial reconnaissance missions over Iraq and Syria to assist US-led forces there. One of the biggest Bundeswehr deployments is in the West African state of Mali on behalf of a UN peacekeeping mission.

One of the most important developments has been the creation of PESCO, the Permanent Structured Cooperation, in which twenty-five of the EU's twenty-seven member states have started more than thirty joint military projects. They include drone warfare, space surveillance, helicopter training, medical command, rapid cyber response and maritime anti-mine countermeasures. A common spy academy is also to be established. Not entirely cleverly perhaps, the Joint European Intelligence School will be under the aegis of Cyprus and Greece, member states that have close relationships with Russia and China. One of the aims of PESCO is jointly to 'develop defence capabilities and make them available for EU military operations'.[32] In early 2019, Ursula von der Leyen, then German defence minister, declared: 'Europe's army is already taking shape.'[33] The French and Germans disagree on the strategy. In 2018, Macron spearheaded the creation of a European Intervention Initiative (EI2), which would plan for future crises. France sees the EU as a potential military force. Germany is more cautious. Merkel has resisted setting the EU up as an alternative to NATO. She has enough trouble with the Americans as it is.

Strategically, however, the biggest conundrum for German international relations is China. Duisburg is one of several cities in the heavily industrialized Ruhr area that has fallen on hard times. A few years ago, its mayor came up with a regeneration plan that has transformed the city. The starring role is played by China. In the city's ornate *Rathaus*, town hall, I meet Duisburg's China spokesman. Johannes Pflug tells me how he took up the post. As a member of the Bundestag, he led a delegation to China a few years ago. The group was invited to watch a PowerPoint presentation. It went straight to a map of Germany, which pinpointed two cities – Berlin and Duisburg. He had no idea why. 'I told them, ever so politely, that perhaps they meant Hamburg or Munich. Perhaps they had made a mistake in the transliteration and intended to write Düsseldorf.'

This was no error. The Chinese had already staked out the place. They wanted to make Duisburg their most important destination in the whole of Europe. Just as imperial Germany had planned a Berlin to Baghdad railway, so the Chinese have their Belt and Road. Why Duisburg indeed? Location has always been the town's greatest asset. In the sixteenth century, the Flemish cartographer Gerardus Mercator spent the last thirty years of his life in Duisburg, where he published a book of maps of Europe, the first 'atlas' to carry that name. A statue of Mercator stands close to the *Rathaus*. Indeed, if you stuck a pin into the middle of a contemporary map of Europe, it might end up somewhere around here. Duisburg stands on the confluence of the rivers Rhine and Ruhr. Motorways come at it from north, south, east and west. It has Europe's largest inland port. It is not far from Düsseldorf international airport. And it is at the centre of the continent's railway network.

Launched by President Xi Jinping in 2013, the Belt and Road is known variously as a twenty-first-century Silk Road or China's Marshall Plan for the rest of the world. It is a grid for Chinese business and influence – a 'belt' of overland corridors and a maritime 'road' of shipping lanes, taking in seventy-one countries, half of the world's population and a quarter of global GDP. It is scaring the life out of the West.

Duisburg was identified as its end point. It was cheap, perfectly located – and desperate for investment. From here goods could be transported by road, rail, ship or barge across Europe and beyond. The town's mayor was quick to sign up. A year later, during a state visit to Germany, Xi made a special stop in Duisburg. Timed to coincide with an incoming freight train festooned with red ribbons, his arrival was greeted by an orchestra playing traditional mining songs and local children holding banners in Chinese. Thirty trains a week now travel between China and Germany on the Belt and Road. They take the northern route from Shanghai, Wuhan, Chongqing or Chengdu via Almaty in Kazakhstan through Moscow and Warsaw. They bring clothes, toys and electronics. The trains then go back the other way carrying German cars, Scottish whisky, French wine and more. Banners proclaim: 'We are Germany's China city.'

Chinese money had an immediate effect. Duisport, the company that was created, is expanding to such a degree that it is challenging Hamburg as Germany's premier port. A business centre is being built nearby, creating a foothold for firms to embed their links in European markets. It is hard to find criticism of Belt and Road in Duisburg, not among politicians, not among the media. Martin Ahlers, a reporter at the *Westdeutsche*

Allgemeine Zeitung, the regional paper, says it is all about jobs. Then he refers back to the NSA's bugging of the chancellor's phone. The US telecoms company Cisco, which manages much of the German government and security forces' data, was suspected in the German media of providing back-end access to the Americans. 'People only talk about Chinese behaviour. Why not American? It was Cisco that did Merkel in,' he says.

The Duisburg investment is part of a bigger picture. Across Europe, China is consolidating its economic and political power. It has poured €1 billion into a railway between Budapest and Belgrade. It has bought the strategically vital Greek port of Piraeus. It is building a new city in the forests on the outskirts of the Belarusian capital, Minsk, to create a manufacturing hub between the EU and Russia.

Exports are vital to Germany's economic success. They are also a projection of Germany's global brand. Decades ago, the country placed a long-term bet on China. It is now more exposed than most to the vicissitudes of China's global ambitions. From the moment Deng Xiaoping opened up China, German companies flooded in. China was the gift that kept on giving. China wanted cars, high-end engineering and know-how. Germany saw a reliable partner and an inexhaustible market, as hundreds of millions of new consumers emerged. German entrepreneurs proclaimed that, with one political ideology and one economic model triumphant, they could do business anywhere. After 'recapturing' the GDR market and consolidating in Eastern Europe, they went further afield, into Asia in particular. They left the politics to the politicians, although they were guided by the motto *Wandel durch Handel*, change through trade. They assumed that the more China traded, the more it would open up.

Two decades later, two events threw this approach into doubt. One was local, the other global. In 2016, one of the darlings of

Germany's high-end industry was the object of a hostile take-over. For all the rhetorical allegiance towards the free markets, the Germans have jealously guarded their national champions. KUKA was one such firm. It started out in the pretty southern town of Augsburg in 1898, a typical story of a family company starting with a single product – designing and building street lights. A century later, it had become one of the world's leading developers of industrial robots. The Chinese were on the lookout for acquisitions that would meet the requirements of two long-term government plans, Made in China 2025 and its own version of Industry 4.0 (culled in large measure from Germany's). These projects were designed to transform China's economy from low-cost, labour-intensive imitations into a global leader in innovation. Beijing pushed Chinese companies to go out and invest in foreign targets to increase their technological capabilities and seek new markets as its own economy slowed. In the course of that year, Chinese companies announced or completed purchases of German firms worth €11 billion.[34]

Out of the blue, the Chinese company Midea, which made fridges and air conditioners, offered €115 per share for KUKA, valuing the firm at €4.6 billion – a premium of nearly 60 per cent. In spite of protests, by shareholders, some of the management and the trade union, and unsuccessful efforts to find another purchaser, Midea secured a stake of more than 90 per cent of the company.[35] The private buyout was regarded by many market participants as the blueprint for a successful Chinese outbound acquisition. Despite calls to intervene, Merkel did nothing. The Economics Ministry announced it had no grounds to stop the purchase. One of the jewels in Germany's business crown became a Chinese company overnight. Two years later, the German CEO stood down. Business leaders were alarmed. The Chinese were about to steal their lunch. No German company was safe. What about others in the *Mittelstand* (the small and medium-sized enterprises)? What if China went for the car industry?

The BDI, the employers' federation, produced a detailed report on China's strategy. At the heart of its investigation were the ramifications of the 19th Party Congress in 2017 when Xi made clear that the Communist Party would maintain its leading role in business and politics. 'We realized that convergence wouldn't lead to democratization alongside markets. That was just an illusion,' one business leader told me. 'Also, that meant that the state would be subsidising business. The Chinese were paying higher than the market price for acquisitions, based on state subsidies. These were market distortions.' At one BDI seminar they looked at three broad options. Option one was that business could say it had no choice but to accept the reality. It could use the next five to seven years to make profits in the market before being muscled out. Option two was to bail from China immediately. The third option was to come up with a new modus operandi. Business could define where it could work with China and where it couldn't, protecting the system from as much damage as possible. They opted for number three, the compromise. But still that was a big shift. When the paper was published, it caused a storm. It spoke of China as a 'systemic competitor', noting that the West was in a 'contest of economic systems'[36] with China's state-subsidized capitalism. It made more than fifty policy proposals, including more proactive use of EU subsidy laws.

At the same time, parliament passed a law that would give the government the right to scrutinize and potentially block all investments in sensitive industries in which a non-EU company acquires more than 10 per cent of a German business. The previous threshold had been 25 per cent. The law applied to defence and security companies, and businesses that operate 'critical infrastructure' such as energy, power and telecommunications, as well as media. The economics minister Peter Altmaier introduced a 'National Industry Strategy 2030,' creating national champions in strategic industries from aerospace to green technologies, from 3D printing to, of course, cars.

The EU followed suit with a ten-point plan that marked a shift towards a more defensive industrial strategy. Germany was becoming more openly protectionist. The first Chinese takeover to be blocked was of computer chip manufacturer Aixtron. A year later, the government scrambled a new tactic to prevent another purchase from happening. A state-owned bank was instructed to buy a 20 per cent share of the power-distributing company 50Hertz, thwarting a bid from the State Grid Corporation of China. The Economics and Finance ministries said they had a 'strong interest to protect critical energy infrastructure'.[37] For Germany and for other Western powers, the problem was a classic one of economic investment buying political acquiescence. Chinese purchases of raw materials led Australia into a period of economic and political subservience. That trend has now established itself within part of the EU, particularly in Southeast and Central Europe. In June 2017, Greece blocked a statement at the UN Human Rights Council criticizing China's human rights record, the first time the EU had failed to make a joint statement. Three months earlier, Hungary had refused to sign a letter denouncing the reported torture of detained lawyers in China, also breaking consensus.

Merkel was strongly behind the EU's tougher line, although she was careful to act diplomatically. Two complications ensued. President Trump's decision to go after China on trade, slapping tariffs on a wide range of goods and denouncing it for undervaluing its currency and other sharp practices, was a potentially devastating blow. The other problem was business itself. No sooner had they agreed to take a tougher line than corporate bosses started to have second thoughts. Some called the BDI paper excessively strident. Just one of many examples: VW makes more than half its global profits in China. As other corporations have found, getting on the wrong side of the Chinese government never pays. Daimler Benz had to apologize profusely and repeatedly for an Instagram advert that quoted the Dalai Lama. In so doing they were no different from Christian Dior or the US National Basketball Association. Chinese citizens were told that any purchase of a Mercedes car would be deemed an unpatriotic act.

China is doing everything it can to condition the story that is told of it around the world. Companies are required to become cheerleaders for it if they want contracts. When Merkel made the latest of her twelve official visits to China in September 2019 (almost one per year since she took office), she took with her a delegation of business leaders. On the way there, they gave her a list of sensitive issues to bring up with the Chinese prime minister Li Keqiang, including market access restrictions and the risk of espionage through technology back-end access. When she did just that, they then refused to back her up. According to a senior German security official, who told me this story, she was seething at how German business leaders had left her dangling.

Merkel had another dilemma. Digital infrastructure has fallen behind. The OECD ranks Germany's 4G speeds at twenty-fourth out of twenty-nine countries. One company offered the most effective solution: Huawei. The Chinese company already plays a major role in European telecommunications. Deutsche Telekom has been using its technology for years. Huawei handsets are the second-most popular in Germany, behind Samsung but ahead of Apple's iPhone. The only 5G rivals to Huawei are Cisco, not everyone's favourite in Germany after the eavesdropping scandal, and Ericsson or Nokia from within Europe. Huawei's proposal is said to be the most technologically advanced and cost-effective. Yet the security implications were considerable. For months the government was split. Merkel's Chancellery and the business-oriented Economics Ministry were in favour of giving the contract to Huawei. The Interior and Foreign ministries were hostile. Merkel, without giving her cabinet prior warning, announced that the government would not preclude any company from entering the bidding process. It seems she had been got at by the business lobby. 'She was influenced by car makers,' one senior MP told me. 'She was scared of economic retaliation.' The parliamentary backlash was strong and she was forced to reconsider. On this at least Merkel could reassure herself that she was not alone. Other governments around Europe were facing the same quandary. They had to decide what was more important: China's cost-effective technology or the wrath of the Americans? In Britain, Parliament approved Johnson's decision to proceed with Huawei, subject to certain conditions. That did not go down well in Washington, but it seemed Trump's complaints were too late.

Divide and rule is China's biggest weapon. It has preyed on countries in Southeast Europe still struggling to recover from years of war, neglect and from the humiliations of the debt crisis. It is hovering around populist-nationalist states of Central Europe like Hungary. Merkel has tried to tread a delicate path, but too often Germany has been reticent to speak up, whether on the mass imprisonment of Uighurs in Xinjiang province or the destruction of the pro-democracy movement in Hong Kong. Merkel was desperate to use Germany's presidency of the EU to conclude an investment agreement with China. She achieved that, after years of stalled negotiations, but the concessions she made did not reflect well.

It has become a commonplace, in Berlin and beyond, to criticize Germany's foreign and security policy as weak and confused. The refusal to meet NATO's spending requirements is clearly a problem, undermining the country's professed commitment to the Western alliance. The deterioration of military hardware undermines its ability to take part in campaigns, even defensive ones. Both need to be addressed.

How far has Germany's place in the world really changed since reunification? One intriguing analysis was given to me by Jan Techau of the German Marshall Fund. He argues that Kosovo was not the breakthrough it appeared at the time. 'The moment we start rationalizing military decisions through national interest, and not through Auschwitz, we'll have really changed,' he says.

Germany remains in its post-war shell, reluctant to get involved in military action. From the 1950s to the 1980s, this position was acceptable, indeed demanded of it. But since reunification, and with the power of other Western powers waning, that is no longer tenable. 'The demand side of security, for us to step up, is increasing faster than we can supply,' he adds. 'We think we've gone to our limits, whereas others think we have fallen behind.' Others have another explanation. 'German pacifism comes from a negative feedback loop – public, media, politics,' suggests Ulrike Franke at the European Council on Foreign Relations. 'It's a source of moral superiority and pride.' Virtue signalling in lieu of foreign policy? Franke's view is not uncommon among German foreign-policy experts. The German position, according to this analysis, does not reflect caution or under-confidence, but a view that unlike the more gung-ho

Anglo-Saxon countries they have 'got over' being aggressive. Perhaps there is some faux superiority, but that should not be overplayed. As ever, the past intrudes. Techau compares Britain and Germany. 'You believe you are on the right side of history, even if you mess up. You Brits have given into your own complexes; you build your identity around a greatness of yesterday. You're comfortable winging it. We need rules. Germans have zero confidence that when they take a risk they'll end up on the right side. That's why they don't want to take risks.' That seems to me to be the most compelling argument. A Germany at war – with anyone – is not something voters want to think about. Have they perhaps learnt the lessons of the past too well?

In any case, how many more conventional military interventions will the world see in the coming years? When Syria's opposition desperately needed help, Obama set red lines but then failed to act. The British parliament refused Cameron's request to send troops. It is doubtful whether the UK has the military capability or the clout to do much anymore, except on the coat tails of the US. Meanwhile, Trump's 'America First' approach is a crude reaffirmation of national interest over any other concerns. A willingness to go to war is only one aspect of foreign and security policy. The flip side of Germany's caution has been a deliberativeness often lacking in the more hubristic political cultures of the US, UK and, to some degree, France. Germany has put a strong onus on peacekeeping and multilateralism.

Germany is already bracing itself for a more uncomfortable future. In May 2017, at a party rally in a beer garden in the suburbs of Munich, Merkel said something remarkable. 'The times when we could rely on others are over. That is something I've learned in recent times. We have to take our destiny much more into our own hands in the future if we want to be strong.'[38] She later elaborated on the point, suggesting in an interview that ties had weakened with the US not so much because of her relationship with Trump but more because of America's changed priorities. 'Europe is no longer, so to say, at the centre of world events [. . .] The United States' focus on Europe is declining – that will be the case under any president.'[39]

With or without Trump, is this the end of *Pax Americana*?

The United States provided the glue for post-war Germany. No matter how vocal anti-Americanism was among some, most Germans appreciated the role Uncle Sam played in enabling the country to rebuild and prosper, safe in the knowledge that someone else would defend it. American forces, on the ground in Germany for so long after the war, enabled Germans to trust in themselves again. Without them, the European project would not have got off the ground. As ever in modern Germany, times of upheaval produce a stream of soul-searching. 'One could almost be grateful to Donald Trump,' wrote *Die Zeit* commentators Bernd Ulrich and Jörg Lau. 'The fact that the constants and principles of German foreign policy – European integration, multilateralism, engagement in the name of human rights and the rule of law, rule-based globalisation – are questioned by the American government constitutes an enormous intellectual and strategic challenge. In the future, Europe now, out of necessity, has to do this by itself without the aid of the US, or perhaps even against the US government.'[40]

The idea of Germany setting itself up as an adversary would have been unthinkable prior to Trump. Germans watched helplessly as the values they held dear were systematically undermined by the man who was supposed to be the leader of the free world.

Once in a while, someone says or does something that encapsulates a moment. This was the case when Thomas Bagger, head of the German president's foreign-policy department, penned an article in late 2018 in a relatively obscure academic journal, the *Washington Quarterly*. He started by saying that Fukuyama's thesis, or rather a simple reading of it, had set the tone of reunified Germany. 'Towards the end of a century marked by having been on the wrong side of history twice, Germany finally found itself on the right side.' People desperately wanted to believe that the Cold War was over, democracy had won, and everyone could calmly go about their business. They did so because that is what they had to fall back on. Shorn of its history, this was German identity. 'While others can go back to their respective Gaullist traditions of foreign-policy thinking, with a more or less clear set of defined national interests that do not depend on integration with others, there is little of that in Germany that has not been contaminated.' Since 1945, Germans have had a thoroughly linear expectation of the future. It was based on a number of assumptions, which were reinforced from 1990. Countries would gradually reform into open market, liberal democracies. The Helsinki Final Act of 1975 – the recognition of borders and the respect of human rights – was the great milestone. After the collapse of communism, Central and Eastern Europe undertook a catch-up in Western Europe's image. China would follow. The Arab Spring would reinforce this trend. Setbacks were temporary: 'Since there was no room for authoritarianism in our imagination of the imminent end of history, these could only be last gasps and aberrations.'[41]

Sitting with Bagger in Schloss Bellevue, the president's office, I discussed Brexit with him – inevitably – but also what had gone wrong more generally with Europe. I noted that Trump criticizes Merkel and Macron with alacrity, while embracing the leaders of the populist illiberal right, from Orbán to Le Pen, from Italy's Matteo Salvini to Jaroslaw Kaczynski in Poland. 'The

Trump challenge goes much deeper than just policy disagreements,' Bagger said. 'His approach pulls the rug from under the feet of German foreign-policy thinking. Germany has lost its moorings.' He then offered something that stays with me: 'Our problem is that we expect everyone to learn the same lessons as we do.'

Joe Biden will be a very different kind of leader. Yet the threat posed by nativist-populism around the world has not abated. Trump himself may struggle to mount a challenge in 2024, but, like a virus, his politics may mutate into something else, at least as dangerous.

That is Germany's biggest challenge. Merkel's offer to her people was stability. She provided that. But as she leaves the world stage, her successor will have to convince voters that the comfort blanket will need to be removed; the end of history was a mirage, the survival of liberal democracy is no longer a given. That task begins at Germany's frontiers.

To understand Germany in Europe, you have to come to the beautiful border city of Aachen. I meander through the narrow streets. The road signs point you to the small town of Vaals in the Netherlands or Kelmis in Belgium, just a short cycle ride away. 'EUREGIO' train tickets connect the three countries. It is a place of beauty, learning, science, culture and tragedy – the German and European story in microcosm. This was the front line where the Germans sent troops into Flanders at the start of the Great War and where American tanks crossed the Siegfried Line in October 1944. For a full six months before Hitler's capitulation, this small sliver of Germany was under Allied control. The city became a test bed for post-war democratic reconstruction.

Aachen presents itself as the centre of Europe, the cradle of Western European culture. It is synonymous with Charlemagne, or Karl der Grosse, as the Germans call him, the Frankish king of the ninth century who brought most of Europe under his wing. In subsequent centuries many of Europe's great warriors, leaders, thinkers and churchmen, from Otto the Great to Napoleon, drew on the Charlemagne name. They projected whatever they wanted onto him: benevolent monarch, holy defender, imperious conqueror. '*Je suis Charlemagne*,' declared an invading Napoleon in 1806 as he surveyed his new domain. Hitler tried to appropriate him too.

In 1949, a local businessman by the name of Kurt Pfeiffer proposed a prize to honour statesmen in service of Europe. Pfeiffer was no major figure. He took over his parents' clothing business in the 1920s, backed various democratic parties during the Weimar period but then, at the prompting of friends and colleagues, joined the Nazi Party in 1933. He refused to join the boycott of Jewish businesses and was forced to resign the chairmanship of the local retail association. He was still deemed tainted, and straight after the war his immigration application to Canada was refused. The Americans, however, still chose him as one of nine citizens to run the city's transitional government. Pfeiffer suggested to a reading group that he should found an international prize 'for the most valuable contribution in the services of Western European understanding and work for the community, and in the services of humanity and world peace. This contribution may be in the field of literary, scientific, economic or political endeavour.'[42] In 1950, the city made its first Charlemagne award. In its restored Gothic town hall, a multilingual screen gives a brief biography of the winners of the prize. The roll call of Charlemagne laureates is a who's who of the European project. The first decade included Jean Monnet and Robert Schuman, alongside Adenauer and Churchill. They were followed by Jacques Delors, Bill Clinton, Pope John Paul II and

Václav Havel. Also on the list are Roy Jenkins, Ted Heath and Tony Blair. Those were the days when people dared to dream of a Europe with Britain playing a pivotal role.

From the town hall to the city museum, my last destination is the cathedral. The dean takes me to the coronation throne, made of marble said to have been transported from the Church of the Holy Sepulchre in Jerusalem. Here thirty German kings were crowned. The magnificent building, with its famous octagon roof, has been rebuilt many times, after fire engulfed the city in 1656 and after Allied bombing during the Second World War. It houses spoils from across Europe, from Byzantium to Ravenna in Northern Italy, an amalgam of the whole continent from east to west, the dean tells me. When we bid farewell, he offers this: 'If St Peter's in Rome belongs to the world, and Cologne Cathedral is Germany's, then Aachen is truly Europe's home.' As if on cue, just outside in one of the main squares, a group of men and women, young and old, with rucksacks, cycle helmets or baby holsters, hold hands and sing along to the European Union's anthem – Beethoven's 'Ode to Joy', blaring from a loudspeaker. They still invoke the spirit of Charlemagne and a united continent.

From Adenauer to de Gaulle, Macron to Merkel, French presidents and German chancellors have chosen this city to seal their reconciliation and renew their European vows. Europe was an attempt to solve the German question, once and for all. For the French, it was about ensuring that it could never again be threatened on its eastern border, while not repeating the mistakes of reparations and Versailles. Industrial interdependence and energy security were required, alongside political reconstruction and collective defence. The plan, conceived by Monnet and presented by Schuman in 1950, proposed the creation of a European Coal and Steel Community. This begat the European

Economic Community under the Treaty of Rome in 1957, the Single European Act of 1987 and the Maastricht Treaty of 1992.

The chances are that almost no Brits, outside the rarefied world of foreign policy, know much about these European milestones. By contrast, the EU is an integral part of the German syllabus. Students are taught at the start of high school about the four pillars – the Commission, Parliament, Council and Court. They have a fairly good idea of what is decided at national level and what powers are transferred to Brussels. Germans, I have found, are generally not starry-eyed about Europe. They accept that all countries have legitimate, and sometimes divergent, national interests. They know they are still the object of suspicion. They know that their entire post-war reconstruction and rehabilitation is based on the notion of Europe, for which compromises on sovereignty are unavoidable. Take currency: the Deutschmark was venerated, and alongside Mercedes or BMW it was possibly Germany's proudest global brand. To give it up, as they did in 2002, for the sake of European integration was nothing short of remarkable. Germany has always accepted its role as Europe's paymaster – contributing far more than the UK once Thatcher had secured her rebate. Monetary union exacerbated the imbalance between rich and poor states, between prudent and profligate (in the eyes of the beholders) and between north and south. The debt crisis that followed the global financial crash of 2007–8 revived in the eyes of many in Europe the spectre of an over-weaning Germany. Contagion hit not just Greece, but Ireland, Portugal and others. Between 2011 and 2012, governments collapsed in just under half of Eurozone member states. The European Central Bank and IMF were the main actors in engineering a bailout for Greece, but only under the most stringent terms. Behind the scenes, the key player was Germany. After all, it would be Germany that would stump up most of the money. A broader debate emerged immediately afterwards about the causes of the crash, the failure of economies to improve living standards since, the rights and wrongs of trade surpluses and of austerity versus Keynesian economics. What is beyond dispute, though, is that Greece endured severe economic pain and that the Germans were caricatured not just in Greece, but across much of Europe, as belligerent Teutons. The visceral public hostility in Greece – a poster in Athens of Merkel with a Hitler moustache scribbled on – was painful for Germans. Most opinion polls, however, showed broad support for the tough line their government took. Germans struggle to understand, let alone sympathize with, those they deem to be financially irresponsible.

The most important relationship for the success of the European project, on which most depends, is the one between Germany and France. Underpinning this relationship of mutual dependency, and the centrality of Europe, is the Élysée Treaty, now sixty years old. With a troublesome and distant America, and with the UK now out of the loop, Germany needs France as never before. Tensions between leaders are not new, but whenever required, the countries have come together at crucial moments. Schmidt and Giscard d'Estaing did so in the late seventies over the global monetary crisis; Kohl and Mitterrand on reunification; Schröder and Chirac over Iraq.

Merkel worked closely with presidents Nicolas Sarkozy and François Hollande. During those periods the German chancellor was always first among equals with the president. Since Emmanuel Macron swept to power with his centrist *En Marche* revolution, Merkel has struggled. She resents his grand gestures. She sees his flamboyant overtures to Trump and Putin as naive and untrustworthy. He did not bother to run them past her, or even tell her what he was about to do. In turn, he has become frustrated with her deadening hand, her refusal to engage with his attempts to forge a new Europe.

The irony is that the one partner the Germans have probably most aligned with in policy terms is the UK. As a result, the pain surrounding the UK's departure from the EU is real, but they have already got over it. At a British-German dinner in Berlin in 2019, the justice minister at the time, Katarina Barley, gave this painful prediction: 'Even if we agree with you in the future, we will always be more distant, because family comes first and you are no longer family.' She should know, being half British. Her father's side comes from Brexit-supporting Lincolnshire. Within weeks of Brexit taking place, Barley's warning seemed to come true. British diplomats and others saw how quickly they were shut out of important discussions – or relegated to an afterthought.

Germany needs a united Europe, not just for trade but for its sense of purpose. As Merkel herself noted wistfully: 'I see the European Union as our life insurance. Germany is far too small to exert geo-political influence on its own.'[43] Germany will have to ensure that, whatever the squalls of Brexit and the populist right, the EU will survive. At the same time, America's withdrawal from Europe will not end with Trump.

Germany remained the protected child far longer than it should have been. That is over. With the credibility of the US and UK undermined, Germany has found itself in the deeply uncomfortable position of being the standard-bearer for liberal democracy. It is the cornerstone of Europe. It has a big role to play – and will be required to make tough decisions. That will be the biggest challenge of all for Merkel's successor and for future generations of Germans.

5

The Wonder

The economic miracle and its aftermath

An industrial estate in Neuss, on the outskirts of Düsseldorf, is the epicentre of European sushi. Or so Tim Hornemann insists. I have just been picked up from the airport by one of Hornemann's old school friends, Tom Bolzen, in his Porsche. In the parking area of the factory, his car holds its own alongside the various latest model Mercedes, BMWs and Audis. After a quick introduction, Hornemann leads us onto the factory floor. It takes me a bit of time to manoeuvre my frame into the paper-thin disposable overalls, hairnet and mask. Rules are rules. No germs must get between the maki roll and the customer.

Hornemann's company is quintessentially German. It may be global in reach, but it is local in its loyalties. It is one of hundreds of thousands of small and medium-sized enterprises (with turnover of under €50 million and up to 250 workers) in towns across Germany. The *Mittelstand* employs around three quarters of the country's workforce and produces more than half the economic output. It is the backbone of the economy and the backbone of society.

Hornemann has cornered much of the market in low-cost sushi sold at the counters of the big supermarket chains Edeka, Rewe, Aldi and Lidl. He was supposed to follow his father in the sausage trade but a trip to California led him astray. Impressed by the sight of bars selling raw fish in department stores, he brought the exotic product back home. It didn't start well. He and his brother named their operation the Tsunami Sushi Bar. 'Nobody knew what the word meant at the time.' That was 2004. To be fair, he was only twenty-eight years old. Now he is king of the sea. Natsu, as his company is called, imports frozen salmon and prawns from Norway. State-of-the-art machines defrost the fish, steam the rice (from Valencia) and administer the wasabi (from China). Workers, mainly from Eastern Europe, arrange the mathematically cut slices at high speed. Then off it goes in lorries and containers across Germany and Europe, as far as Scotland.

We talk business and ethics. I tell Hornemann and Bolzen that wherever I go, I'm lectured about how socially aware German bosses are. I'm getting a little sceptical. I shouldn't be, they insist. A big difference between Germany and other countries is that owners here feel a strong sense of local loyalty. 'When I think of selling my company, I get stomach cramps,' Tim says. 'You wouldn't be respected by your neighbours,' Tom adds. 'You'd be running away from your responsibilities. You'd be called a coward.' Nor should company bosses lord it over others. Seek to be part of the best organization; don't try to be the best individual. Don't boast. The term they use is *demütig*, humble. They admit they have had it easy, particularly compared with their parents' post-war generation, who had to rebuild companies and communities from scratch. I wonder about the behaviour of the management at Volkswagen during the emissions scandal. 'Those people were assholes,' they reply. 'They ruined their reputation, they played God.' Multinationals, they say, are one thing. The *Mittelstand* is quite another.

Local companies are required to act as good citizens. They are not thanked for sponsoring sports teams and music clubs. It's required of them. *Mitmachen*. Loosely translated: get stuck in. It's required of me too. I spend a long weekend immersed in the mores of small-town Germany. Each place seems to merge with the next. The Porsche has taken us to Mönchengladbach. Bolzen is an architect who designs apartment blocks that are either carbon-neutral or carbon-negative. He takes me to one such building and shows me the solar batteries in the basement. Residents can sell back any surplus energy they don't use in return for reduced rent. Tom's home, in a pristine residential neighbourhood, is picture-perfect, modern, stylish and eco-friendly. I don't have the heart to ask him how this squares with the Porsche, Lexus and two other family cars.

The third member of this *Mittelstand*-manager-mates' group is Roger Brandts. Mönchengladbach has been known since the mid-nineteenth century as a textile city. Most of the production is long gone, offshored to cheaper producers in countries such as China and Turkey. Now it is known for a number of specialized engineering companies. One of the father figures of the textile trade, Franz Brandts, learnt how to use the power loom in England and brought machines over that would industrialize the work. But Brandts was the opposite of a Dickensian employer. In the 1880s, during the Bismarck era, he set up an association for the welfare of his staff and their families, steeped in Catholicism – the first to establish workers' rights, including housing, schooling and medical care. It was paternalistic and a precursor to present-day German concepts of the social market. Roger is a fourth-generation descendant. We are sitting in the building that once housed the family firm. Now it resembles a safari tent. The family business was wound up some time ago, but there was no question of changing the line of work. After studying textile technology (what else?), he got a job on the fast-track management scheme at the department store Peek & Cloppenburg. In 1998, he was sent to South Africa on a six-month internship. He happened to watch the film *Out of Africa* and decided he wanted to create a clothing line that harked back to the clothes the characters were wearing in the film.

'My father wouldn't talk to me for six months,' Brandts explains. It is hard for outsiders to understand but few Germans give up a good, safe job on a whim. He reckoned he would need 60,000 Deutschmarks (around £20,000 then), to purchase a clothes collection, a car and a computer. He had to borrow from the bank. They don't like taking risks either, so they set him a high interest rate of 7 per cent, giving him five years to pay it back. He called his company Fynch-Hatton after one of the lead characters in the movie, the aristocratic English big-game hunter Denys Finch Hatton. I ask Brandts what image he is seeking to reproduce in his clothing line. 'Drinking a gin and tonic and relaxing in the open air under an acacia tree at sundown'. Very colonial, oh so British. It has proved popular. Fynch-Hatton is now exporting to fifty-five countries from Russia to China, New Zealand to Pakistan.

Mönchengladbach is a neat, unspectacular city, with its share of social problems – drug abuse, late-night anti-social behaviour and a high street blighted by rows of boarded-up shops that cannot compete with the indoor shopping centre. With a good public transport system covering the whole region, many people use it as a dormitory town for commuting to wealthier places such as Düsseldorf. The one place where everyone congregates is Borussia Park, the local football club's stadium. They call the town the Manchester of Germany: textiles, industry and football. While Borussia Mönchengladbach is not the team it was, and is not a touch on City or United, it has a fan base that never wavers. Brandts and Hornemann have executive boxes, as their companies are sponsors. I go with Bolzen and his teenage son and daughter to the terraces. I am transported back into the seventies or eighties. This is good old standing-only. People are smoking (one of my pet hates about Germany), and servers come around with a giant beer keg on their backs to fill up supporters' pint glasses. Big money is coming into the game, but still all but two of the German Bundesliga clubs are majority-owned by their fans. The idea of selling to any old Russian or Emirati oligarch would be seen as betrayal.

I am south of Frankfurt, in the largely forgettable industrial town of Mannheim. I have come for a meeting with Markus Schill, founder of VRmagic, a company that specializes in health care. After studying physics at the university in nearby Heidelberg, he did a postgraduate degree in modelling how soft tissue behaves under pressure. He was looking at craniectomy, a surgery that involves removing part of the skull to relieve pressure from a swelling that follows a head injury. In those days, he explains, it would take up to four days to train surgeons in the procedure. His supervisor, a hard taskmaster, told him he needed to speed up the training process, to real time. As it happened, Schill was reading a book about virtual reality. He decided to build a simulator, similar to the type used for flight pilots. Before this, surgeons had to practise on their patients and they regarded failures as part of the learning process. In 1998, Schill applied for his first grant, but the German Research Foundation turned him down. They read his business plan, but were not convinced he could bring it into being. 'The bank asked me what I thought the market size was. I said I had no idea. I hadn't thought about it.' He found another way to raise money, via venture capitalists and local family foundations. Three years later he started his company. It was tough to begin with. 'We built one machine. The first version had all manner of technical errors.' He keeps it in the office for posterity. His investors stuck with him. 'The financing scene in Germany is conservative. You have to know someone who knows someone. They are slow in picking up opportunities, but quite often it's the case that if it's succeeded somewhere else, then they'll invest.'

Along with regionalization, family ties and social responsibility, another key aspect of the *Mittelstand* is its emphasis on specialization. Many of the most successful entrepreneurs find a single product – a particular machine tool or a household appliance. Theirs is a narrow expertise, but they often then end up cornering the global market, focusing relentlessly on acquiring and expanding their customer base, and making sure they stay ahead of the competition. Schill's surgical simulators dominate the market in most countries. VRmagic supplies and operates hundreds of models for cataract operations around the world, with seventy employees in Mannheim and a base in the US, in Cambridge, Massachusetts. I ask Schill when, or whether, he will sell the company. He looks at me askance. 'I love the science. I feel what I'm doing is helping medicine. I'm not doing it for the money.'

Two statistics stand out. Some 80 per cent of German GDP is derived from family businesses. Two thirds of successful global *Mittelstand* companies are based in places with fewer than fifty thousand inhabitants. If one just looks at western Germany, small towns there have suffered some depopulation, but the exodus to larger cities is much less than in other countries, such as France, Britain, Poland or Spain. It is not just family firms that stay put. Multinationals are spread around the country – Mercedes and Bosch are in Stuttgart; Siemens and BMW in Munich; ThyssenKrupp is in Essen; VW is in Wolfsburg, on the western side of what was the old inner German border; Adidas is in Herzogenaurach, north of Nuremberg; BASF's headquarters is in the Rhine port town of Ludwigshafen; and software giant SAP (one of the few early German tech successes) is south of Heidelberg in a place called Walldorf. In many other countries in the Western world, industrial and business operations have become very much centralized towards the major cities, whereas in Germany, advanced manufacturing, international footprint and regionalism go together.

Most of all, it is the smaller firms that set Germany apart. The business strategist and author Hermann Simon has coined the term 'hidden champions'. These are companies, like the ones I've mentioned, that devote themselves to a niche. These are success stories of globalization and free trade. The individuals in charge are classic monomaniacs, single-minded and devoted to a single cause or product. They usually shun the limelight. 'Deeply hidden under the headlines of sensational business successes lies a completely unnoticed source of leadership wisdom,'[1] Simon writes. He lists 2,700 such firms worldwide. Half of them come from Germany. The US, Japan and China follow, a long way behind. Other European countries are nowhere in sight.

Ludwig Erhard's radical reforms of 1948 had an instant effect on revitalizing the German economy after the war. Germans were missing roughly ten hours of work a week as they scoured their neighbourhoods for food and other basics. Within a few months of the reforms being put into place, that number was down to four hours. On the eve of the currency reform and lifting of price controls, industrial production was about half of its level in 1936. By the end of 1948 it had risen to 80 per cent.[2] Henry Wallich, a Yale University economist and later Federal Reserve governor, wrote in his 1955 book, *The Mainsprings of the German Revival*: 'The spirit of the country changed overnight. The grey, hungry, dead-looking figures wandering about the streets in their everlasting search for food came to life.'[3] In 1958, industrial production was four times higher than it had been just one decade earlier. The economy grew an average of 8 per cent a year over this period (the levels the present-day Chinese have regarded as the benchmark for an emerging power); the figure was twice as fast as any major economy in Europe. By 1968, barely two decades after the end of the war that had left the country in ruins, West Germany's economy was larger than that of the UK. The trend continued remorselessly. In 2003, it became the largest exporter to Eastern Europe. In 2005, it surpassed the US as the leading source of machinery imports into India. It is the largest exporter of vehicles to China. Most impressively, in 2003, Germany overtook the US to become the biggest total exporter of goods in the world – a position it lost only in 2010, to China.

Data such as these tell only part of the story. The economic miracle was also a social project. Erhard, who was economics minister from 1949 to 1963 and chancellor from 1963 to 1966, is known as the father of the *Wirtschaftswunder*, or what became known internationally as the Miracle on the Rhine, the economic transformation of Germany in the second half of the twentieth century. Underpinning it was the idea of the social market, a term coined by an economist and sociologist, Alfred Müller-Armack. He sought a 'new synthesis' of market freedom and social protection. According to the theory, policymakers guide the market to produce the maximum wealth, which is then redistributed in the name of social justice. Or to put it another way – it's about everyone feeling they play a part. At the heart of corporate governance is the practice of co-determination. This was enshrined in law in 1976, requiring large companies to ensure that half of the seats of the supervisory board are given over to workers' representatives, elected usually via the trade union. In the case of medium-sized companies, the quota is a third. Just as workers do not feel out of place in the boardroom, many German bosses would not think twice about having their lunch in the canteen.

In other countries, notably the United States and Britain, such a division of power between employers and unions is generally seen as dangerously socialist, but Germany has had variants on this theme since the early years of the Industrial Revolution. The only concerted attempt to stamp out organized labour was under the Nazis. Then, during the 1980s, in the heyday of Thatcherism and Reaganism, some in Germany were having second thoughts about their system, wondering if the Anglo-Saxon 'hire 'em, fire 'em' approach wasn't more conducive to growth and productivity. Helmut Kohl tried two industrial relations moves: one to reduce the coverage of collective bargaining, the other to reduce the power of works councils. Both were scuppered early on – by the employers. They had long concluded that a system with strong unions and regulated input was preferable to weaker, angrier and less predictable worker representation.

I talked with a couple of people who were familiar with both models. Jürgen Maier was born in Austria but went to Leeds at the age of ten when his mother remarried an Englishman. (He remembers being bullied and called names ... German, Austrian, it was all the same thing.) He worked his way up on the floor of the Siemens factory in Congleton, Cheshire, before becoming its boss and later the head of the company's large UK operation. He enjoys the informality of the English workplace. But he lists several attributes that set Germany apart – leadership, social fabric, training and long-termism. 'I was predicting from the early nineties that the German model was going to fail,' he says. 'I have been proven wrong, time and again. The German model does ultimately work.'

A recent research report by MIT, UC Berkeley, and the German Institute for Employment Research compared medium-sized German companies that had workers on the board with those that didn't. The study's finding is striking. Firms in the first category had stocks of fixed long-term capital which were about 40–50 per cent larger than those of companies in the second group. In other words, putting workers on the board leads to significantly more investment. Wages rose more at the companies with shared governance, but only in line with workers' productivity. Revenue growth was about the same for both groups, and profitability at the companies with workers on the board was either slightly higher or equal to the other group, depending on the measure. In short, co-determination proved neutral to strongly positive on all the measures of corporate success. And yet classic free marketeers generally expect workers on boards to be self-serving, blocking change and extracting higher wages for themselves.

At the employers' federation in Berlin, the BDI, I discuss 'responsible capitalism', a term that has become common parlance only recently in other countries. Stefan Mair, a member of its executive board, extols the virtues of unions. He also talks of redistribution. German bosses, he says, regard shareholder value as an important goal, but not the only one. 'Social cohesion is a good investment decision,' he says. I invite him to explain. Set a market-friendly frame but build institutions and norms that lead to equitable distribution of economic gains, he says. And look after your employees. During and immediately after the financial crash, German companies did everything they could to avoid getting rid of workers. People were put on short-time work, told to bring forward annual leave, invited to take unpaid leave – anything not to disrupt the chain. They assumed that orders would eventually increase and did not want to start recruiting or training new people. Workers accepted the short-term sacrifices to keep their jobs. 'This helped us to recover relatively quickly. It was a rational decision.'

Manufacturing and engineering; exporting; solid public finances; a high skills base; social solidarity. The German way.

Germany has experienced recent economic dips but has ridden through them. Throughout the 1990s and 2000s, growth was lower than the Eurozone average. The shock of absorbing the East German economy, with sixteen million people, thousands of outdated smokestack factories and a fifty-year legacy of central planning, would have brought any other economy to its knees. At the time, everyone began to deride Germany as a dinosaur. *The Economist*'s famous editorial of June 1999, which policymakers and politicians in Berlin seem to know by heart, said: 'As economic growth stalls yet again, Germany is being branded the sick man (or even the Japan) of Europe.'[4] Strengths were suddenly seen as weaknesses. The yearning for stability had led to a labour market that was too inflexible and a welfare state too generous.

Germany's sense of worth took a knock. In 2003, Gerhard Schröder followed up his surprise re-election with a radical package of economic reforms, the likes of which had not been seen since Erhard in 1948. The country was hurting: unemployment had risen to 9.5 per cent, and the budget deficit was approaching 4 per cent of GDP.[5] Economic growth had ground

to a halt. The labour market was strangled. The unemployed
were entitled to refuse any offer of work unless it was in their
existing profession. The jobs market was barely functioning.
The government's answer was to establish a commission. The
fifteen-member group was chaired by Peter Hartz, Volkswagen's
HR director. Many of the reforms it proposed, on training, tax
and national insurance, were uncontroversial. It was the fourth
of five elements – welfare benefits – that was most divisive. In
putting forward the reforms, Schröder received more support
from the opposition CDU than from his own party. He had to
face down the SPD by threatening to resign. He appreciated all
the help he could find. The leaders of the Protestant and Roman
Catholic Churches in Germany took the highly unusual step
of publicly expressing their support for the government's proposals, saying they could see no other way of getting people
back to work.

The measures passed through the Bundestag in December
2003 and took effect in January 2005. Even now they are a source
of heated argument. The package put unemployment and social
assistance into a single system; curbed incentives to retire early;
and made it easier to employ part-time and contract workers.
Most controversially, unemployment benefit was instantly cut
to 50 per cent of a worker's last salary; it had previously been
two thirds. It would be paid only up to a maximum of one year,
whereas prior to that they could get benefits indefinitely. Even
a single failure to turn up to a job centre meeting could lead to
a partial loss of money. The slogan was *Fördern und Fordern*
– support people and make demands of them. Schröder, like
his friend Tony Blair, was enamoured of global jargon, so the
reforms were peppered with 'Denglisch' terms like 'Jobcenter'
and 'Mini-Job'.

Schröder pushed Germany more towards the harsh realities

of global markets and away from the social consensus. The SPD paid the price. Schröder lost the election he called in 2005. Many on the left looked for scapegoats. While on the campaign trail, the SPD's chairman, Franz Müntefering, attacked foreign investors whose 'profit-maximising strategies' posed a threat to democracy. 'They have no face, fall like a plague of locusts on companies, stripping them bare before moving on to the next one,'[6] he declared. The word locust was standard Nazi anti-Semitic propaganda. Müntefering had to apologize.

On succeeding Schröder, Merkel reaped the economic benefits, while distancing herself from the politics; she was smart enough not to align herself with his handiwork. Competitiveness and productivity increased. Unemployment fell. Investment flowed back. German companies made a beeline for Eastern Europe and the BRICs, countries booming and flushed with credit. Exports soared again. In the seven years before the financial crisis, Germany's exports increased 75 per cent, compared with only 20 per cent for its rivals.[7] Once again, Deutschland AG was taking over the world. It had done so by adopting its own model of capitalism, a social market that, in spite of its faults, had managed the twin achievement of consistent economic growth alongside relatively greater social cohesion.

In 2005, the economic historian Werner Abelshauser published a seminal book called *The Dynamics of German Industry: Germany's Path toward the New Economy and the American Challenge*. He maintained that the two dominant economies of the twentieth century, the US and Germany, were closely aligned until the 1980s, only starting to diverge with deregulation and the get-rich-quick culture ushered in by Reagan and Thatcher and their guru Milton Friedman. He later argued, in an interview with *Die Zeit* headlined 'Are we not the richest?', that the 2008 financial crash had proven both the morality and efficacy of the German way, suggesting that Germans did not rely as heavily on individual acquisitiveness as they do in other states in order to be content. Instead they looked to a sense of commonwealth, to use the original turn of phrase. 'In Germany, the state is traditionally regarded as the guarantor,'[8] he said.

The evidence backs this up. Germans do not participate in the stock market nearly as much as people in other countries. They save and they save, irrespective of extremely low and sometimes negative interest rates. Almost all of that saving goes into pensions and life insurance. More than 100 million policies have been bought – more than there are people. Value creation is not derived through high-risk investments. Of course, one can overdo the differentiation. German banks have proved no less voracious; Germany has its fair share of tax dodgers; Germans love their domestic luxuries and their holidays; they venerate the car. These caveats aside, the German social state is a culture shock for those with a free-market Anglo-Saxon mindset.

Even after the Hartz reforms, everything has been designed to mitigate risk. *Langsam aber sicher*. Slow but sure. The search for consensus in the boardroom could be seen as preventing spontaneity or speed. Germans see no contradiction between economic success and social cohesion. What is so remarkable about the country is that, apart from a few short periods, the economy has remained consistently strong, seemingly without people being obsessed with work. France has its thirty-five-hour legislation, which prevents employers from forcing anyone to work more than the maximum hours, although they can by mutual consent supplement that by a certain amount of over-time. It was introduced in 2000 to increase employment and productivity. The results have been mixed, depending on the criteria used. Germany does not have that rigidity, but in some ways it is going further than France. With the presence of trade unions on the boards of companies, it is doing so without the seemingly endless wave of strikes that have epitomized French industrial relations for decades. When strikes are called in Germany, they are invariably a measure of last resort – and they usually result in a compromise.

In early 2018, however, a concession was won by workers that marked a new departure. IG Metall, the largest union, secured a deal in which all workers in the electrical and metal sectors could opt to go down to a twenty-eight-hour working week for two years in order to look after children and elderly or sick relatives – alongside a hefty hourly pay increase.[9] Their employers are required to restore their full-time status (if the employee wants it) when the term comes to an end. This had a domino effect across industry with the railway and transport union EVG next in line with a similar agreement. Tellingly, workers at Deutsche Post were given the choice between a 5 per cent pay rise or an extra hundred or so hours of holiday over two years. When the union representing them and other services workers polled its members, 56 per cent opted for more time off, against 41 per cent for more money.

The Germans call it *Entschleunigung*, literally slowing down, or what others refer to as work–life balance. It has been achieved without affecting output. German productivity has been the object of envy for years, not least from the British, who work some of the longest hours. In 2017, business secretary Greg Clark noted that, 'It takes people in Germany four days to produce what people in the UK take five days to produce. And that means that they can pay themselves better, or they need to work fewer hours. This is a long-standing challenge of the British economy.'[10]

Bizarrely, for a country that prides itself on its social market, it took until 2015 for Germany to introduce a national minimum wage. That was a full forty-five years after France and sixteen years after the supposedly cut-throat UK. Not only did employers resist (they usually do everywhere), but so did the unions. German unions saw the idea as undermining their negotiating power. They argued that while it was necessary in other countries, because workers had no other protections to fall back on, in Germany they were already covered by co-determination. Given that union membership is decreasing, albeit at a slower pace than elsewhere in the world, this was a position guided more by self-interest than by principle. Before the legislation was finally passed in 2013 and introduced in 2015, an estimated 10 per cent of Germans, almost all non-unionized, were earning below the introductory level of €9.90 per hour.

The definition of personal comfort and social stability in Germany is not just confined to take-home pay. Many workers have traditionally looked to their employers for guidance and protection. Companies have insulated them from some of the vagaries of market forces, providing insurance, social clubs and a sense of belonging. 'The social market economy works well for those citizens who are on the treadmill,' explains Christian Odendahl of the Centre for European Reform. 'If you fall outside, you end up in the services sector, where you are regarded as a second-class worker.' He means those in the gig economy, working on informal contracts or zero hours as cleaners, security guards or delivery riders. Self-employment or freelance work is considered risky, not what Germans are about. More generally, many people look down on the services sector. There are some exceptions. The insurance industry is regarded as grown-up. Banking too, although public sentiment is hardly sympathetic, as everywhere else in the world. In Britain, services account for 80 per cent of output, a far higher figure, and many see services as the future, and industrial production as 'legacy industries'. The UK's creative industries collectively bring in over £100 billion a year to the economy.[11] To Germans most of this is 'entertainment'. High culture is another thing. Classical musicians for instance are hugely respected, but their worth is based on their artistic talent and not judged on the basis of economic utility.

Germany is slow to innovate. In many digital areas the country lags behind – from cashless payments to e-government. 'We are usually the incumbent,' Siemens' CEO Kaeser tells me. 'That produces a defensive environment in the face of disruptive innovation.' We discuss the social stigma of failure. I cite the example of a South Korean entrepreneur, barely in his mid-twenties, who declared proudly at a conference that he was on his fifth start-up. The others had all gone under, but this time it had worked. The term 'fail fast' is common boardroom talk in the US and Asia. Kaeser notes that Americans can apply for Chapter 11 bankruptcy on one floor of the district judge's office and then go upstairs to open a new company. Not so in Germany. The youngest company on Germany's DAX stock market index is software giant SAP, founded in 1972, which perhaps helps explain why Germany was initially slow to embrace technology and start-up culture. The market value of the world's largest company, Apple, is now the equivalent of all those listed on the DAX.

Yet the Germans are catching up. In the course of the mid-2010s, Berlin has had the highest percentage of start-ups of any city in Europe. Venture capital investment in German-based tech has been increasing on average 60–80 per cent, year on year, over the past few years. Most of that goes to the capital city which is now vying with London for Europe's brightest minds. Frankfurt and Munich are also becoming more attractive for investors. There is no shortage of German success stories, particularly in e-commerce and blockchain: online fashion retailer Zalando, food service Delivery Hero, music-sharing service SoundCloud, alongside investors and angels such as Rocket Internet and Cherry Ventures. The granddaddy of them all is price comparison website Idealo, which began back in 2000, when pretty much nothing was kitted out for the tech sector. Now everyone has piled in. Bill Gates has put money into a science network; his successor at Microsoft, Steve Ballmer, opened an accelerator in the heart of Berlin. Corporate Germany is joining in. Springer, the once fusty newspaper group, has joined forces with Porsche to open an accelerator called APX. It, and others like it, are based in a backwater Berlin street close to where Checkpoint Charlie was situated. Inside is the usual array of millennials and Generation Xers in their hoodies and T-shirts. It is hard to tell who is German and who is not as everyone is speaking English. Katy Campbell, a Scot, is running a course for female entrepreneurs every Monday evening. She wouldn't swap Berlin for anywhere else, she says. Other cities have been and gone.

Berlin's particular vibe cuts both ways for the tech sector. Google has a major presence in the centre of the city, but it would like to expand further. Its plans to build its seventh Campus (hubs for tech entrepreneurs such as those it has in London, Madrid, Tel Aviv, Warsaw and elsewhere) were thwarted after two years of protests. It had identified a disused electrical substation in Kreuzberg. This, it assumed, was the perfect location; Mozilla, WeWork and others were already there. But it didn't reckon on the locals who refused to have Silicon Valley mega-corporations invading their space. Instead they have the Factory. I'm walking through a former Agfa camera plant with Martin Eyerer. He is chief innovation officer by day but also one of Germany's best-known DJs. The place is a mix of the corporate (Siemens, Audi, Daimler) and the achingly hip. Meeting areas include a bed of squashy balls to lie on. A third of the four thousand people who have joined the Factory, at either of its two sites in the city, are German. The rest come from seventy countries. The original Kreuzberg hippies resent the recent influx of the hipsters. They are seen as too 'capitalist', Eyerer says, before adding: 'This is where 1968 meets the old GDR.'

His frustration is understandable. Change is resisted not just by the elderly, but also by a sizeable section of the young and the left. Yet a small part of me respects the idea that many local communities, in Berlin and other cities, refuse to be taken for granted. The social market, the sense of belonging to community, is deeply embedded.

Germany is less unequal than many countries, but more unequal than might be assumed. The Gini coefficient, the accepted data set that measures inequality country by country, has Germany roughly halfway down the list of thirty-six OECD states, just below the Nordics, but much better than the US and UK, and marginally better than France. Since Schröder's Hartz reforms, inequality has increased. In 2019, *Forbes* magazine listed 120 German dollar billionaires, more than double the number in Britain and equating to one for every 727,000 Germans, not far from America's tally of one for every 539,000. Ireland, whose per capita income is not far below Germany's, has only six billionaires.[12] A recent report by the German Institute for Economic Research (DIW) came to the attention-grabbing conclusion that forty-five of the wealthiest households in Germany commanded as much wealth as half of the population.[13] In the United States and other countries, the ultra-wealthy devour the rich lists that are published by *Forbes*, or in the UK by the *Sunday Times*. They feel affronted if they have gone down a notch, and yet there is a difference in Germany. Whether they follow the rankings or not, the super-rich on the whole do all they can to keep out of the public eye.

Very little of such wealth is 'old money' – much of that was wiped out by the Nazi dictatorship and two world wars. Many of the super-rich have made their money from the *Mittelstand*. Number three on the German rich list is Dieter Schwarz of Lidl. The owners of supermarket rival Aldi, the Albrecht family, come in fifth. Tenth on the list is the Würth family, whose company, based in Künzelsau, a small town in Baden-Württemberg, makes screws and other hardware. Many of these owners have kept their companies private. Some have family trusts and foundations. They are likely to have a fleet of cars, large houses, country homes and the usual accoutrements of wealth, but there's very little ostentatious flashing the cash in public. That would be seen as distasteful.

The des-res in Germany is a nice family home surrounded by good, solid neighbours, who do not cause a fuss and are neither too rich nor too poor. Streets should be neither down at heel nor ostentatious. Average household net income per capita is approximately €30,000 a year, roughly 10 per cent above the OECD median. Domestic consumption does not reflect that. Apart from the ubiquitous car, the sensible household gadgets and the summer holiday in the sun, Germany is not a particularly consumerist society, as the restrictive shopping hours attest. What matters is to husband your resources carefully. German families squirrel away almost twice as much as US and UK households. The typical German household has £8,600 in savings and investments, against £5,000 in the UK.

Almost half of the population say in surveys that if they ever had to buy anything on credit they would be embarrassed. Contrast that with other countries, particularly the US and the UK.

In Britain, as of December 2019, overall personal debt had risen from £180 billion to £225 billion in a decade. On average, every adult is sitting on £4,300 of overdrafts, personal loans and credit cards.[14] To Germans that would be anathema. What matters to them is not risk-based asset purchasing (home ownership is among the lowest in the Western world) but securing one's future without risk. The retirement system is relatively standard, with three pillars – the mandatory state pension, company schemes and private plans. As in other countries, the German government is trying to deal with the problems of an ageing population without causing too much social upheaval. The retirement age is gradually due to go up to sixty-seven, with some mooting the possibility of sixty-nine. Contributions are also to be increased, while the maximum pension will eventually be reduced to 67 per cent of net pay, from 70 per cent. The decisions have all required considerable deliberation.

Since the financial crash, a key cause of public hostility has been wage stagnation. The bottom half of earners have suffered most. The flip side of decisions not to lay off workers has been agreement on pay restraint. Fears of unemployment and inflation are still stoked by memories of the Great Depression of the early 1930s. The emphasis on exports has also had an effect. One of the reasons why Germany has dominated so many markets has been by keeping unit labour costs down.

The first _Tafel_ opened its doors in Berlin in 1993, distributing vegetables and fruit to the homeless. _Tafel_ means table and it was Germany's first food bank. Its organizers say that demand has grown exponentially since the Hartz reforms. Around half of those who are fed by its outlets are pensioners and children. Public donations have steadily risen, but they are more than offset by the increase in recipients, whose number has been swollen by the post-2015 migrant influx. The impact of this sudden wave has produced a double challenge for politicians – dealing with the actual needs of the refugees, but also the politics. In 2018, there was a furious row when a food bank in Essen stopped giving out food to migrants in order to prioritize locals. Even Merkel stepped into the fray, saying it was 'not good'[15] to distinguish between the needy. 'We won't let ourselves be reprimanded by the chancellor for what is a consequence of her politics,' shot back a furious *Tafel* chief, Jochen Brühl. He reminded her of Germany's 'enormous poverty problem', 'unbelievable low-wage sector', 'inadequate basic welfare' and 'half-cocked immigration policy'.[16]

Some twelve million Germans, just over 15 per cent of the population, are classified as poor, as defined by the standard international measure of an income below 60 per cent of the household median, giving them less than €900 per month.[17] This is the highest number since the difficult early years of reunification. Many belong to the so-called 'working poor'. Welfare payments top up their income but not by a large amount. As of 2015, there were just under three million children and young people living in Germany at risk of poverty, just under a fifth of the overall total. The real hidden poverty is in respect to old people. The number of pensioners living in poverty has risen by 33 per cent in the last ten years, an increase that is much higher than in other groups.[18]

In the UK, the buzzword of the Johnson government is 'levelling up', addressing the chronic gap in investment and standard of living between North and South. Post-war Germany has always done that. Equalization payments were established to ensure fairness between the centre and the regions and between the regions themselves. Reunification took that to another level, with the Solidarity Tax. In spite of its best efforts, however, the regional mismatches are increasing – and they are not just between East and West. Over the past decade, poverty has fallen in thirty-five out of ninety-five districts, including many in the East. But in over a quarter of districts, poverty has increased by more than 20 per cent over the same period.[19]

The northern city of Bremen, the smallest state, has the highest poverty rate – 22 per cent of the population – due mainly to the closure of its shipbuilding yards and the failure to provide sustainable new jobs in the area. Aside from the states of the former GDR, other regions with high poverty rates include Hamburg (which also has some of the wealthiest areas) and Schleswig-Holstein in the north and northwest. The central state of Hesse has gone from comparative affluence to hardship. North Rhine-Westphalia, Germany's most populous state, remains the number-one problem region. It is not hard to see why. What is remarkable about the three firms in the Mönchengladbach area described at the start of the chapter is that they are doing so well in this deprived area, which in general has a lack of *Mittelstand* companies. In the past, cities like Dortmund, Bochum and Gelsenkirchen constituted Germany's industrial heartland, based on the production of chemicals, steel and coal. Essen was the proud home of the nineteenth-century industrialist, steelmaker and weapons maker par excellence, Alfred Krupp.

The Ruhr area was one of the main targets of Allied bombers. 'Here lies the heart of Germany's industrial might,'[20] wrote Henry Morgenthau, US Treasury secretary, in a memo to President Roosevelt. 'This area should not only be stripped of all existing industry there, but so weakened and controlled that it cannot for the foreseeable future become an industrial area again.' The Ruhr was duly flattened in numerous bombing raids. Four fifths of its buildings were destroyed or heavily damaged. Many of those inhabitants who survived fled to other regions. After the war, in spite of the *Wirtschaftswunder*, the towns of the

Ruhr followed the classic cycle of post-industrial poverty and demoralization. Their populations have shrunk; unemployment is twice the national average. A number of districts have become no-go areas. Their city councils have sought the usual routes out – building tech parks, giant retail outlets or bidding to house new federal quangos. Some of these schemes have worked but many others have not.

Frankfurt faces different challenges. The financial heart of Germany has been pulling out all the stops to attract global bankers in the wake of Brexit. The marketing is slick, proclaiming many of the benefits of its business, social and cultural life. The city is getting a little livelier – albeit from what was a low base. The new Old Town (the oxymoron is lost on no one) has made it more attractive. The airport can take you anywhere in the world. The international schools are high quality. The housing stock is good. Countryside is easily accessible.

But there is a problem. Germany's banks, global and local, are a mess. A combination of poor governance, bad lending decisions, poor tech investment and bureaucracy have over the years stopped Frankfurt from challenging London and New York as a global financial centre. At every level the banks have been found wanting. Deutsche Bank used to be seen as a national champion. For the past decade it has been a national embarrassment. Its fall from grace is similar to that of other banks around the world, but hubris, risk-taking and incompetence were not supposed to be the German way. The rot set in when it decided in the late 1980s to take on the sharks of Wall Street. It began with the acquisition of blue-blooded British merchant bank Morgan Grenfell. It pushed into European markets, buying Banco de Madrid. In 1999, it snapped up New York-based Bankers Trust. Flotation on the New York Stock Exchange was the inevitable next step. Deutsche then did what they all did and became embroiled in the sub-prime mortgage scam. It continued to sell toxic mortgage-based investments even as the market fell. It began betting against these increasingly worthless products itself.

As the net tightened on wrongdoers, the bank responded not by apologizing and learning the lessons, but by trying to intimidate the whistle-blowers. An internal investigation found that it hired private detectives to spy on people it considered a threat to the bank – including a shareholder, a journalist and a member of the public. In 2008, the bank reported its first annual loss for five decades, losing €4 billion. 'We have made mistakes, as everyone did,'[21] said its Swiss chief executive Josef Ackermann, with a classic mix of understatement and buck passing. He was removed, but only after a decade in charge. The problems piled up. In 2016, the bank was fined a record €2 billion by US and UK regulators for rigging the key Libor interest rate. The following year, it was fined another €500 million for failing to prevent Russian money laundering. In 2019, the US Congress subpoenaed the bank to hand over documents relating to its dealings with Donald Trump. Deutsche was one of Trump's biggest lenders, sticking by the real estate mogul even after US banks refused to lend.

A once venerable bank, 150 years old, was in a downward spiral of declining revenue, outdated technology, a brain drain and heavy fines. With the blessing of the government, it put together a plan to take over Commerzbank, one basket case merging with another, but then it realized that this wouldn't help either. Instead, it began a series of cost-cutting exercises, shedding more than a fifth of its worldwide staff and paring down its investment divisions. Both Deutsche and Commerzbank saw their share prices halve, making them a potentially attractive proposition for outside investors.

It wasn't just the multinationals that were in trouble. Germany had prided itself on its system of regional banks, the *Landesbanken*. They too were lured by greed into investing in what turned out to be junk. The job of these banks had been to provide reliable capital to local companies. They were where the public put their savings. Nobody imagined that they would ever default. In order to save the banks, the regional governments, many of whose members had places on the boards and went along with the racket, had to bail them out. Some collapsed; some merged, others were privatized. With interest rates negative, confidence low and caution gripping the sector, Germany's banks were pretty much out of the global game. It was lucky that the still-healthy general economy was cash-rich and could function almost irrespective of the banks' woes.

Transparency International's annual survey over the past twenty-five years rates Germany generally quite highly. In 2019 the country was ninth least corrupt in the world – predictably after the Nordics, plus the likes of New Zealand and Singapore, but higher than the UK and significantly higher than the US and France. When scandals hit, however, they tend to be spectacular. The Wirecard affair exposed not just malfeasance, but alarming structural weaknesses of the state. When the *Financial Times* began reporting on fraud and creative accounting at the Munich-based payments company, the response of the financial supervisory authority BaFin was to attack the journalists and investors. It then issued a temporary ban on short-selling in Wirecard after €10 billion was wiped off its stock market valuation. Even more outrageously BaFin filed legal complaints against two FT journalists. The initial response of much of the German media, rather than to rally to their own, was either to stand back or support the regulator.

In June 2020 Wirecard eventually filed for insolvency, with

debts of €3.5 billion. Its CEO, Markus Braun, was arrested on suspicion of falsifying accounts. Its COO fled the country. Some €1.9 billion disappeared from its balance sheet – it may be that the money was invented to inflate the accounts. So what went wrong? All the way through, even as the evidence mounted, the supervisory board did nothing. What was the role of the auditors, EY, and why did they not spot anything?

This was a high-profile, chronic and deeply worrying episode. It demonstrated a failure of regulation. BaFin lacks teeth and conviction. All the agencies that should have policed the company failed in their duties; almost all are overseen by the Finance Ministry. The Finance Minister and the SPD's candidate for chancellor, Olaf Scholz, announced an overhaul of the system, but many fingers were pointed at him.

Wirecard pointed to broader weaknesses in corporate governance. Appointments to supervisory boards are all too often part of a revolving-door circuit of business old-timers who know each other too well. The paradox is that Wirecard was supposed to be part of a new generation, a company seeking to speed up the cashless, tech-oriented society, one of the darlings of the Dax-30.

Another structural weakness is affecting the economy and people's standard of living: Germany's infrastructure is creaking. The problems are taking their toll: run-down school buildings, crumbling bridges (one in eight of the country's forty thousand bridges along major roads and highways are said to be in a substandard condition), unreliable Internet and underfunded army. And then there are the trains . . . which absolutely do not run on time. I can vouch for that. On one visit to Germany, six of the seven journeys I took were delayed by twenty minutes or more. And to make it worse, the passengers alongside me just shrugged their shoulders. 'Happens all the time', was the standard response to my agitated questions about German punctuality. The main reason, it seems, is the overloaded and complex network, which has seen the number of services increase by a quarter over two decades, with intercity services, regional and freight all forced to operate on existing tracks. The Germans look to France's TGV with envy. Even the Spanish, they note, have high-speed lines. The rail industry and passengers themselves do what they do in other ill-served countries – they build slack into their schedules. It is hardly the most efficient way to carry on, and it goes against Germany's obsession with punctuality. At least the carriages themselves are comfortable.

Every country has a history of *grands projets* going wrong, failing, spiralling massively over budget. Britain has a long list, from Wembley Stadium to HS2, from the Dome to Crossrail. Spain has its ghost towns that were built and never occupied. France planned a huge airport outside Nantes that never saw the light of day. But Germany? One project is so notorious it has even inspired a board game. The object of the 'crazy airport game' is to waste as much money as possible. Players pick up cards with instructions such as to build escalators that are too short. Each of the examples it uses is based on what actually happened.

The idea was straightforward enough. Divided Berlin had two airports, both built straight after the war, Tegel in the West and Schönefeld in the East. Both are hopelessly outdated. The capital cannot accommodate large jets. The main hub for intercontinental flights is Frankfurt, with Munich as a second option. So small and overloaded is Tegel that the government is forced to keep its official jets at Cologne Bonn airport and fly them in whenever needed. In 2006, with Berlin experiencing a building boom, the central government and region decided on a new site for a new airport, in the southeast close to Schönefeld. It was to be called the Willy Brandt Berlin-Brandenburg airport, BER for short. The construction was signed off as completed in 2012. Invitations were sent out for the grand opening, with the chancellor to give the keynote speech. Suddenly, the local official responsible for certifying the building's fire safety called a halt. He had discovered that the supposedly sophisticated system of smoke detectors and automated alarmed fire doors was not working. Amid much embarrassment, the start was delayed. A new management was brought in. It discovered half a million faults, including dodgy cabling, all of which had to be removed.

In the intervening years BER became a laughing stock, a Potemkin city that had to be kept going in order not to conk out. Its railway station ran one ghost train a day. In the airport hotel, a skeleton staff dusted rooms and turned on taps to keep the water supply moving. Luggage carousels were given a daily rotation. Indicator boards were switched on and off; they showed flights arriving and departing but were using data from other city airports. So irked was the Brandt family that they asked for his name to be removed. Much has been written and said about the causes of the fiasco. Most of the chaos seems to have stemmed from having multiple layers of management. Nobody had the authority to make things happen. At the end of October 2020 it finally opened. There was no fanfare; it took place in the middle of the second wave of the pandemic when few people were flying, and there was nothing to celebrate.

Then there is Stuttgart 21, a project for a new railway station and European main-line hub that, as its name suggests, was supposed to ring in the twenty-first century. The plans were agreed in 1994, but it took fifteen years for construction to begin. The project is more ambitious than anything tried before, burying an entire railway station under a functioning city. It involves putting a seven-storey, 15,000-tonne building onto an entirely new foundation made of forty pillars several metres high – just to dig a tunnel. It also requires the creation of 60 kilometres of tunnels through surrounding mountains. Locals wanted a smaller-scale scheme and protested in court and on the streets against the demolition of the northern façade of the original station. The controversy was eventually settled by a referendum. The project won't be completed before 2024. In the meantime, the area is a noisy mess.

These may be the two most egregious examples of failure and delay, but Germany has also had its regeneration success stories. The rebranding of Bonn as a centre of culture, with its impressive Museum Mile, was a smart piece of thinking by the city and state authorities, given that the building work had begun before reunification took place and the seat of government was moved. Across the East, road and rail provision has been transformed, as have many of the city centres. Perhaps the most impressive example is Hamburg. Alongside the working port, an entire new district has emerged. HafenCity (Harbour City) is Europe's biggest inner-city development, taking a large swathe of dockland to the south and the world's largest warehouse district, called the Speicherstadt, where buildings sit on timber-pile foundations. Its landmark is the stunning new concert hall for the Elbe Philharmonic, the Elbphilharmonie, better known by its nickname, the *Elphi*. Cranes abound, but all construction projects are subject to two rigorous requirements – flood protection and social housing provision. That Hamburg, Germany's second-largest city, is so liveable is a testament to city planners over the years. A third of the city was burnt in a fire in 1842 and then it was razed by Allied bombing in the war.

Still, an infrastructure that was once the envy of the world is not what it was. Some of the problems can be put down to maladministration; some to a refusal by central government to spend money. Many put it down to the *schwarze Null*, the Black Zero, a sinister-sounding term for a law meant to ensure fiscal probity. The story goes back to the 2000s, when Germany was struggling with high unemployment and weak public finances. Straight after the 2008 financial crash, the government passed a law on balanced budgets prohibiting the sixteen states from running budget deficits and limiting the federal government's structural deficit to 0.35 per cent of gross domestic product. Since 2014, each year, the government has balanced the books. In 2018 alone, the Treasury ran a surplus of €54 billion.[22]

The debt brake, a fiscal straitjacket the likes of which few countries have introduced so methodically, was one of the few truly conservative policies of the Merkel era. It forced the regions into endorsing a German version of austerity. What is most curious is that the chancellor's partner in the grand coalition, the SPD, endorsed it. That is the party that at the same time was desperately trying to dissociate itself from the Hartz welfare reforms. As the economy slowed, calls increased for a change of tack. Merkel initially would have none of it. The proverbial Swabian housewife would not spend beyond her means. Germany's shrinking pool of young people 'could not be burdened with rising debt',[23] she insisted. Yet with her power waning, her hand was being forced. The SPD's finance minister, Olaf Scholz, made it clear he wanted to free resources for small towns struggling to pay for public services and infrastructure, by allowing them to pass on their debts to the federal government. A mantra of saving, not spending, was about to be broken.

It is tempting to conclude that, with all the problems laid out like this, Germany is heading for a fall. The years of continued high growth are certainly over. Whenever Germany is in the doldrums, other countries gloat. This time is no exception. Germany's economic model is broken, its detractors insist. No, it isn't. But it does need to make changes. In 2019, Germany fell four spots to seventh in the World Economic Forum's global competitiveness report (Singapore took top spot from the US; the highest EU country was the Netherlands at fourth; the UK was ninth). This annual report, which has been produced for the past forty years, assesses performance in twelve areas such as economic stability, health, infrastructure, innovation and tech. Germany, for sure, needs to be more tech-savvy. It has been slow off the mark on quantum computing and artificial intelligence. It needs to sort out its financial services. It needs to incentivize the right kind of risk – not reckless bankers but digital innovators. It will have to navigate the choppy waters of exports with China and Trump's trade war with Beijing. It will have to boost domestic consumption and infrastructure spending. Most important, it needs to imbue among corporate bosses, directors and unions a sense of impatience to adapt to future trends and technologies. Marcel Fratzscher, head of the DIW economic think tank, argues: 'Stability is not what we need over the next 20 years. What worked over the last 150 years isn't necessarily suited to now.'

Stability on its own will, for sure, not be enough. But it is not a bad starting point. Germany's inbuilt resilience will get it through the next difficult period. Spending on research and development has for decades been higher than equivalent countries. Productivity, although it has taken a dent, remains high. Germans may over-engineer; they may be excessively deliberative; they may be slow to embrace change; but their industrial muscle, cash reserves and highly skilled labour force will enable them to catch up – and one might wager that they will eventually overtake their rivals even in areas where they are currently lagging behind. The demographics of Germany will work both ways. An ageing population requires continued productivity growth in the workforce and increased spending. The next generation of employees will have it good because there is a narrow pool to choose from. Economically, the country has no choice but to fill labour market shortages with workers from abroad. Yet the political dangers of that approach are clear.

In 2014, Stewart Wood, one of the chief advisers to former British prime minister Gordon Brown, provided this compare-and-contrast analysis:

> We cannot copy the German economy or transplant the culture in which it is embedded. But we can learn much from the institutions and policies that have helped produce the most successful high-wage, high-skill economy of the modern era. What is most inspirational about the German economy is not the policies it has pursued, but the consensus of values on which the economy is based. Germany is committed to a free market economy, but one in which capitalism is organised and responsible. This 'social market' rests on widely accepted rules and practices: to encourage long-termism; to promote collaboration rather than conflict in the workplace; to incentivise employers to invest in the skills and productivity of their workers; and to try to ensure prosperity is available to Germans in all regions rather than just one.[24]

Amen to that. Germany pursued a mix of economic growth and social inclusion long before it became fashionable in the Anglo-Saxon world. It created wealth without recourse to untrammelled free markets and Thatcherite excess. It realized long before others that countries cannot be successful if regional imbalances are not tackled. Germany has had its longest un-interrupted run of growth for half a century, with the highest levels of employment since reunification and surging tax receipts. It has run surpluses since 2014 and paid down large amounts of debt, while still increasing spending and ensuring near full employment. For all the anxieties, the country continues to outperform its rivals. It rode out the financial crisis with relative ease (investing rather than retrenching). It has absorbed one country. It has allowed in one million of the world's most deprived. Such is the proven strength of Germany's engineering base, its long-termism, the emphasis on skills in education and apprenticeships and other in-work training, the country has already shown that it can adapt to disruption and change. Any *Schadenfreude* may be short-lived.

6

The Dog Doesn't Eat the Dog

A society that sticks together

Every year for the past three decades, the Association of German Language, the equivalent of the Académie Française, has chosen a Phrase of the Year. In 1991, it went to *Besserwessi* (the West German know-it-all); in 1998, it was *Rot-Grün* (Red-Green, the colour of the first coalition containing the Green Party); in 2003, it was *das alte Europa* (Old Europe, the term used by George W. Bush for those European states that refused to go along with his war against Iraq). In 2007, it chose *Klimakatastrophe* (which other country was talking about climate catastrophe so early?). In 1982, the Association chose *Ellenbogengesellschaft*, the elbow society, which more figuratively translates as 'dog eat dog'. The eighties were the era of Wall Street, Gordon Gekko, and greed is good. Free-market zealots dominated the discourse in the US and UK; flushed with hubris, they sought to export the mantra around the world. Germany was fascinated but also petrified. Capitalism as a principle of creating production and wealth was not in question. The debate in Germany was how. What role did society play? The Germans, the creators of the social market, were being told they were too soft. It was time to put on those braces, take some risks, stop worrying about the poor and feckless. You don't make an omelette without cracking eggs.

That wasn't the way Germans saw it. Yes, they realized that sometimes the way they did things was stultifying. Living in Germany, I was often frustrated by the slow pace of change. I was more of a child of Thatcher than I realized. Now everyone in the US and UK is talking about reviving communities, equalling out regional imbalances, setting basic incomes, a shorter working week. The Germans just got there first. Or rather, they were the ones who stood their ground. While in the US, France and the UK, regional inequality was the result of wilful neglect, a refusal to help communities ravaged by the demise of heavy industry, many although not all of such problems in Germany have stemmed from reunification, from inheriting a moribund Eastern economy.

Consumption is not the primary leisure activity. Its leaders would be loathe to say, as Gordon Brown once did when he was prime minister, that shopping was a patriotic duty. Germans buy things when they need them. The country's restrictive shopping laws date back to 1956. Closing time was 6.30 p.m. on weekdays and 2.00 p.m. on Saturdays. When I first encountered it in 1980s Bonn, I often felt dispirited. The town reminded me of my childhood. Dark winter Sunday afternoons; nothing was open; nobody was on the streets. Even on Saturdays, Goddammit, the shops closed shortly after lunch. As for weekday evenings – when working people actually had time to go out and shop – that was no better. I could always console myself in the pub. When I returned recently, I was pleasantly surprised to see that Bonn is a little more dynamic. It built a cultural quarter from scratch, the Museum Mile, in the 1990s, just as the government was moving out. The plans had been approved just before the Wall came down when everyone assumed the status quo would remain for a long time. But it is still far too quiet.

From the 1990s, successive incremental reforms relaxed the rules, but late-night shopping isn't that popular; supermarkets can close early if there aren't any customers; and nothing has changed when it comes to Sundays. It wasn't always like this. The novelist, poet, translator of Shakespeare and sometime travel writer Theodor Fontane was, like his contemporary Heinrich Heine, less than enamoured of 1850s England. Of the many frustrations of life there, the worst was the Sabbath: 'The great tyrants have all died; only in England one lives on – the English Sunday.'[1]

Almost nobody I have met, from any walk of life or generation, advocates tampering with the sanctity of Sunday, and yet almost nobody cites religion to make their case. Rather, they talk about quality of life, family and community. Again, Germans stayed the same while others changed. Robert Putnam's seminal book, *Bowling Alone*, published around the millennium, demonstrated a deeper malaise in societies like the US that had dispensed with community ties and sought to replace them with the superficial allure of bling.

Germany is not immune from the manifestations of the atomized society, but, although it is hard to measure, there is ample evidence to suggest that social capital – to use Putnam's term – has not declined as fast in Germany as elsewhere. This has always been at the heart of the government's agenda. Which other country's Interior Ministry would, in its official documents, put social cohesion as one of its top priorities?

> For society to function, it must share values such as human
> dignity, freedom, democracy and sovereignty of the people,

based on the cornerstones of individual responsibility and social engagement. This is why the Federal Ministry of the Interior supports civic education and social participation. For example, the programme to encourage social cohesion through participation in rural and less developed regions promotes vigorous and democratic communities through long-term support for organizations and clubs.[2]

The *Verein*, the social club, is still a key part of daily life, and every town, large or small, has dozens of them. You would be expected to put your child in the one for music, or handball, or even Carnival preparations. There are not just book clubs, which have become fashionable in other countries, but clubs for dog owners, singles, smokers, stamp collectors. In order to fulfil the requirements for registration, the club needs at least seven members (who must elect a Board). It must have a statute and a purpose ('for the enjoyment of hill walking on a Sunday' etc.). Bureaucracy aside, they are wildly popular. Whereas in 1960 there were 86,000 of them (in East as well as West), in 2016 the number surpassed 400,000. Nearly every second German (44 per cent of the population) says they are a member of at least one club.[3]

Then, of course, there is football. On one freezing midweek January evening I joined Andreas Fanizadeh for a training session at his club Blau Weiss Berolina. A cultural journalist with the *Taz* newspaper, he volunteers to train his under-seventeens team twice a week, with a match at the weekend. The boys are from the poorest and wealthiest parts of Berlin, alongside one from Puebla in Mexico and another, a refugee from Afghanistan. Their artificial grass training ground is in the heart of the Scheunenviertel, Berlin's swanky art district. On one side is an expensive new gallery and apartment block, on another more traditional homes and restaurants. The pitch, however, is sacro-sanct. It was a bomb site, but the East Berlin city council would not allow it to be rebuilt. The authorities in united Berlin have continued that policy, refusing proposals to develop it in spite of the huge revenue they would get for it. How many other cash-strapped cities would show such restraint? How many sports pitches have been sold off elsewhere? Fanizadeh, whose mother was Austrian and father Iranian, takes his responsibil-ities incredibly seriously, as does his newspaper, which gives him time off. He sees his task as part sports, part social. 'My aim is to bring these boys together,' he says. 'We don't talk backgrounds. We don't talk politics.' I ask him about trainers for other teams, particularly those from rougher neighbourhoods. Can he tell which ones belong to the AfD. 'You don't ask. But you just know,' he says. 'And I try to respect them anyway.'

Football is the great leveller, in many countries. What is particularly German is the role the local fire station plays. Of Germany's two thousand towns and cities, only a hundred are served by fully professional fire services. The rest rely completely or in large part on volunteers. Just under one million Germans are registered and trained as volunteer firefighters – an extraor-dinary figure. It is simply what people do. Indeed, it would be frowned upon not to do it. Contributing to one's local commu-nity is an important part of belonging. A number of towns are seeking to enlist the new wave of immigrants, partly to plug gaps, partly to help both groups to get on better.

One of the most German of all customs is *Kehrwoche*. Sweeping week means what it says, and more. It dates back to late-fifteenth-century Swabia, the area that roughly comprises present-day Baden-Württemberg. *Kehrwoche* is a national insti-tution, at least for those who live in apartment blocks, which is most people. It comes in one of two forms: residents are either

required to muck in for one week a year to do some heavy lifting on behalf of the neighbourhood. Or, more commonly, each
household is given roughly one week a year in which they are
responsible for either putting out the rubbish, sweeping the
streets of leaves or gritting in the event of snow. Or they have to
do indoor jobs such as clearing up the communal staircase and
entrance hall. Sometimes a sign hangs on the appointed family's door. More often than not, the details are online. Drudgery
such as this is but one example of a sense of duty to the local
community, and of belonging too. Germans take their fetes and
festivities incredibly seriously, and they often involve food or
drink. There always seems to be something going on whether
it's celebrating (inevitably) beer, wine, schnapps or sausages
– or, something that seems an obsession across the country,
asparagus.

Spargelzeit is asparagus season, but it is the white variety,
which grows under the earth and doesn't see the light, that the
Germans are fond of. They call it white gold; it is calculated that
in an average year some 125,000 tonnes of it are consumed.[4] It
is served everywhere, from the poshest restaurants (caked in
butter, with boiled potatoes and ham) to stalls outside railway
stations where queues inevitably develop. But it would be sac-
rilegious to serve asparagus outside the season, which begins
in April and ends precisely on the Christian festival of St John's
Day, 24 June.

The traditions of *Karneval* seem to represent a bygone era.
Carnival starts on the Thursday preceding Ash Wednesday,
called 'Old Women Day' or 'Women's Day'. During the celebrations, women storm the neighbourhood, scissors in hand,
wildly snipping off men's ties. They also kiss unsuspecting men.
The tradition stems from washerwomen taking the day off work
on that day. Rose Monday (*Rosenmontag*) is the start of the main

spectacle, when people of all ages parade the streets, ride floats, play in marching bands and dance. The floats are meticulously designed and of the moment, often lampooning politicians. At the 2020 parade, one bore a monster with the words 'Facebook', 'hate' and 'radicalization'; another depicted the AfD's mastermind in Thuringia, Björn Höcke, doing a Nazi salute, his outstretched arm held up by Merkel's CDU and the FDP. One of the more light-hearted ones was of Boris Johnson's chest covered in the Union Flag, wearing a kilt and EU socks marching away from him. Carnival culminates with costume balls on Shrove Tuesday. It takes place everywhere but is strongest in the West and centre of Germany, and is primarily focused on Cologne, Düsseldorf (which begins its celebrations with a person emerging from a mustard pot) and the ancient cathedral city of Mainz.

Such traditions are adhered to meticulously and I think there are a number of reasons why: firstly, football aside, Germans feel they cannot rally around national celebrations. The second point is that wherever they are from, Germans are from somewhere local, be it Bavaria, or Hamburg or the Rhineland or Saxony. Dialects vary and food and drink and customs do, too, and celebrating them is an important part of local pride. Thirdly, there is the sense that Werner Abelshauser's argument about the importance of community over the individual really does hold in Germany.

All countries, of course, have local traditions and festivities. In the UK, locals gather for the village fete, St George's Day tugs of war, cheese rolling, inter-village ball games etc. Distinctiveness is celebrated, but it should be seen as complementary to, not in competition with, other identities. In 1993, John Major, trying to reassure voters that membership of the EU did not detract from tradition, mused that the country would in fifty years' time still be known for the 'long shadows on county grounds, warm beer, invincible green suburbs and dog lovers'.[5] He lost the argument about the EU but the Germans have kept all their local quirks – while remaining proudly European.

On several fronts, Germany is happy to display its feminist credentials. It has had, in Angela Merkel, by far the most influential female leader since Indira Gandhi or Margaret Thatcher. Women outperform men at university and at the early stage of their careers, as they do in other countries. Germany's anti-discrimination legislation ranks alongside the Nordic countries in its scope and detail. Female representation in the boardroom has always been woefully low, but a law was passed in 2016 requiring public-sector boards to contain a minimum of 30 per cent women. Men still outnumber women by 350 to 40 on the boards of the top companies listed on the DAX. Such is the scramble to recruit female members that their remuneration is increasing 7 per cent faster a year than men's, albeit from a lower base.[6]

In 2013, a movement called #Aufschrei (Outcry) started on Twitter, four years before the much more famous American-initiated #MeToo campaign. It arose when a female journalist wrote an account of a conversation that she had had with a former economics minister, Rainer Brüderle. She alleged that he had made sexual advances to her and told her, while looking at her breasts, that she 'could fill out a *Dirndl* well' (the traditional dress worn by women in Bavaria).[7] Two years earlier the CEO of Deutsche Bank Josef Ackermann said he regretted the fact that they had not been able to find a woman for the senior management team, adding: 'But I hope it will become more colourful and prettier one day.'[8]

Yet it is a curious mix. When it comes to bread-and-butter issues of taxation and childcare, the German state is far behind equivalent countries. All manner of impediments, from tax to school hours, are put in the way of working mothers. It is surprising that this is not more of a hot political issue. Only about 14 per cent of German mothers with one child, and only 6 per cent with two children go back to work full-time, far lower than the EU average.[9] Such is the pressure on working mothers that most professionally ambitious women decide either not to have children or to stay at home most, if not all, of the day. Labour participation has increased steadily for women, but almost all of it is part-time. The problem is both social and economic. Traditional Germans have a term for women who return 'too quickly' to the workplace. They are *Rabenmütter* – raven mothers – female ravens who abandon their chicks in the nest. Although few would admit to using the word now, the sentiment prevails, particularly in small towns. Added to that are day-to-day logistics. Only recently did the government start to reform the half-day school system. Pre-school, which is called *Kita*, is heavily subsidized and good quality, but the days are even shorter. As for private childcare, the market barely exists. Parents, if they use an outsider, end up paying back in tax almost as much as the extra income they would earn. Now, more men are taking parental leave. One of the partners can take twelve months' leave, the other two months. Many middle-class parents take their child on holiday in that shared part – not quite the consequence that was intended.

The tax system also has much to answer for. Katharina Wrohlich at the DIW has been monitoring gender economic equality for nearly two decades. The crucial element that holds women back is called 'married couple splitting'. In essence, if both the man and the woman earn roughly the same, they end up being taxed more than having only one income, or if one person vastly out-earns the other. In other words, there is a considerable tax disadvantage in both partners working full-time. 'Other countries have abolished the splitting rule, such as Austria, Sweden and Italy, but nothing has changed here,' Wrohlich says. With none of the parties lobbying for change, she adds, 'there seems little prospect of any movement now.'

Women were more emancipated under the old regime in the East. Children were sent to state nurseries at a young age and both parents went to work, one of the very few pluses of the old system. Merkel has always been reluctant to be identified on 'women's issues'. In January 2019, she gave a rare interview on the theme to author Jana Hensel in *Die Zeit* that was typically Merkel-esque. She talked about the obstacles that women face, including those she had experienced during her time as a physicist. Then she added: 'I'm not just the chancellor for women in Germany. I'm also not at all certain that women expect me to address them specifically.'[10] Perhaps because she hails from the East, Merkel has always underestimated gender inequality. Given that such reforms tend to emanate from cosmopolitan big cities, perhaps this is one of the few negative consequences of the preponderance of small towns in Germany. More likely, this is a generational question and that change will come, albeit more slowly.

To be seen as part of the productive economy and wider society, it is assumed you have had either tertiary education or a skills-based apprenticeship, depending on which route you have followed. The education system selects early. The academically gifted go to grammar school, *Gymnasium*. The *Realschule* caters for the middle ground, while pupils who go to *Hauptschule* usually end up in manual/technical jobs. At the age of ten or eleven, a child's career trajectory isn't set in stone – people can and do change direction at school and after it – but the system is quite prescriptive. Education policy falls under the states rather than central government and as a result the system varies from region to region. Some regions, for example, have comprehensive schools, called *Gesamtschule*, in which all groups are catered for. Some states are more sympathetic than others to private schools, a small but growing sector. The curriculum isn't uniform across the country either. In more traditional Bavaria, religious education takes up two slots, one for Protestant belief, the other for Catholic. Berlin's more liberal syllabus contains items on diversity, gender equality and 'democracy education'. Students are taught about conflict resolution and migration. Schools everywhere find time for classes on Europe and the European Union.

Andreas Schleicher is regarded as the global guru on comparative education systems, his brief at the OECD's headquarters in Paris. He is also responsible for the OECD's Programme for International Student Assessment (PISA) reports testing educational attainment in thirty or so countries. When the first results came out in 2000, Germany went into a state of shock. It thought it would be at the top of the tree. Instead, it tested near the bottom in maths, science and reading and was declared the most unequal in school performance. The PISA shock, as it was known, led to a public outcry. A number of educationalists challenged its methodology. Yet it succeeded in spurring policy-makers into action. The school day, which was one of the shortest in industrialized countries, was lengthened. Early years education was given higher priority. Performance in lower-achieving schools was required to improve. More comprehensives were introduced, ensuring that struggling students – including some of the 22 per cent whose mother tongue is not German – would be helped more. The education system, which is in the hands of the regions, was required to adopt national standards. Subsequent tests, which have taken place every three years, saw an immediate and sustained improvement in Germany's position in the table, although the most recent one saw a drop.

Schleicher tells me that too many young people were receiving an education based on the needs of a specific local employer rather than identifying unique talent that would serve them well in an era in which creativity and artificial intelligence come to the fore.

Policymakers are discussing a new raft of reforms. As ever, these will take time, as consensus is sought across the education sector and among political parties. Teachers in Germany are generally well paid and well qualified. But school buildings are often in need of repair and modernization. Curbs on regional spending have exacerbated the problem. Yet, as Schleicher and other experts point out, it does not all come down to budgets. For example, the Netherlands spends less per pupil than Germany, France or the UK but achieves better outcomes, with more emphasis on twenty-first-century skills.

Around half of German school leavers go into vocational training.[11] When I was first told that a shop assistant might be required to undergo training that could last three years, I dismissed the story as an urban myth. But it's true. I had assumed Schleicher would scoff at this absurdity, but he doesn't. He points out that people who work in bakeries are invited to take advanced maths in the evenings. 'It's not such a terrible idea. Learning for your current job is only part of the task. The German approach puts you on a path; it looks at your long-term career trajectory. China and Japan are the most advanced in this.' The skills acquired are often disconnected from the immediate requirements of the employee. You rarely hear the term 'over-skilled' in Germany. There is a premium on the future, rather than the present – all based on the assumption that the employee is likely to stay for a while. Schleicher compares this to the UK: 'There only 5 per cent of the labour force have higher skills than what's required for their present job. That is a huge threat to productivity.'

In 2015, just as Germany abolished tuition fees for university students in most parts of the country, the Higher Education Policy Institute in London published a pamphlet entitled 'Keeping up with the Germans?' It provides a detailed comparison between the German university system and that of the UK and others. In fact, it notes that there are more parallels between Germany and Scotland than with England. In essence, German universities are less autonomous and less well funded, but more equal. Some have better reputations (Heidelberg and Munich, for example) than others, but there is no equivalent to the hierarchy of Oxbridge and the Russell Group. As in many countries in Europe, most students go to a university either in their home town or nearby. Unlike France, where the drop-out rate is high, students tend to stay for the duration of the course. The institutions perform less well in global league tables, because research is often done in separate specific institutes. US Ivy League universities reign supreme in the tables, with a smattering from the UK (Oxford and Cambridge, Imperial). Many continental European educationalists dispute the methodology behind such tables. The other inbuilt advantage is the English language. A number of German universities have introduced courses in English in order to compete in the highly competitive market of students from China, India and elsewhere. According to the last available figures, just over 250,000 international students were studying in Germany in 2016, which puts it in fourth place behind the US, UK and Australia.[12] That figure has steadily risen and will continue to rise.

Professor Martin Rennert was president of Berlin's University of the Arts (UdK) for fourteen years, until standing down in early 2020. A Jew from Brooklyn, as he proudly tells me, he went to New York's famous Juilliard School. He is passionate about the German approach to higher education, particularly arts education. Admission to UdK is highly competitive, but once you are in, it is all free – and that applies equally to international students. 'This is a cultural-political intervention – an offer to the world, an investment in international relations, a successful demonstration of soft power,' he tells me. Rather than pulling up the drawbridge, the government has further loosened restrictions on foreign graduates staying in the country. Anja Karliczek, the education minister, said foreign students represent 'significant and growing potential' to meet Germany's demand for skills. Rennert gives a less utilitarian justification. 'Isn't higher education for the benefit to the whole nation? Here you don't have to make the intrinsic case for the value of learning.' Students can take many years over their learning, moving from an undergraduate degree to a masters to a PhD. Some Germans enter the workforce only in their thirties. Slow and slothful, or considered and long-termist? Probably all these things.

The Theater am Marientor in the town of Duisburg had fallen on hard times. Its next planned performance, based on the Scottish independence fighter William Wallace, was not selling at the box office. The show was cancelled; bankruptcy beckoned. The theatre was therefore the perfect location for a COVID testing centre.

Germany, like everywhere else in Europe, did not appreciate the importance of the pictures that were being beamed from Wuhan in China in January and February 2020. But when reports came in from Italy, of hospitals being overrun in Bergamo and other towns, the response was quick. In Duisburg, a poor town in a poor region, elective surgery was cancelled. Hospital beds were cleared. Extra capacity in operating theatres was found. Meanwhile, a testing centre was set up straight away. Hundreds of volunteers were drafted in. When the first batches of disinfectant and hand sanitizer ran out, they made their own and distributed it to hospitals and old people's homes. Regions and towns did it themselves, coordinated by the health offices, but they communicated with each other and learnt from each other.

During those difficult months of spring 2020, Germany coped as well as any country. The number of deaths, at 9,000, was very low as a proportion of the population. Supplies of personal protective equipment, of breathing equipment never ran out. Hospitals were, in their worst moments, hard pressed, but the health service managed. Impressively.

When I was shown around the Duisburg theatre, just as the second wave was about to begin, I couldn't believe my eyes. Jointly run by the fire service and the local health office, the centre had three entrances – for people told to get tested by their doctor; for those who had been tracked down to a location of infection; and for those who had just arrived from a high-risk country. They came, they were processed, they went, like clockwork, up to 400 a day, I was told. When I told them of all the woes back home in the UK, of the equipment shortages, the failures of track and trace, of tests hard to come by, they smiled an embarrassed smile. Luck, they said. That's all it was.

Self-deprecation might be an endearing trait, but it doesn't help to tell the story.

No area of public policy demonstrates more acutely a state's resilience and long-termism than its health service. Germany's is by no means perfect. It is costly. It is bureaucratic. Like France, it does not have the primary care system that has served the UK well. Yet survival rates for some of the most common diseases, such as breast, cervical and colon cancer, are among the highest in the industrialized world, although progress has stagnated in recent years.

At 11 per cent of GDP, spending is relatively high, but by no means the highest in Europe. Healthcare is provided through mandatory public insurance: employees pay 7 per cent of their pre-tax salary, a sum that is matched by their employers. One in ten of the population, the wealthy, self-employed and civil servants (a curious combination), are required to pay into private schemes, although they access the same services. They expect high standards, access to specialists without having to wait long, and to screening and medication almost on demand.

In the round, Germany's state health service, the oldest in Europe, has served its people comparatively well. When it was put to the ultimate test, with the COVID-19 pandemic, it was in an enviable position. At the start of the crisis, Germany was much better prepared than other countries, with more testing facilities, more ventilators and more protective equipment. This was due to a combination of long-term planning and an industrial base at the heart of the economy, led by a strong network of biotech and pharmaceutical companies able to quickly respond to emergencies requiring highly specialized know-how.

The system was also more resilient to shocks, with more hospital beds per patient than in most equivalent countries. In Germany the ratio was 8.2 per 1,000 population, whereas in France it was 7.2, with the EU average at 5.2. The UK was a lamentable 2.7, thanks in part to chronic under-funding and short-term planning, but also a tendency to discharge patients quickly in order to free up space instead of allowing them to convalesce in hospital. Efficiency and cost-saving had been the mantra handed down from the UK government to managers for decades. Most winters, hospitals found themselves on the edge of coping with seasonal flu. There was no slack in the system to deal with anything worse.

Germany had a total of 28,000 intensive care unit beds, against Britain's 4,100[13] – a massive difference in capability when it was most needed. As for staff, the difference was similarly stark. For every 1,000 people, Germany had 4.1 doctors, compared with the EU average of 3.5 and the UK's 2.8. The figure for nurses was 13.1 per 1,000 in Germany versus 8.2 in Britain. Behind these dry statistics lie stories of care delivered well in Germany and not so well elsewhere. And that's just in normal times.

Germany's post-war constitution, with its checks and balances on central power and strong devolution, could have produced chaos during the pandemic. Instead, Merkel moved quickly to ensure joined-up decision-making. She succeeded most of the time. Regional leaders maintained their autonomy, giving them far greater flexibility in urgent procurements. But it was all coordinated. Personal protective equipment (PPE) was quickly sourced and provided to front-line medical services. Overall, with some regional variations, the system coped admirably.

Britain prides itself, with justification, on its National Health Service, now more than 70 years old. It is one of the few institutions around which the country can coalesce. But it is also bureaucratic, heavily centralized and financially insecure. At every step of the way, the British system was found wanting with not enough vital equipment and little emergency planning. Johnson called on companies to start building ventilators to supplement the country's paltry stock of 8,000, blithely dubbing the scheme 'Operation Last Gasp'. By that point Germany had already ordered 10,000 from an existing manufacturer, supplementing its existing 20,000. As for virus tests, both countries entered the crisis working roughly in tandem. Within weeks,

Germany's laboratories were running at more than five times the British rate. NHS workers were recognized as national heroes. People came out onto their doorsteps and balconies every Thursday evening to cheer them. But they were being sent into the frontline with inadequate protection. A month into the crisis, barely 5,000 of the NHS's 500,000 frontline workers had been tested.

Britain lurched from one decision to the next during COVID. The government was slow when locking down, trying to keep the country as open as possible, but doing so with such incompetence that neither citizens nor the economy benefited. Its one saving grace was the speed with which it began the vaccination process. By early 2021 some of the gloss had come off Germany's response. The death rate rose sharply, hospitalizations too. Access to the vaccines was frustratingly slow. But even at its worst moment, the German system avoided the chaos of Johnson's Britain and Trump's America.

All governments and voters have reassessed their priorities in light of the pandemic. Globally, countries allocated billions to tackle the economic consequences of COVID-19. In Germany there had long been a consensus around the principles of generous contributions directly from the pay packet in return for high-quality service. There is similarly broad support for the principles underlying higher taxation and the role of the state – that you are paying not just for your own benefit, and that of your family, but for the needs of society at large. That way of thinking has been in place in Germany for decades.

Regional imbalances, a sense of small towns left behind by the big cities that have it all, exist in Germany, most potently in the Eastern states. But in one important respect Germany is different. Its capital city does not dominate. There is no comparison between the power of Berlin and that of London and Paris, which are central to much of their countries' politics, business, science and arts, attracting disproportionate investment, money and talent. Smaller countries have similar problems. Without Athens, Greece would lose 20 per cent of its GDP, while for Slovakia and Bratislava the figure is 19 per cent. The figures for France and Paris are 15 per cent, and for the UK and London 11 per cent. Germany is the only country where GDP per capita is lower in the capital than in the country at large. Germany without Berlin would be 0.2% richer.[14] In other words, Berlin acts as a drag on the rest of the country. It polarizes. Indeed, many in richer cities such as Hamburg and Munich look down on it as inefficient and grubby.

One place epitomizes the idiosyncrasy of Berlin. Tempelhof Field is the site of what was once the most important airport in the world, the place where the *Humboldt* balloon was launched in 1893, where Albert Speer planned a grandiose gateway to a new Nazi 'Germania' and where the Western Allies made their daring missions to circumvent the Soviet blockade. Norman Foster called it 'the mother of airports'.[15] The last three aeroplanes flew out of Tempelhof in November 2008, a month after the airport's official closure. From that point on, they didn't know what to do with an area one and a half times as big as the principality of Monaco.

Now it seems just a tatty mess; and yet most Berliners couldn't be prouder of it.

Any other global city would have slavered at the space available for development. Think of all those high-rise luxury flats, or grandiose hotels or art galleries or shopping malls. Post-reunification Berlin was desperate for more space and this site, just a few miles to the south of the city, was a dream for property developers. In 2011, developers submitted plans for a mixed-development site of offices, nearly five thousand homes (including considerable affordable housing) and a large public library. The mayor at the time, Klaus Wowereit, insisted that only a quarter of the site could be built on.[16] Even that was too much for the locals who organized to stop the scheme. As soon as it was turned over to the public in May 2010, the site became an instant hit with urban gardeners, yoga enthusiasts, hipsters, dope smokers, yummy mummies, barbequers and sports fanatics. The area was renamed *Tempelhofer Freiheit*, Tempelhof Freedom. In May 2014, after years of infighting, Berlin held a referendum (a rare event in a country that fears exercises of direct, as opposed to representative, democracy). Just under two thirds of eligible voters chose to keep the site unchanged. The Tempelhof Conservation Act now prohibits construction anywhere on the former airfield and ensures only limited development, until 2024 at least.[17]

Some of the original airport buildings – landmarks in civil engineering – have been put to use. The 72-metre radar tower is still used by the German army to monitor flight traffic. The cavernous Nazi-era terminal, including the curved hangars that stretch for nearly a mile under a column-free roof, is mostly leased out to a hundred or so disparate tenants. The Berlin police have used a part of it for training programmes. There's a central lost property office, a kindergarten, a dancing school and one of the city's oldest revue theatres. Tempelhof is also home to Germany's largest refugee shelter. A series of white containers on the side of the field, supplemented by part of one of the aircraft hangars, have become a small refugee village which is used as a first stop, before they are relocated across the country.

During the forty-five years of division, and the semi-occupation of the Western half of the city by the three Allies, West Berlin was unlike anywhere else in Germany, or the world.

It was an alternative island, where you didn't have to do national service like the rest of West Germany, where (a few exceptions notwithstanding) the staid and wealthy would rather not live. Much of that, of course, has changed in the last thirty years of 'normality'. Since reunification, much of the central area has been given over to glistening (or antiseptic, depending on your point of view) government buildings. Potsdamer Platz, rushed back into life in the early 1990s, is a hideous monument to glass-fronted globalized tat. But Berlin continues to look and feel different. To those who prefer orderly, manicured medium-sized towns, it is anathema. All the other big cities work so much better. Hamburg and Munich vie in glossy magazines such as *Monocle* and *Forbes* with places like Vienna and Copenhagen for the top spot in Europe in terms of quality of life. Hamburgers pride themselves on their restraint. Munich has, in summer, a sultry, languid sense of well-being.

Neither city has the grit of brusque Berlin. The capital has been de-industrialized twice – both at the end of the war, with division, and with the dismantling of the GDR economy by the *Treuhand*. Apart from the burgeoning tech sector, it isn't known for *making* or *doing* anything and has a reputation just for politicians, journalists, lobbyists, artists, students and hippies: degenerate subsidy junkies. At least, that's the view of many a bourgeois burgher from Bavaria. Berlin's attractions are completely at odds with the overall strength of the country. Doing the basics isn't easy. The bureaucracy, which is expected to work like clockwork elsewhere in Germany, frequently falls short. Many recent arrivals, and even some Berliners themselves, exchange anecdotes about the various inefficiencies. The most common one relates to getting your car registered. Apparently, it is quicker to take a day off work and drive to Hamburg and do it there. 'We are no longer quite as poor, but still sexy,' says

Michael Müller, Berlin's present mayor. Berlin is becoming more like other capitals around the world, but it still has a long way to go. Many Berliners, or at least the originals rather than the many incomers, are determined that it should stay the way it is. Their key battleground is housing – dominated by a visceral animosity towards gentrification.

Germans are not obsessed by the housing ladder. Few people buy homes before they have children. They see no point, because rent is usually manageable, and homes are well maintained. Germany has the lowest home ownership proportion (the ratio of total owner-occupied units to overall residential units) across the OECD, apart from Switzerland. The figure is just over 50 per cent. Britain, the US and France are around two thirds – although both have seen owner-occupation fall and renting go up since the financial crash. The highest figure in Europe is, strangely, Romania at 96 per cent. In Berlin, by contrast, only 15 per cent of properties are owner-occupied, and few people would dream of buying a place purely as an investment rather than as a home or as security for their family.[18] There are, of course, plenty of landlords (some private, some housing associations or other groups) and plenty of Airbnb and similar apartments available, but one would rarely hear in polite society a discussion about profits to be made from 'buy to let'. Those who indulge in such money-making ventures tend not to tell their friends about it. There is, rather, the shame of the absent landlord. In countries like the US and UK, the ratio between earnings and assets has long been out of kilter, and annual salary differences pale into insignificance compared with those who have bricks and mortar in areas of growth.

Where else in the world, or at least in the Western world, would the expropriation of property become part of the mainstream? In Berlin, in 2019, this became a serious political goal, and it hasn't quite disappeared as an option for the city. Residents (and, according to the *Tagesspiegel* newspaper, a majority of them) expressed their support for a citizens' initiative to hold a referendum on seizing private property. Launched at a 'rent insanity' protest, the aim was to gather signatures to force a city-wide vote on whether to oblige companies that own over three thousand properties to sell them back to the city. Although this would have cost billions in compensation, the goal was to have the properties run by a public board. The private developer Deutsche Wohnen was the main target. It owns 167,000 units across Germany, and among them are over 100,000 apartments acquired in Berlin from the mid-1990s. The cash-strapped city council started privatizing swathes of infrastructure, from water to half of its electricity utilities. It sold 65,000 units of housing for the cheap price of €400 million, offloading a sizeable amount of municipal debt to private investors. Each apartment was valued at only around €30,000. In total, 200,000 units were sold off between 1989 and 2004. Deutsche Wohnen grew and grew. The company made a $2 billion profit in 2017 and has become the whipping boy for opponents of hard-edged capitalism.

The concept of *Enteignung*, expropriation, relies on a novel interpretation of two clauses in the constitution. The campaigners argue that Article 14 allows for property to be taken back into public ownership if it is being misused: 'Property entails obligations. Its use shall also serve the public good.' This, they say, is corroborated by the subsequent Article 15, which states: 'Land, natural resources and means of production may for the purpose of socialization be transferred to public ownership or other forms of public enterprise by a law that determines the nature and extent of compensation.' The mass-circulation *Bild* tabloid went into overdrive in its opposition to the idea. 'A spectre is haunting Germany, the spectre of expropriation,'[19] it declared. In his *Hart aber Fair*, Hard but Fair, chat show on ARD, presenter Frank Plasberg said that he couldn't quite believe they were discussing such an idea. Conservative commentators denounced what they called GDR state socialism by the back door. But it was being seriously discussed, and it had a lot of supporters, and it is one of those moments when as an outsider you really do have to blink, as you realize how different are many Germans' concepts of society and capitalism. The idea fell away (for the moment at least) when the biggest part of Berlin's coalition, the SPD, voted not to proceed. The decision put it at odds with its two junior partners, Die Linke and the Greens.

Over the past decade, rent in Berlin has risen by more than 100 per cent, according to several estate agent surveys, with the annual pace of increase most recently at 20 per cent – the fastest anywhere in the world. Meanwhile, the city's population has been growing by forty thousand people a year, most of them upwardly mobile people from other parts of Germany and abroad. As a result, low-income residents have been pushed further out.

It is a familiar story across the world. Large swathes of Manhattan are virtual no-go areas for 'ordinary' people. In London, developers pay lip service to requirements for social housing. They pare down the amount of affordable homes to a minimum, sometimes building separate entrances for them, known as 'poor doors'. Rich neighbourhoods are often deserted as they become merely the boltholes of wealthy Russians, Chinese and Emiratis whose properties are left vacant for weeks on end, while workers fight onto overcrowded trains taking them on commutes of up to two hours into the city. In Paris, the social tensions of the *banlieues* are well documented.

Berliners prided themselves that they were different, that they shielded themselves from the worst excesses of globalization. In some ways they still have. At the same time as the seizure of property was put on hold, the city authorities agreed on a controversial law designed to cap rents. It means that 1.5 million homes in the capital will have their rents frozen for five years. Landlords cannot charge rents higher than what the previous tenant paid and, if tenants' rent is above the limit set out in a rent table, they can even apply to have it lowered. The law on the rent cap, *Mietendeckel*, is not unique to Berlin. In the last few years, Spain and the Netherlands have introduced nationwide rent control measures, as have four states in the US: California, New York, New Jersey and Maryland. Canada has had some form of rent regulation since 2006, while Paris is planning regulation, once it has seen how Berlin's experiment works out. The Berlin law gives a legal definition to 'extortionate rent', setting it at 120 per cent of the value set out in a rent table it has produced. If the rent is above that, tenants can sue to have their rent lowered, and any surplus payment given back, regardless of what it says in their contract.

Much of the housing shortage in Berlin, and therefore the pressure on price rises, can be put down to the failure of city planners in the 2000s to predict its popularity, hence population growth – both people coming to live and to visit. It had already become one of the most popular European destinations for weekenders. City authorities reckon that around a third of visitors come for the clubbing scene alone. The tourist influx put further strain on accommodation and services.

Munich is the most expensive city for housing, both for sales and rental. It is followed by Frankfurt, Hamburg and then Stuttgart. Berlin is fifth. A few years ago, it was only eighth of the fourteen cities annually surveyed. Two cities of the former GDR feature in the list and both have leapfrogged over some in the West. Dresden is tenth, while Leipzig has moved up to twelfth. When Berliners complain about affordability, they have a point

– until one compares it with comparable capital cities in Europe and around the world.

In Moabit, an up-and-coming district of Berlin, less gentrified than places like Prenzlauer Berg, I visit a state-run housing company called Gewobag. The name stands for the Trade Union, Housing and Building Cooperative. But this is no 1968-socialist-woke company. It has just celebrated its centenary as an arms-length body of the Berlin government that builds and rents at affordable prices. They plough back any profits into new builds. They and the other big state companies, Degewo and Gesobau, focus mainly on mixed-development properties. They are doing this on a scale that puts other capital cities to shame. Johannes Noske gives me the low-down on the city's housing problems. The city will continue to grow, he points out, but there is only so much the council can do, with its limited resources. One of the problems, he says, is baby boomers, 'people who moved into places like Charlottenburg in the 1970s when they were run down and shabby. They are now chic and highly desirable, and they will stay and stay.'

Some of the strain has been alleviated by the fact that more than 300,000 people – mostly millennials starting families – have moved out to the suburbs and beyond. Berlin is the centre of a doughnut, surrounded by the state of Brandenburg. Some of the area is rural and semi-rural, with heathland, forests and dozens of lakes. One of the most popular areas is the Spreewald to the southeast. Some of it is less prepossessing and already built up. The Germans have their own take on the term commuter belt – they call it *Speckgürtel*, the bacon belt, denoting people who have got a little too comfortable with life. Population growth in the suburbs is at least as fast as in the cities, which doesn't leave everyone happy. 'There are far fewer empty spaces than before,' Noske adds. 'Germans love empty spaces.'

*

The town of Wittenberge, in Brandenburg, is not a place at the top of any holidaymaker's must-see list. I decided to visit it during the most evocative of weeks, the celebration of thirty years since the fall of the Wall. Wittenberge is well beyond the bacon belt. For nearly half a century it was situated on the heavily fortified inner German border, on the eastern side of the Elbe river, separated from towns and villages in the Western state of Lower Saxony. Founded in the thirteenth century by the Saxon King Otto I, its heyday was in the nineteenth century as a thriving industrial town, with a huge textile factory, oil mill and rolling-stock engineering plant serving the railway between Berlin and Hamburg. Its station was one of the most economically important in the land. Its most evocative building is a giant sewing machine factory. Visible from miles around, it sports the tallest clock tower on the continent of Europe (Big Ben is slightly higher). It was built at the turn of the twentieth century by the American company Singer, as part of its most important factory outside the US. Between 1904 and 1943, it is said that 6.5 million sewing machines were made here. After the war, the factory machinery was taken by the Soviets as reparations and transferred to their own sewing machine plant in Podolsk, near Moscow. The factory was eventually re-equipped and restarted in the 1950s by the East Germans under the name of the state enterprise Veritas. Since reunification, Wittenberge has lost a third of its population, an entire generation who went West. The disused factory, and its clock, stand as monuments to a forgotten era.

I'm walking through the centre of town, past row upon row of derelict buildings, with Frederik Fischer. The scene is particularly forlorn as it is bucketing with rain. A year and a half ago, this young Bavarian entrepreneur had an idea about housing to help the town. Why not build one or two hubs, or rather rural retreats, for digital nomads away from the city of Berlin? They could help regenerate impoverished and depopulated communities. So he wrote an open letter, inviting expressions of interest from mayors across the East, about his plans to build creative hubs. Young people would help develop the tech skills of local residents in return for cheap living and office space, and access to the countryside. 'My mailbox exploded,' he tells me. He then invited bids from people he calls 'pioneers', choosing twenty to join him in these empty surroundings.

The local council gave him the rear part of a disused oil mill (the front was turned into a hotel). Some of his pioneers have moved in already, paying a mere €150 per month, subsidized by the local authority, for a six-month trial period. He explains that he wants to bring urban infrastructure to the countryside, while giving his techies a co-working space plus access to nature. He has coined the word *Co-Dorf*, Co-Village. The community has its own beach bar by the Elbe (for the hot summers) and bikes which can take them into the middle of nowhere within ten minutes. This is still the most thinly populated part of Germany, but the railway connections were important too. Wittenberge was designated the only town in the old GDR to have a dedicated ICE intercity station on the fast train from Berlin to Hamburg, so the new residents can be back in a shot to Hipster Central for the weekend, if they want to. 'This is just one counter-narrative to rural decay,' Fischer says. He has toured fifteen or so other towns with a view to implementing similar projects and is under way with a second project in the town of Wiesenburg, southwest of Berlin, taking over a disused timber works next to the station.

Fischer and his project have become a hit in the media, a change of fortune for Wittenberge, which has only had terrible write-ups over the past thirty years. 'Places like this lack self-confidence. They thought only one or two people would last the course. But people are really enjoying being here. This is the place where the future is born,' he tells me, with an optimism that is infectious and, in the East, somewhat hard to find.

In April 2013, David Cameron visited Angela Merkel. The British prime minister was only the third European leader to be invited to the chancellor's state residence at Schloss Meseberg, to the north of Berlin and not far from her home town of Templin. This was to be a family weekend occasion, with Cameron's wife, Samantha, and their three children being joined by Merkel's husband. Alongside them was a smattering of cultural and political figures with links to the two countries. Cameron had only a few months earlier announced his commitment to a referendum on Britain's membership of the EU. There was much to discuss. The hostess wanted to do it in the most convivial and informal way possible.

By way of small talk over dinner on the Saturday night, Merkel brought up the arts. She discussed the operas she had enjoyed most at Bayreuth. She mentioned the theatre performances and art exhibitions she had sneaked into. She asked her guest what he would recommend on show in London. Cameron stuttered and said he liked watching TV. He added that he would have loved to go to concerts but whenever they venture out like that prime ministers get hounded by the press as elitist, one of the 'luvvies'. This moment highlighted a wider gulf between Germany and political reality in much of the rest of the world. Germans feel comfortable talking about culture, particularly high culture. Politicians' association with the arts is not just tolerated in Germany; it is required of them.

One of those who despairs at the disparity is the British

architect David Chipperfield. I worked with him building Turner Contemporary in Margate in 2011, a rare British commission for his company. He is, by contrast, a public figure in Germany, responsible for many important buildings across the country, most famously the Neues Museum in Berlin, for which he was awarded the Order of Merit. His most recent opening, the James Simon Gallery, also in Berlin, was attended by the chancellor. One of his many commissions was the reconstruction of Mies van der Rohe's Neue Nationalgalerie in the western part of the city. At a dinner to mark its closure, attended by arts and political figures (the German culture minister Monika Grütters was there; her British equivalent was invited, but did not bother to come), Chipperfield talked of the importance of the public realm in Germany: 'It's refreshing that architecture is subject to such robust debate here,' he says, lamenting the lack of such discourse in Britain. 'They really hold your feet to the fire, which is painful at the time, but the work is better for it.' He added: 'Clearly the war and the fact that Germany had to reconstruct itself spiritually as well as physically means it is a much more reflective society than ours. Ours is a success-based culture. Whereas here there is a lot of discussion of what things mean.'

Public funding of culture is strong and consistent in Germany. The city of Berlin subsidizes workspace rents for artists of all disciplines to the tune of €7 million per year. It also invests a further €7 million in acquiring and converting new workspaces. This could be seen as sticking plaster, because the steep rise in rents has produced a parlous situation for many of the city's eight thousand artists. Although quite a few have been forced to move out to smaller towns, or to cities in other countries (Athens and Lisbon have proven particularly popular), Berlin remains very attractive for musicians, artists, designers, architects and others who have long been unable to operate in New York, Paris or London.

Other German cities spend even more per head on artists (and subsidizing audiences) than cash-strapped Berlin. While much work has been done in France and Britain on culture-led regeneration (in Margate, Nantes, Gateshead, Marseilles), Germany's decentralization has ensured a more equitable distribution of funds and talent from the outset. Cultural and education policy belong to the *Länder*, with the federal government having only a coordinating role. Wherever one looks, small and medium-sized towns have a plethora of museums, theatres and concert halls of renown – both *Mittelstand* companies and culture helping to embed a sense of local pride and place. Saxony, for example, has a total population of only three million people, yet it has two of the world's finest orchestras in Leipzig's Gewandhaus and Dresden's Staatskapelle.

The cultural community, I would argue, is more radical in Germany than certainly in the UK and across much of Europe too. The aesthetic, political and intellectual expectations of an artist are higher. That is one of the reasons why the British theatre director Katie Mitchell upped sticks more than a decade ago for Cologne and Berlin. She was accused by one critic of displaying 'a willful disregard for classic texts',[20] something that would not be frowned upon in Germany. She has argued that audiences in the UK are too frequently served up nostalgia and safety, whereas in her adopted home theatregoers expect to be challenged, to have their views and sensibilities threatened. 'German critics are always instinctively sceptical when a play looks too polished – they fear it may cover up a lack of depth,'[21] she has said.

In various conversations I have had with cultural leaders, a number of common strands can be identified. As ever with Germany, the strengths and weaknesses are stark, and the flip side of each other. German arts institutions do not have to fret every few years about whether they can keep the lights on. Many of them receive money from companies and family trusts, so their directors and boards do not have to devote a disproportionate amount of time to fundraising, as they do in the US, UK and elsewhere. Freed from the emphasis on commercialism, they can experiment more readily. I sense when in Germany, in Berlin in particular, a convulsive passion, a thirst for political activism among artists that is sadly seldom seen in the UK. For sure, there is much written and performed around personal issues of identity, but on the biggest issue of the last many decades – Brexit – the British cultural scene has lost its nerve, desperate to ingratiate itself with government and not to cause trouble with funders.

In Germany, it would be considered entirely appropriate for a cultural leader to take a political stand and have influence over the government. At the same time, the government also feels entitled to have a role in culture. Nowhere was this displayed more acutely, than at Berlin's Volksbühne. This is one of those best of Germany, worst of Germany stories. The theatre was founded in 1914. The slogan above its door was: *Die Kunst dem Volke*, Art to the People. During the period of the Weimar Republic, this was a hotbed of experimental performance, an unashamedly left-wing theatre with tickets priced low in order to attract a working-class audience. Great figures such as the director Max Reinhardt worked there. It survived the GDR by staying just within the bounds of acceptability, but towards the end of the regime dissidents flocked to its subtly subversive productions. After reunification, it had a new lease of life and a dynamic director, Frank Castorf. From 1992, he led the theatre for twenty-five years, turning it into one of Germany's most innovative, and making no concessions to convention or commercial success. He didn't care if the critics panned his shows or if people didn't understand. This was art as didacticism and to hell with the rest. In 2013, at the cradle of opera, Bayreuth, Castorf was booed by the audience at the end of his adaptation of Wagner's *Ring* cycle. The louder the well-heeled operagoers expressed their disapproval, the more he seemed to enjoy it, giving them a thumbs up and ironic applause. Eventually in 2015, the Berlin government eased him out. Traditionalists and radicals (often in Germany the same thing) were horrified. That turned to fury when his successor, Chris Dercon, was announced. Dercon is a larger-than-life man from Belgium, someone who knows his mind and has been a ubiquitous figure on the London visual arts scene, and that for many in Berlin was the problem.

As he was serving out his notice and before he took up his post, more than 150 actors and other employees published an open letter expressing 'deep concern' about his appointment, which represented 'historical levelling and razing of identity'.[22] Bizarrely, they saw Dercon's previous employers, Tate, as a Trojan horse of Anglo-American cultural dominance. His appointment was a hostile buyout, the start of a 'corporatist' approach, and worst of all, he was a 'neoliberal'. Castorf cocked a snook at his successor-to-be by staging a version of *Faust*, as his valedictory, themed on colonization and takeovers. Dercon didn't help his cause by dismissing what he saw as nostalgia: 'That Berlin is over. Berlin is becoming a normal city with normal issues.'[23] When he arrived, some staff tried to stop him from entering the building, and then mounted a six-day sit-in. A petition against the appointment was signed by forty thousand people. Dercon lasted less than a year. His first season, which opened with a dance performance in an alternative venue, a hangar at Tempelhof airport, and a play by Samuel Beckett, didn't go down well. In August 2017, faeces were left at the door of his apartment. One man poured beer over his head at a party. Another shouted,

'You dog!' at him on the street. Dercon had joined a theatre with a strong identity and an equally strong reluctance to change. Dercon was out and found himself a happier home running the Grand Palais in Paris.

Neil MacGregor, one of the greats of the UK's museum world, is, like Chipperfield, a figure of considerable renown in Germany. His *Memories of a Nation* exhibition at the British Museum brought together two hundred objects exploring six hundred years of German history. The exhibition later transferred to the Martin-Gropius-Bau in Berlin. MacGregor published a book of the same name, which, like the exhibition, was highly acclaimed. After leaving the British Museum (where he was succeeded by a German, Hartwig Fischer), MacGregor began work on what he called 'Europe's most important museum project'. The Humboldt Forum in Berlin will be one of the continent's biggest displays of anthropology, ethnology and art from around the world. While few of the contents will be German, the building itself is being recreated in the style of the Stadtschloss, the Prussian baroque palace that stood on the site until it was bombed in the war and demolished a few years later by the Soviets. In its place, in the 1970s, they built the Palast der Republik. Therein lie the roots of so much disquiet and discussion. That monumental glass-fronted modernist building housed the Volkskammer, the rubber-stamping pretend parliament of the GDR. It was somewhat perversely a building of pride for East Berliners. The foyer was a glamorous (in its own terms) place to meet for coffee; there was also a bowling alley and a concert chamber. Many people didn't buy the story that the Palast der Republik had to be knocked down after reunification because of asbestos, believing it to be a ruse to demolish it. When demolition work began a few years later, protesters tried to block the cranes. Some of its internal exhibits were preserved and later shown at the Kunsthalle in Rostock, the only museum to be built under the GDR.

Work on the new, or rather old, Berlin palace didn't begin for another decade. Many East Germans wondered why they needed to build an edifice that celebrated German power and colonialism, costing €600 million to boot. MacGregor's task was not easy, to say the least. As he himself wrote, with reference to the 1905–7 suppression of a revolt in Tanganyika (now Tanzania) and the annihilation of indigenous tribes in Namibia, dubbed 'the first genocide of the 20th century': 'Now there is a groundswell of demand that Germany's colonial crimes, deemed by some to be comparable to the Nazis', be publicly acknowledged and researched with equivalent commitment.'[24] The German Lost Art Foundation, which has been responsible for investigating Nazi-looted art, announced it would widen its remit and give grants to museums for colonial provenance research. The Canadians and Australians are doing such work; President Macron has challenged France to return objects stolen from colonies. While some in the UK are beginning to discuss the British Empire in such terms, it is still referred to in much public debate with a myopic reverence.

MacGregor had other, more immediate tasks. He had to bring five independent museums under one umbrella and deal with a labyrinthine governance structure and some big egos. He wanted the new space to be free to visit (as many museums in the UK and other countries are), as did the federal government, but the city authorities had a different view.

MacGregor and I talk about the specificities of the German museum world, and the arts world more generally. The accent, he says, is still very much on research and learning. Curators are king. They enjoy what is termed 'sovereignty of interpretation'. In other words, they pretty much dictate what will be shown in their particular galleries. To make changes, to get things done, he adds, you cannot as a director of an arts institution dictate decisions. You have to bring the last person along with you and with most employees being civil servants, it is hard to move them. We discuss another term: *verharmlosen*. This is best described as taking the sting out of an issue. In the visual arts, as in the performing arts, change is made incrementally.

The Natural History Museum, at the north end of the centre of Berlin, is the preserve of Johannes Vogel, the bearer of possibly the most elaborate handlebar moustache in Germany. Vogel, who is married to Sarah Darwin, a descendant of Charles Darwin, was for many years at the equivalent museum in London. Vogel had a different immediate problem from Dercon or MacGregor. His museum was literally falling down. They were losing birds and insects. Entire sections were becoming unsafe. Less than a tenth of the exhibition space was being used.

He takes me through the storeroom in the bowels of the building, where posters of Erich Honecker are still on the wall and a flag of the FDJ (the communist youth league) stands on a derelict desk. 'I said we needed €400 million to restore the building and create something fantastic. I went to parliament three times. It didn't work. Then in 2018, between April and November, Germany didn't have any rain. And the museum in Rio [the National Museum of Brazil] burnt down.' A few days after that tragedy, Vogel wrote a comment piece in the *Financial Times*, drawing a link between the safety of museums and public funding. Over one night's horse-trading, he was given a staggering €740 million until 2030 – for an organization that has an annual running budget of only €17 million. He now wants to turn the museum into one of the world's great homes for science and nature, with an accent on digital learning and interaction.

It is not regarded as pretentious in Germany to begin a

conversation about high art, as Cameron found out to his embarrassment when dining with Merkel. The counterargument is
that German institutions do not try particularly hard to broaden
their appeal. Some institutions are beginning to change, with
free entry on Sunday, cheap seats and school outreach, but many
are not particularly fussed if their audiences come from a fairly
narrow social stratum. Diversity and access have some way to
go. Panels at cultural (or other) conferences can frequently be
the preserve of white males of a certain age and background.

Germany's political and literary space is rich in argument.
Like the French and Italians, Germans are at ease with the
concept of public intellectuals. Broadsheet newspapers and
magazines have changed little over the years (for good and ill),
with rigour and intelligence prized more highly than chasing
circulation. The feuilletons, the review sections of newspapers,
are not dumbed down. I recall one Sunday paper devoting its
entire front page to an analysis of African development ahead
of an EU–Africa summit. You might see that in France but, I
wonder, where else? One midweek afternoon, back in the late
1980s, I remember watching a quiz show. It wasn't supposed
to be highbrow. Fingers on the buzzer: 'Who is the leader of
the opposition in the UK?' Both teams immediately shouted
their answers, one a fraction before the other: 'Neil Kinnock'.
How many Brits or Americans would be able to name any
leader of the opposition (or even head of government) from
another country? I say that not to mock – and German TV's
Saturday-night fare contains oompah bands, celebrities kicking
footballs through hoops and its own version of *Love Island* – but
to suggest that in Germany there is more of a requirement to be
ultra-serious and outward-looking. The most striking cultural
difference is the approach to language. Whereas Britain is mired
in monolingual mediocrity, its reference points extending to the

US and not much further, most Germans are taught two foreign languages at school. Perhaps as a result, I am always struck by a cultural curiosity that is truly international.

If the positive of German journalism is its refusal to dispense with intelligent argument, the negative is a reluctance to probe too deeply. When Merkel was seen in 2019 shaking at public events on at least three occasions, most newspapers in Germany deemed it improper to investigate further. In justification for such stand-offishness, the standard response among editors and TV executives is to differentiate between the private (health, love life) and the public (use of funds or policy decisions).

As with so much of German life, the past influences the present. Anything that impinges on privacy, whether governmental or commercial, is taken incredibly seriously. I was struck when addressing a conference on free expression a decade ago run by the SPD's think tank, the Friedrich Ebert Foundation, when one participant said she would rather have a publicly run social media platform than one from Silicon Valley. Don't trust Facebook or Google with your data, she declared. That remark felt old-fashioned at the time, another example of Germans' excessive caution. Yet some would regard that now as having been prescient as concerns about privacy have increased. Not many politicians have popular Twitter or Facebook accounts. Posts are often dull and formal. It is changing – although none of the country's prominent politicians would want to do a Donald Trump and replace conventional methods of government announcements with mouthing off on social media while sitting on your bed watching *Fox & Friends*.

One person who has been on both sides of the fence is Ulrich Wilhelm, formerly Merkel's top aide. 'Bombastic journalism is seen more as a threat to democracy than a reinforcement of it,' he says. 'It was as used an instrument of aggression and hostility to democracy during the rise of Hitler.' He argues that the character assassinations of senior figures in the Weimar Republic by pro-Nazi propagandists have left their mark.

Polls suggest that trust in traditional media remains higher in Germany than in comparative countries, in spite of the AfD's best efforts to undermine faith in mainstream institutions. The most recent survey by the Reuters Institute says that 47 per cent of Germans trust what they read, online and offline. That is slightly down, as it is everywhere, but it is still higher than equivalent countries. Out of thirty-eight countries, the German media is twelfth in terms of public trust. The UK is twenty-first, the US thirty-second, and France is second-bottom, with only 24 per cent believing what they read. Some 70 per cent of Britons say they fear fake news, whereas only 38 per cent of Germans do.[25] Still, there is much room for concern. Germany's established parties are hopeless at social media.

Germany is one of the world's wealthiest countries, yet many Germans see something vulgar in the Anglo-Saxon emphasis on acquisition. Perhaps the fact that the shops are not always open, rather than being a cursed inconvenience (my first reaction), might be seen as demonstrating a more balanced set of priorities, with community at its heart. German high streets, unlike their counterparts in many other countries, still feel distinctive; independent shops are not priced out of the market by high rents. One of the joys is that in many small and medium-sized German towns, alongside the concert hall and the museum, one can stroll into a bookshop occupying pride of place.

As for authorship, how many countries could boast a head of state who is a prolific writer on philosophy? Two years after stepping down as president, Joachim Gauck, like Merkel one of few East Germans who made it to the top, published a book about the Enlightenment value of tolerance, why it matters and how it is threatened. He traces its history from the religious wars of the seventeenth century to Voltaire to Mill to Kant and Goethe. He delves into the limits of individualization and the need for a broader notion of shared endeavour. It became a bestseller. Where else, but Germany?

7

No More Pillepalle

Climate and cars

Germany's Green movement, one of the world's oldest and most influential, originated half a century ago in a village called Wyhl, on the edge of the wine-growing region of Kaiserstuhl in the southwest of the country.

In 1960, West Germany passed the Atomic Energy Act, designed to promote nuclear energy. Experts had been discussing how to develop the new technology since the late 1950s, but it took the oil crisis of the early 1970s to bring home the urgency of the task. They began a search for sites, identifying Wyhl, a tranquil spot in Baden-Württemberg on the border with France, as a perfect location. They encountered misgivings locally, but they were confident that these would be easy to overcome. Planning permission was quickly granted; the site was cordoned off and the first digging began in February 1975. That was the start of the trouble. On the following day, local inhabitants occupied the site. Television coverage of police dragging away farmers and their wives through the mud turned it into a national news story. Local clergy and wine-growers took back the fields that had been requisitioned, reinforced by students from the nearby university at Freiburg. Plans to remove the protesters were abandoned. Just over a month later the construction licence was withdrawn. The plant was never built, and the land eventually became a nature reserve.

The protesters' success at Wyhl brought the issue to a wider public and inspired the creation of citizens' groups wherever a nuclear project was mooted or whenever a transport of nuclear waste was planned. It is this link between anti-nuclear and the wider environmental agenda that makes the German approach so distinctive. The nuclear issue produces far less passion in France, the UK and the US. Indeed, for many, the French and British nuclear deterrents enable those two countries to continue to regard themselves as global powers. Their seats at the UN Security Council (valid perhaps in 1945 but absurdly anachronistic seventy-five years later) are due in large part to their nuclear status. Germans' concerns about nuclear warfare and energy long preceded the climate change debate. Now they go hand in hand – a double dose of existential anxiety.

In early summer 2019, I was walking past a school in Mönchengladbach and towards its contemporary art museum when a repeated booming sound almost knocked me off my feet. I asked a passer-by what it was. That's the nuclear siren going off, she told me, in a matter-of-fact way. Apparently, it gets tested once a month on a Saturday. They take their nuclear warnings extremely seriously here. 'Close your windows and doors tight, switch off all heating and air conditioning appliances. Take your iodine pills. Look quickly for a cellar or another space indoors where you can ensure adequate radio reception.'[1] This advice is from the instructions sent out by the city authorities in its brochure, published in October 2018. There are twenty-two pages of it, available online or in printed form. All around this region, in the population centres close to the Belgian border, locals prepare drills and keep a ready supply of bottled water and non-perishable food. Some have protective suits kept in cupboards and under beds.

Seventy miles to the southwest in the small Belgian town of Huy stands the Tihange nuclear power plant, a vast structure that has been striking fear into residents for years. In 2012, ultrasonic tests on reactor pressure vessels at Tihange and Belgium's other plant, Doel, further away near Antwerp, revealed mysterious cracks deep inside the steel. One reactor in each of the plants was shut down in March 2014. Reactor pressure vessels are vital components of nuclear power plants, essentially steel cocoons containing the fuel rods and the site where the nuclear chain reaction takes place. Tests had revealed that the number of cracks had risen to sixteen thousand. If one of the vessels were to burst, a nuclear meltdown would result. Just a few hours after such an accident, prevailing west winds might blow the radioactive cloud into the Netherlands and Germany.

Residents of the region believed the damaged reactor at Tihange would not be allowed to go back into service. However, Belgium's Federal Agency for Nuclear Control (FANC) reversed its decision. In November of 2015, the authority granted permission to the reactor's operator to restart Tihange 2 despite the concerns. FANC and the plant operator Electrabel had come up with a new explanation for the cracks. The company announced that inspections had revealed the cracks had been there from the very beginning and were not the result of the plant's operation. They were, the company said, 'hydrogen flakes that were produced during the forging process'.[2] The expanding number of cracks, the statement said, was the result of the increased sensitivity of the testing equipment, which had improved over the years. FANC insisted that the structural integrity of the vessels in question was 'only slightly reduced' and was still 1.5 times greater than the limits imposed by law. It failed to acknowledge that Tihange was already more than four decades old; it was built to have a lifespan of only thirty years.

The Belgian government, which relies on the plants to provide half of the country's electricity needs, has pledged that it will go non-nuclear by 2025. The locals in Mönchengladbach fear they won't have that long to wait before a meltdown. They don't trust the Belgian ruling. The region has become home to one of the largest anti-nuclear movements. The black-on-yellow slogan 'Stop Tihange' can be seen everywhere: on car stickers, as flags flying from apartment windows. Aachen, the beautiful cathedral city, lies only 40 miles away from the reactor. Public opinion in Belgium is mixed. As in France, many voters see nuclear energy as an important, cleaner technology and insist that the Germans and Dutch are scoring political points by questioning its safety. But hostility to the plant has only grown. A report by the Dutch Safety Board suggested all the countries potentially affected were failing to coordinate their responses in the event of an accident. The result, it noted, would be 'confusion and unrest'.[3] German politicians have struggled to reach a unified position. Merkel is seen to have enough problems on her plate regarding EU cohesion without falling out with the Belgians. The German regional government dèmanded that Tihange be shut down, only to then realize that its pension fund had invested €23 billion, in bonds and index certificates, in the company that owns the plant. It quickly sold off the assets.

When Germans think of nuclear power, they think of Chernobyl and Fukushima. Both disasters seemed to affect their psychology more profoundly than other countries; after all, divided Germany was at the epicentre of a Cold War between two nuclear powers. Perhaps it is also a combination of the general aversion to risk, suspicion of large corporations – and the lessons of history. Nuclear weapons and nuclear energy are regarded as another manifestation of the danger of giving humans untrammelled power to cause terrible harm.

The first nuclear accident to affect the German population took place on the other side of the world. When a reactor partially melted down in 1979 at Three Mile Island, near Harrisburg, Pennsylvania, around 120,000 people took part in a rally outside government buildings in Bonn. But despite the numbers involved, and the initial success at Wyhl, the protesters haven't always prevailed. Over the years, energy companies have lobbied the government hard and to date Germany has built seventeen nuclear power stations. The most violent clashes in the protests against their construction took place in the northwestern coastal tip of the country. In February 1981, some 100,000 people took part in confrontations with police at Brokdorf, northwest of Hamburg. More than ten thousand police were mobilized against them, up to that point the biggest police operation in the history of West Germany. Many dozens on both sides were injured, but eventually five years later the plant went ahead regardless.

The Chernobyl disaster of 1986 was the game changer. It sent the whole of Europe into a panic, particularly in Germany, which was directly in the line of the radioactive cloud spreading from the east. At the time I was based in Moscow. For days, most Soviet citizens had no idea what had happened. I recall landing in Milan about a month after the accident and realizing to my shock that we were required to leave the plane one by one at a remote part of the airfield, where we were checked by men in protective suits with Geiger counters. As the radioactive cloud swept across the continent, Germans went to great lengths to deal with the contamination. Regions, cities and villages cobbled together emergency plans. Crops were incinerated; firemen wearing protective gear cleaned cars as they crossed the border from other countries; school playground sandpits were replaced. Politically, from that point it made the construction of new nuclear facilities almost impossible.

Chernobyl turbocharged Germany's Green movement. The party had been inaugurated in 1980 when 250 or so citizens' action groups came together in the town of Karlsruhe. This motley collection of ecologists, feminists, students and counter-cultural networks issued a programme calling for the dismantling of both the Warsaw Pact and NATO, the demilitarization of Europe, and the breaking-up of large economic enterprises into smaller units. They wanted it to be an 'anti-party' party, shunning conventional structures. To foster equality and a flat power structure, members elected to state or federal assemblies were required to step down halfway through their terms, to be replaced by the next person on the list. That policy was subsequently dropped. Gender equality was rigorously enforced, with 50 per cent of all leadership positions occupied by women, and that has remained. Membership grew steadily. The party emerged as a hybrid of two different forces – radical urban and student types, and more conservative rural dwellers. They were united in their alienation from industrial capitalism and their search for a slower-paced, more traditional way of life. It was still considered fringe. Its political breakthrough would come shortly after, but it was clear that something was afoot in Germany that was hard to discern in most other countries.

My time there in the mid-1980s was the first time I had been exposed to any serious discussion about the environment. I found it inspiring but also annoying. Germany embraced recycling early, but often enforcement seemed an excuse for meddling and the exercise of petty rules. On one occasion, I answered my doorbell to a dustman wearing thick gloves. He proceeded to deliver a stern lecture on how I wasn't separating the glass, plastic and paper properly. The Brits weren't doing any recycling then and I didn't know why he was getting so worked up. This felt to me like the nanny state writ large, plus rank hypocrisy. How did they reconcile their environmental credentials with one of the most fervent car-driving cultures in the world?

Which takes me from Mönchengladbach to Munich. Most people my age remember the Audi TV ads of the 1980s with the closing phrase, *Vorsprung durch Technik*. But the slogan that best describes Germans' love affair with the car isn't so much Audi's but BMW's *Freude am Fahren*. Joy in driving. To understand it, you have to go to one of the temples to the car, BMW World, on the edge of Munich's Olympic Park. It is the most visited tourism destination in Bavaria and one of the most popular in the country. Opened in 2007 (a year late, so it missed coinciding with the football World Cup) it is part museum, part theme park, part showroom, replete with cringe-making marketing-speak such as 'This is Tomorrow. Now.' I visited on a hot summer's day, mingling with excitable German families and groups of visiting Chinese and Emirati. They gawped at the various models, running their fingers over the paintwork; they sat on the motorbikes outside. They bought souvenirs from the retail store, but the real business was taking place in the meeting rooms upstairs where potential customers (the sales team can tell the serious visitors from the chancers) discuss their dream vehicle and the specifications to go with it. The deal can be done there and then.

Over in Stuttgart's northern suburb of Zuffenhausen,

Porsche's headquarters is almost as popular. Here, next to its own museum with its multi-touch wall and mixed-reality screens, you can also buy a car. But you have to wait for a Porsche as the cars are built only to specification. No matter how fast the company grows, demand has outstripped supply. When the new electric Taycan was announced in 2015, there was a long waiting list for a car that costs upwards of €100,000. Staff are allowed to lease the cars at a heavily subsidized price taken directly out of their monthly salary. In the German car industry you do everything you can to hang on to your best engineers.

Andreas Kraemer, founder of the Ecologic Institute in Berlin, explains to me Germany's obsession with the car. He starts with the history. In 1876, an engineer called Nikolaus Otto invented a new generation of internal combustion engines, the precursor to the modern petrol version. He collaborated with the designer Gottlieb Daimler but the two later parted company, becoming ardent rivals – the rest, as they say, is the history of the German automobile industry. Seventeen years later, German engineer Rudolf Diesel came up with the prototype of a different kind of more fuel-efficient engine, the one that bore his name for more than a century and is now the object of such opprobrium. According to Kraemer, the best place to understand the psychology of the car as a status symbol is in the company car park. 'In many professions people think: "If I don't turn up for work in the latest BMW I won't be taken seriously." The car establishes a pecking order. It also denotes solidity, respectability. A doctor is saying to his patients, a construction engineer to his business partners: "You can trust me, I drive a Mercedes,"' Kraemer says. 'For decades, the car was the rite of passage. It signifies freedom. It is a source of pride.'

More than half of German households are members of the ADAC, the automobile association. The print run of its subscriber magazine is eleven million, by far the largest circulation for any publication in the country. A car was the standard gift for a young person coming of age at eighteen or passing their school-leaving exams, the *Abitur*. They would do their driving test at seventeen, in anticipation. Now that is changing. Kraemer says his daughters and their friends would rather have a computer or a trip abroad. But it is changing only in the major metropolitan areas. Just as it is stressful, slow and expensive to drive in New York, Paris or London, so it is in Berlin. In small towns and villages though it is business as usual.

It is on the *Autobahn* that Germany's often stifling rules are cast aside. The 12,000 kilometres of concrete race track provide for many people, particularly older generations, a freedom they feel they otherwise don't experience. Successive attempts, right up to the present day, to impose a speed limit have been rejected. Specific restrictions are imposed in urban areas, both for curbing noise and for safety, but this covers less than 30 per cent of the network. Where they do exist, the fatality rate has been cut by a quarter. 'Of all the individual measures, it is the one that would have the greatest impact on the environment. And it costs nothing,' says Dorothee Saar, of Deutsche Umwelthilfe, a not-for-profit environmental organization. 'But when it comes to cars the debate tends to become irrational.'[4] Michael Cramer, a long-standing Green MEP, made a comparison that I've heard from others, particularly the young. 'For the Americans, it's the rifle, the gun lobby. For the Germans, it's the gas pedal, the car lobby.'[5]

What German business leaders, politicians and economists agree on is that if the car industry goes, the German economy goes. The car industry is seen as a barometer of the economic health of the nation, much more than the financial services are to the US and UK. It is only from this perspective that one begins to understand the Volkswagen controversy. 'The car companies believed that the government depended on them, not the other way around. There was an aura of invincibility,' says Stefan Mair at the BDI, the employers' federation. Much of German business and politics, and many consumers, are still in denial about VW. Without the Americans, the emissions scandal might not even have been uncovered. In September 2015, the US Environmental Protection Agency discovered that certain diesel-fuelled cars had been manipulated so that their emissions controls functioned only during laboratory tests. Once they were on the market, the control programme stopped, allowing harmful nitrogen oxide levels to exceed those permitted by US regulators. Over a six-year period, some eleven million cars had been sold on the global market with the so-called 'defeat device' software installed.[6]

VW's chief executive, Martin Winterkorn, resigned. He was charged with fraud and conspiracy by the Americans but is unlikely to face trial there. German prosecutors eventually went after him and Rupert Stadler, head of sister company Audi. Winterkorn, his successor as CEO, and the company's chairman were later charged with stock market manipulation for their alleged failure to reveal the scandal. Prosecutors allege that Winterkorn knew that cheating was taking place at least a year before it was brought to light. His defence insists that, while he may have received relevant emails, he may not have read them. VW has so far paid out €30 billion around the world in fines and costs.[7] In September 2019, it faced an unprecedented legal challenge. For the first time, the German judicial system went down the American route of class actions. In a case brought by VZBV, the Federation of German Consumer Organisations, tens of thousands of customers sued the company for mis-selling. The company has refused to pay its share of putting right the tech on cheating cars. That part is now being paid by the government. A scandal such as this would have destroyed many companies. VW and its offshoots have suffered, but not that much.

The bigger damage Germany's car industry did to its prospects was succumbing to complacency. It assumed it would always remain a world leader and forgot to worry about the competition. In the United States and Asia, research and development of hybrid and electric cars gathered pace while VW, Mercedes, BMW and Audi were sleeping. A decade on, the German brands have started to gain market position in the new technologies, but they are facing an uphill struggle. Tesla, the upmarket American insurgent, is pulling out the stops to build a 'Gigafactory' to the East of Berlin. The plans have split opinion. Advocates point to the creation of twelve thousand jobs and fifty thousand cars using the latest green technology. Opponents are protesting about the felling of a huge area of forest and other environmental damage. The idea of America building a next generation of cars in the heart of Germany is painful for some. But the cars are proving popular with the German consumer.

The air quality in dozens of urban areas is so poor that courts have started imposing temporary bans on diesel. The worst-affected city is the car mecca, Stuttgart. In 2004, citizens took legal action seeking redress. The regional government banned trucks from driving through the centre. But that had little effect. More suits were filed. Little was done. Public opinion was split. Just as many people were infuriated by the idea of a ban on diesel vehicles as were worried by air quality. In 2013, Stuttgart elected a Green mayor. He began to take action, introducing a 'fine particulate matter alarm'. On days when air pollution exceeds EU limits, residents are urged to stop using their wood-fired fireplaces and use public transport rather than cars. Tickets are reduced to half price as an incentive. Again, the measures seemed to stop short of what was required. In 2018, Stuttgart breached the EU's daily permitted PM_{10} levels on sixty-three days – almost double the allowed thirty-five days.[8] It is an exceptional case, in a basin surrounded on three sides by hills, without a ring road to syphon off traffic, but other cities across Germany have experienced similar issues and are not far behind. Now it is not uncommon for owners of SUVs or other gas guzzlers in big cities to find notes on their vehicles that say things like 'Your car is too big' or 'Does your ego need such a flashy car?'

The environment has always been an important political issue in Germany. Now it is on the front line of its culture war.

The Fridays For Future movement started to galvanize the young within days of Greta Thunberg beginning her school strike in Sweden in August 2018. Its German arm is one of the most active, with demonstrations taking place regularly across the major cities. In November 2019, on the consumerist frenzy that is Black Friday, hundreds of thousands took part in protests in more than five hundred German cities and towns. Thunberg is a frequent visitor, speaking not just at rallies but taking part in direct action, such as one in Hambach, west of Cologne, to stop an ancient woodland being demolished. Wherever she goes, she is adored by the crowds, but Germany also has its own super-campaigner, a confident twenty-three-year-old called Luisa Neubauer. So influential has Neubauer become that in January 2020, Joe Kaeser, the CEO of Siemens, publicly invited her to join a new Sustainability Board that the multinational was planning to set up. She equally publicly declined, pointing out that Siemens had just agreed to become a partner in one of the largest coal mining projects in the world, in Australia, where much of the country was being ravaged by forest fires caused by climate change. In any case, she did not want to compromise on her message. Corporate Germany has been quick to jump on the bandwagon, eager to display its new-found green credentials. When Thunberg tweeted to her five million followers a photograph of her sitting in the corridor of an overcrowded German train, during a thirty-hour trek from a UN climate conference in Madrid back to her home in Sweden, Deutsche Bahn immediately sprang into action, insisting it had offered her a seat in first class. The railway service points to a continued increase in passenger numbers, which it attributes in large part to the climate protests. Total journeys in 2019 were 150 million, an increase of 25 per cent in four years, adding to the strain the creaking system is already under. Meanwhile, domestic air travel has gone down 12 per cent.[9]

Germany's Friday rallies are impassioned, but orderly. Sympathetic local authorities help out with stages and sound systems. Parents write permission slips for their children to attend, where they are joined by teachers, artists and scientists. The first such protest took place in Invalidenpark, a spot pregnant with history. The park was used as a barracks for East German police, the VoPos, guarding the Berlin Wall. The climate and transport ministries are here, alongside a number of economic and scientific research centres. 'This is the brains trust of Berlin,' Johannes Vogel, director of the Natural History Museum, tells me. He points out, with a smile, that the surveillance training centre for the BND, the foreign intelligence service, is around the corner too. Vogel is proud of the role his institution has played in the climate movement. It hosts debates after each rally, Fridays For Future alongside Scientists for Future. 'The young protesters have got together with scientists. They have four hours of intensive discussions each time.' He also ensured that the museum hosted an international press conference by the activists which led the main evening television news. 'This is now a place commemorating a revolution,' he says.

Alongside Fridays For Future there is now Fridays for Horse-power. The Facebook group was started by a car mechanic called Christopher Grau. A self-declared 'petrolhead', he posted a video venting his frustration with the climate protests. The picture was shaky and the sound terrible, but that didn't stop more than 150,000 people from watching his hour-long diatribe. According to the group's description, they intend to 'counter the rampant climate mania with some fun'. His closed group exceeded half a million members within days. Grau capitalized on his sudden celebrity by doing a series of media interviews. The group argues that electrification is not the way ahead; alternative fuels like hydrogen fuel or biodiesel should be adopted instead. They are, they insist, more climate-friendly and work in combustion engines. The context behind his popularity is a mix of libertarianism ('get the state off our back') and anti-metropolitanism. His 'Beast Factory' car workshop is situated outside the small town of Nordkirchen, 4 miles from the closest railway station, with only an unreliable volunteer bus service. It is some distance from Dortmund to the south and Münster to the north: in other words, near nowhere in particular. 'You need a car here or you can't get out.' Grau says restrictions on the car are an assault on his community's way of life. He denies he is a climate change denier or that his group has been infiltrated by the AfD. Even if that is not his intention, he has certainly been adopted by them.

His initiative might be relatively harmless, but others are not. Thunberg, Neubauer and environmental activists like them are subjected to relentless trolling and abuse. The AfD works from the assumption that, after immigration and the Euro, climate is the third-most important issue for its base. An internal party paper noted that whenever metropolitan environmentalists come out in support of something, 'the AfD must automatically be against it – and vice versa.'[10]

Now the climate change deniers have come up with a youth champion of their own. She is called Naomi Seibt, a 19-year-old from Münster, who became the darling of right-wing institutes in the US, Germany and elsewhere after she posted a YouTube video expressing her opposition to socialism, feminism and 'climate change hysteria'. In February 2020, she was invited by a right-wing American think tank called the Heartland Institute to speak at the American Conservative Political Action Conference in Maryland. That conference was attended by none other than Donald Trump and Vice President Mike Pence. As in America, as in Germany, the fossil fuel lobby and the alt-right have found common cause.

The city of Cottbus, in the far east of Germany, has a quaint old town and an impressive art gallery with a dynamic director. It doesn't seem to have a lot else going for it. The structure it is probably most famous for lies just outside the city, close to the Polish border. You can see its effect from everywhere around – a thick white cloud hanging in the sky. This is Jänschwalde, a power station that runs on lignite, or brown coal. By some estimates, the plant is responsible for the fourth-largest emissions of carbon dioxide in Europe.[11] Moreover, according to one report, four of the EU's five most polluting plants are in Germany. The environmental case for closing Jänschwalde is unarguable but that is where politics has intervened. Up the road is Lieberose, one of the largest solar power plants in Germany. Opened a decade ago, it occupies the site of a former military training ground covering the space of more than twenty football fields. It produces enough clean electricity to meet the needs of a small town of fifteen thousand households. Its contract to operate is set to last for another ten years, after which it is supposed to be dismantled and the land turned into meadow. The financing has been an astute mix of private and public. So far, so green and virtuous. The problem is that the whole plant needs only around a dozen workers to keep it running. By contrast, more than eight thousand jobs depend on Jänschwalde.

Germany (or rather West Germany) started moving away from its dependency on coal in the 1970s but is not due to be rid of it until 2038. There are three main lignite mining areas: the Lausitz, where Cottbus is situated; the Harz region in the middle of the country; and the heavily industrialized Ruhr to the west. They are poor and politically combustible. Without state subsidy, all the mines would go bust over the next five to ten years, but their life has been prolonged in order to save jobs in areas where meaningful employment is hard to come by. It is a familiar story across the world. Real jobs for real men. When a well-known chain of German pharmacies closed, putting ten thousand mainly women out of work, there was barely a murmur from politicians or media.

Despite Germany's much-vaunted energy reforms, the country is now certain to fail to reach its key benchmark – a reduction in overall CO_2 emissions of 40 per cent by 2030, as measured against 1990 levels. Berlin has all but dumped that original target. Now the government will be content with 30 per cent. Carbon emissions have not decreased for the last decade; transport emissions have not fallen since 1990. Germany is still the sixth-largest emitter of CO_2, accounting for about 2 per cent worldwide. 'We have to draw up a very sober balance sheet. And the fact is, we have now lost an entire decade,'[12] says Ottmar Edenhofer, head of the Potsdam Institute for Climate Impact Research. Even the supposedly gas-guzzling United States has reduced its emissions by a greater percentage than Germany in recent years.[13]

Populist politics and science are butting up against each other. Germany has some of the world's longest-standing and most respected environmental think tanks. There are now said to be more than a thousand researchers working on environment and climate in non-governmental policy institutes – more than in any other country – with an equivalent number working at universities. The first dedicated organization, the Institute for Applied Ecology, the Öko-Institut, emerged from the anti-nuclear movement in the southwestern town of Freiburg as early as 1977. Three years later it produced a text that was way ahead of its time – *Energiewende*, Growth and Prosperity without Oil and Uranium. That term *Wende* was also used to describe the period of reunification, a time of risk-taking and momentous change.

So what has happened? Wasn't Merkel known as the 'Climate Chancellor'? Wasn't Germany one of the countries to give the Green party a role in government? Wasn't Germany one of the first countries to 'go green' and to embrace renewable energy, recycling, cycling and all things environmental?

Part of it was the absence of impending and tangible menace. For years the effects of climate change within Germany were not the main problem. Its effects were further afield. The closest danger was rising sea levels, but even that had more effect on neighbours to the north and west, such as Denmark and the Netherlands. Most of the problem was political. Merkel has faced a number of forces of resistance: the nuclear lobby, the car lobby and the coal lobby. Reunification set back the project, reordering priorities. The politics and economics of the East refocused minds on preserving jobs and social stability, at pretty much all costs. Meanwhile, the chancellor's coalition partners, the SPD, were torn. They needed to keep their core working-class constituency content, while not alienating their younger, more urban, voters.

Germany is energy poor and densely populated. Unlike the

UK or France, or Spain, Portugal or the Netherlands, it has not in the past been able to rely on limitless supplies of resources from colonies. Before the war, coal was the one strategic reserve on which it could rely. It was a natural treasure. It is what made the country great. From 1945, the Americans ensured that Germany became dependent on supplies of oil and gas, on sea lanes it didn't control. It was tied into the Western alliance. Energy security is essential for all countries. A people who had twice in one century witnessed destruction and punishment became adept at husbanding what they had.

In 2000, Germany became the first big economy to place an all-in bet on wind and solar, passing a much-copied law that offered guaranteed high tariffs for renewable energy. The legislation was less about climate change, more about ridding itself of the scourge of nuclear power. Two years later, the 'Act on the structured phase-out of the utilization of nuclear energy for the commercial generation of electricity' took effect, following lengthy negotiations with plant operators. The act legislated for the shutdown of all nuclear facilities by 2021 or so; several closed early, roughly in line with their expected operational life and safety records.[14] In 2005, renewables accounted for just 10 per cent of electricity production.[15] Investors rushed to build wind farms on land and sea. More than 1.5 million solar installations were fitted. This was a time of considerable optimism. One part of the optimism has been justified. The share of renewables has climbed steadily. It now accounts for more than 40 per cent of electricty production, one of the highest proportions in the world. The target is to increase that to 65 per cent by 2030 and 80 per cent by 2050. The programme costs money. Around €25 billion in subsidies flows to renewables each year, mostly through premiums paid by consumers.[16]

Some 160,000 people are employed in the wind power sector

alone. That is eight times the number of workers in the coal industry, although the sense of coal as being intrinsic to Germany's sense of self has meant that one wouldn't know that from the pronouncements of politicians. The renewables boom coincided with other pressures. In the mid-2000s, as Putin was turning against the West, the German government began to wonder whether it could continue to rely safely on Russian gas and electricity. Solar and wind couldn't fill the gap and they began to question the wisdom of abandoning nuclear. In 2008, *Der Spiegel* proclaimed on its cover: Nuclear Power – The Scary Comeback.[17] Merkel and her coalition partners, the centrist FDP, suddenly unveiled legislation in late 2010 to extend the running terms of those nuclear plants that were still operating. This sleight of hand has gone down in environmental folklore as the great betrayal, the great ambush. More protests took place; more court cases ensued. The law was challenged as unconstitutional, because ministers had not consulted the states and had rushed it through the Bundestag. The Greens surged in popularity, taking the lead in opinion polls with 30 per cent of the popular vote, unprecedented anywhere in the world. Three quarters of voters told pollsters they were against nuclear power. Even the government's own experts condemned the move.

Then came Fukushima. The nuclear disaster in Japan provided Merkel with a face-saving opportunity. A new law was adopted three months later setting fixed dates for the abandonment of nuclear: 2021. Such is the deeply ingrained hostility towards nuclear power, and such was the political backlash, Merkel had no choice. In terms of climate change, the move was arguably the wrong way round. Germany should have first closed down coal and other CO_2-intensive sources. Countries currently outperforming the Germans in cutting emissions – the UK, France and Sweden – have a nuclear component in the mix. The chancellor portrayed the U-turn as an act of radical-ism, but she was forced into it.

There is, according to Green activists, one important piece of unfinished business: Tihange and the other nearby plants. Even as Germany moves towards a non-nuclear future, some 30 per cent of the EU's energy comes from nuclear energy, with 130 plants sited in 14 countries. The Euratom Treaty, Europe's commitment to developing peaceful nuclear power, was signed by the founding members of the EEC in 1957. It is intended to 'foster cooperation' and ensure compatible safety standards. Euratom and other international agreements also limit cross-border liability for nuclear accidents. Why not quit these trea-ties when the final German plant closes in 2021, the activists argue? Why should any German government deny its citizens the right to sue for damages after an accident in upwind France or Belgium? And yet, to exit a European treaty would be a very un-German act.

The summer of 2018 brought home the extent of the crisis for the first time. Germany sweltered in dangerously high temper-atures. Crops were ruined. Rivers ran dry. In the second half of the year, the water was so low that cargo traffic on the Rhine ground to a halt for the first time in living memory. The shut-down affected the industrial heartland. The giant ThyssenKrupp steelworks, which dominates the Ruhr area, was forced to scale back production. Chemical multinationals BASF and Bayer were forced to introduce backup cooling systems for their plants because the reduction in flow of the river had caused the water to warm. In the same year, forests caught fire with an inten-sity that the country had never seen before. To many Germans who had previously been lackadaisical about climate change, the burning forests were the clincher. It's hard to overestimate the hold that forests have on the German psyche. From Tacitus's accounts of Germania and the victory over the Romans in the Battle of the Teutoburg Forest, via the Brothers Grimm, to the romantic poetry of von Eichendorff, who spoke of 'a pious dwelling for the soul', forests are regarded almost as a primordial sphere.

With one eye on her legacy, Merkel realized it was time to act. No more *Pillepalle*, she said. Merkel was addressing her parliamentary party in June 2019. No more messing about. It was a strange choice of term for the failure to act on the climate emergency – the thawing of the Arctic permafrost, the blazing forests, the floods and heatwaves, or life-threatening air pollution back home. She might have been addressing the criticism to herself.

The Climate Protection Law was intended to burnish the chancellor's green credentials. As ever, in order to achieve a consensus, the government first asked a commission to investigate. It proposed that all coal-fired power plants be closed by 2038. The biggest energy operators would be required to shut down the equivalent of twenty large power stations by 2022. By 2030, coal production will more than halve. In September 2019, after a fifteen-hour negotiation between coalition partners that went late into the night, Merkel announced a €54 billion package of measures. Companies that produce and sell petrol, coal, heating oil and similar fuels would have to buy certificates to offset the carbon dioxide emissions from their products. Such a system already exists at EU level, though only for heavy industry, aviation and the energy sector. The German carbon price, however, would be significantly lower, starting at €10 per tonne in 2021 and rising to €35 by 2025. The CSU held out successfully against an initial price of €20 per tonne. Other measures encouraged companies and households to reduce their carbon emissions:

rail travel would be made cheaper by cutting VAT, while plane tickets would be taxed more heavily; heating systems that run on oil would be banned from new buildings from 2026; vehicle taxes would be raised for heavily polluting cars, while electric vehicles would be treated more favourably. One million charging points for electric vehicles would be installed by 2030. Reforestation is also a major part of the package. Each sector of the economy is being given a legal responsibility to ensure compliance, with government ministries overseeing the process.

The package is complicated and adoption of all its parts into law is uncertain. But the government was keen to maximize impact. It was announced amid some fanfare. The environment minister Svenja Schulze described it as a 'new beginning for Germany's climate policy'.[18] Many saw it as a missed opportunity, particularly the €10 carbon tax, which they said was set so low it would not change consumer behaviour. Experts have cited other shortfalls. They point out that the continued subsidy for coal has led to surplus production and the export of cheap energy to Germany's neighbours. One of the less discussed issues is the slowing down of onshore wind power production. Local inhabitants have been forcing a change of law in a number of regions, ensuring that turbines are not built within 1 kilometre of any 'settlement' – a deliberately vague term. With many first-generation turbines nearing the end of their life, they may not be replaced. Now the emphasis is on offshore renewables, which can be built only by multinationals.

In her 2020 New Year's message, with an eye on her legacy, Merkel pledged to make the climate emergency the top priority for her last period in office. 'At 65, I am at an age at which I personally will no longer experience all the consequences of climate change that will occur if politicians do not act,' she told the nation. 'It will be our children and grandchildren who have to live with the consequences of what we do, or refrain from doing, today. That is why I use all my strength to ensure that Germany makes its contribution – ecologically, economically, socially – to getting climate change under control.'[19] In those remarks, Merkel appeared to suggest that she knew she had disappointed in recent years, having been such a pioneer on the green agenda at the start of her tenure.

Whatever the pressures from the coal and car lobby and from the political right in the East, her successor knows that Germany has an opportunity to blaze a new trail. It has the technological prowess; it has the political structures. For all the momentum lost, Germans have embedded environmentalism into the heart of communities in a way few countries have done.

Most importantly, Germany could, just could, end up with the first Green chancellor in a new era after Merkel leaves office. Since jointly taking charge of the party two years ago, Robert Habeck and Annalena Baerbock have overseen a surge in its popularity. The Greens now regularly outperform the SPD in regional elections and are consistently ahead of them in national polls. They would then face a dilemma over which of their two leaders would become chancellor. The American magazine *Foreign Policy* recently dubbed Habeck 'Germany's answer to Macron',[20] a description that may be a bit of a stretch but is testament to how much perceptions of the Greens have changed. Like many German politicians, and unlike many in the US or UK, Habeck is not embarrassed by an academic past. He has a thesis on literary aesthetics and has published a book on the enlightenment-era poet Casimir Ulrich Boehlendorff. He continued to write novels until 2009, shortly before entering parliament in the rural northern region of Schleswig-Holstein. There he became deputy prime minister and energy minister. He has talked of redefining politics between open and closed

political systems: 'We now try to become the new playmakers
[. . .] Green parties can also address central questions that don't
fit into the traditional left-right spectrum. How do we establish
a consensus in a diverse society?'[21] He added that the climate
emergency would not be solved by judgementalism or excessive interference in people's lives. 'There can be no politics that
doesn't ban things. We have a highway code, a code of civil law:
the world is full of bans that exist in order to guarantee our
freedom. If you set standards at a broader political level, then
that's a good thing. If you tell people they have a personal calorie
budget for animal proteins, then that's a bad idea.'[22] Baerbock,
more of a behind-the-scenes fixer, is an expert in international
law. A federal MP for Potsdam since 2013, she received the
highest ever vote, 97.1 per cent, for a Green party chair.

The odds are still against one of them becoming leader, but
the very possibility is remarkable. Whether or not they emerge
as the largest party, they are almost certain to form a significant part of the next government, the first time they have been
in power since the days of Gerhard Schröder and the Kosovo
war in the late nineties and early 2000s. The choice will be
either a coalition with the CDU of Merkel's successor – the first
so-called Black-Green coalition in German history (although
it has worked, to good effect, in the regions of Hesse and
Baden-Württemberg). Alternatively, they could form a three-
party centre-left coalition including the SPD and Die Linke, as
is the case in the regional governments of Berlin, Bremen and
Thuringia.

Many more radical younger environmentalists accuse the
Greens of going soft, going mainstream. They certainly have
embraced the ethos of German politics: compromise and the
art of the possible. German businesses, meanwhile, are being
forced, often reluctantly, to rethink their models. A car industry

that fell into ignominy is starting to catch up on electrification, but it has a lot of catching up to do. A country that was one of the first to get to grips with the environmental crisis, and to put it into the political and societal mainstream, may yet see its credentials restored. With the Greens as the new power brokers, very few countries have, in these dark times, a similarly positive story to tell. Very few countries take their politics as seriously as Germany does.

Conclusion

Why the Germans do it better

The world feels more threatening now than at any time in the post-war era. Germans look around them and they see populism, pandemics and the climate emergency at their doorstep. The consequences of COVID-19 will last for years; the environmental crisis for decades beyond that. From the end of the Second World War, Germans lived through division, the building of the Berlin Wall and the Cold War; but they always had others to rely on for their security. Now that sense of stability from the outside has gone. Indeed, many around the world are looking to them.

Much of contemporary Germany's resilience has been wrapped up in the personality of one woman, Angela Merkel. Shortly before pre-announcing that she wouldn't stand as candidate for chancellor at the next election, due by late 2021, she said that Germany 'needs to write a new chapter'.[1] She did not go immediately, leading some detractors to declare that she had outlived her welcome. Yet all through that supposed hiatus her personal popularity rating remained among the highest of any leader in the world and far higher than her own Christian Democrats as a party. Asked about her legacy, she merely says: 'I don't think about my role in history. I do my job.'[2] The harder things became, the more her calmness set her apart from other world leaders. Dour she may have come across to some, dutiful to most, but that was her way. She wasn't going to change.

The responsibilities placed on the new generation of leaders will be immense. What kind of Germany will they preside over? If the past few years of global turbulence have taught us anything, it is not to make sweeping predictions. Yet the immediate stakes are high; 2021 is 'super-election-year' in Germany, with a series of regional elections culminating in the general election in September – the first for a generation without Merkel. Her party went into the year still with no idea about who would take over from her.

After several postponements due to COVID, the CDU finally held its leadership contest in January 2021. Armin Laschet, the premier of the most populous state, North Rhine-Westphalia, narrowly prevailed. The margin of his victory over the more controversial and Conservative Friedrich Merz was narrow, signifying a party uncertain of the way ahead and less-than-thrilled with the result. Would they offer him up as their choice for chancellor? Laschet fits the conventional profile of the German politician, a dealmaker. He eased himself into pole position by cleverly announcing a joint ticket with another contender, Jens Spahn. The two represent both wings of the CDU, Spahn more on the right and Laschet the centrist. Spahn had antagonized Merkel at the height of the refugee influx by criticizing Germany's open-door policy, but the two quickly made up, and she brought him into the heart of decision-making. At forty years old, Spahn has time to wait, but his position as health minister during the pandemic gave him the ultimate grounding in crisis management.

Like Merkel, Laschet is deft at building coalitions, both in the precise sense of forming governments and more broadly across different spectrums of political life. In the 1990s, as an MP, he was a member of the Pizza-Connection, a group of Christian Democrats and Greens who met in the wine cellar of an Italian restaurant in Bonn, where the Bundestag was located at the time, to identify common ground between the parties. At the time the move was seen as eccentric, subversive even. It now seems inspired, with both parties actively preparing for life together in government. He continues to maintain his Pizza-Connection network, with many of the politicians involved at the time now holding leading positions. After spells in the European Parliament and the Bundestag, in 2017 Laschet took over North Rhine-Westphalia, ruling with the small liberal FDP party. His dependable style won him plaudits. That state, whose GDP is larger than many European countries, will have provided a useful test run for national leadership.

A CDU under Merz's leadership would have given more definition. He would have brought back some disgruntled voters on the right, who have gone over to the AfD, but he would have alienated a larger amount in the centre. Another important figure for the future is Markus Söder, the premier of Bavaria and leader of the CDU's sister party, the CSU. By tradition, the two parties form one bloc in national politics, with one joint candidate for chancellor. That decision was due in April 2021, with Söder being encouraged to throw his hat into the ring if Laschet faltered in the polls.

Throughout the final months of her chancellorship, there remained a sneaking suspicion that Merkel – polling better than for many years thanks to her handling of COVID-19 – might not go after all. That was wishful thinking. Germany is facing a period of immense change, but won't have her to steer the ship. Many fear life after *Mutti*. They are right to.

In the UK, government ministers and much of the media shunned public displays of anxiety, hailing the Blitz Spirit to 'defeat' COVID-19. The rhetoric of the Second World War, Britain's obsession, was back – this time with a certain salience. More movingly, the Queen invoked Vera Lynn's wartime song 'We'll Meet Again'. But the more the pandemic continued and the more the nostalgia grew, the more it became apparent that the 1939–45 era was the last time the UK had experienced social solidarity on a national scale. Would it now come back? A generation of political leaders had exacerbated economic divides in Britain, selling short a people whose yearning for community is not so very different from those in other countries.

By summer 2020, some British newspapers that wouldn't have dreamed of saying anything positive about Germany – except their prowess at taking penalties in football – were painfully asking the question: why are the Germans doing it so much better? The pandemic reinforced a sense around the world of Britain floundering. People saw that some of the countries faring worst – the United States and Brazil – were led by charismatic populists of a similar hue. These leaders – Johnson, Trump, Bolsonaro – came to power as campaigners, pursuing culture wars within and beyond their countries. They knew how to identify divisions; they were less adept at bringing people together. Many Germans had got used to criticizing their own more deliberative political culture as dull. The pandemic prompted them to appreciate its advantages once again.

The sense of nationhood the Germans built after the war is based on the horror and shame of the Nazi legacy, and the lessons that needed to be learnt. It has helped the country to navigate the various crises it has faced in recent decades. Values that the Anglo-Saxon world peremptorily dismissed as old-fashioned – such as family, responsibility and the role of the state – have not had to be rehabilitated in Germany at the start of the third decade of the twenty-first century. They simply hadn't gone away.

Financially, an already weakening economy will suffer further, but Germany has an insurance policy that others do not possess. Years of the Black Zero, the austerity requirement that the federal government and regions must balance their books, left the exchequer with a huge surplus. For years, Merkel was attacked for not spending more, even while the German economy was roaring ahead. She resisted. Thrift was her watchword. Just as individuals should save where they could, so should states – for when emergencies strike, as was the case during the COVID-19 crisis when early on the government was able to pump an initial €750 billion to prop up the economy, a staggering amount but one it could more easily absorb than countries that were previously more profligate. The Black Zero might have been shattered. But how vindicated Merkel had been. As the pandemic took hold across Europe, people around the world looked at Germany and wondered why it was coping better than other countries? Germany was giving foreign nationals lifts on chartered planes to get them home. It was treating sick Italians, Spaniards and French. Its rate of virus testing put other countries to shame. It was painful for British politicians to be asked the question: why are the Germans doing it better?

Like its neighbours, Germany vowed to save as many businesses as possible that were driven by the pandemic to the verge of collapse. The difference is that it has much more room for manoeuvre and as a result is likely to survive the global turbulence with less economic and societal damage. The appeal to solidarity could strike a blow to the politics of extremism, denting what had seemed to be the inexorable rise of the AfD. The only regional elections in 2020, which took place in the city-state of Hamburg in February 2020, saw a first setback to the far-right party and re-election of an SPD/Green coalition. Weeks later came an important announcement that was overshadowed by the early stages of the COVID-19 crisis. The Federal Office of the Constitution decided to put one part of the AfD, called the Wing, onto the official watch list. It then quickly disbanded. For the first time, the liberal democratic state was fighting back. It is far too early to declare the AfD's demise – and a prolonged downturn could play into its hands again – but it is just possible that it may have passed its peak.

Germany's long-term challenges remain as clear as before. The methodical economic model is struggling to embrace the next generation of tech. Does Germany have what it takes to catch up with America and China in the development of electric cars, artificial intelligence and computer learning?

And what of its place in the world? As Merkel approached the end of her time in office, *Foreign Policy* magazine gave the thumbs down to her tenure, reflecting a conventional wisdom among conservatives in the Washington Beltway. It talked of a 'loveless grand coalition' presiding over an 'enigmatic' foreign policy.[3] Part of the criticism is justified, at least as it pertains to her fourth and final administration. With Donald Trump causing mayhem and Britain disengaging from Europe and becoming a more marginal power, the path was open for Germany to assert itself more forcefully, not just in terms of national interest but as a moral leader. Merkel did that, to an extent, but much more could have been done, and needs to be done in the future. As for Russia and China, each posing different but significant threats, Germany needs to equivocate less. Merkel was tough on Russia,

weaker on China. Laschet appears worryingly more accommodating to Moscow but may be a tougher adversary to Beijing.

On Brexit, the warning by Katarina Barley, the former
economics minister, became real more quickly than anyone
imagined. Within weeks of Brexit taking place, the Germans
and French began to limit their contacts with the UK on security matters, even though the club of three had previously
cooperated well. Britain went down from Germany's third to
seventh-largest export market. Britain, once a model for post-
war Germany, was dismissed as an offshore annoyance. The
UK's confrontational politics simply hardened that of Germany
and the other twenty-six EU states, which remained remarkably
united. Disengagement from Europe, a continent that Trump
labelled a 'foe',[4] did not bring about the revival of the so-called
special relationship on which Britain so desperately depends
for its sense of international worth.

Meanwhile, the infantile attacks by the early Johnson administration on experts and 'elites' such as the BBC, civil service and
universities were overtaken by the reality of crisis management.
When will the more enlightened Britain – the tolerant, innovative, compassionate, open society that generations of Germans
so admired – be rediscovered? It may take some time yet. Writing in *Die Zeit* on the day the UK left the EU, Bettina Schulz, a
German author, spoke for many: 'When I arrived in Britain 30
years ago, London was freedom for me, a living utopia, a model
for how people from all over the world could live together, work
together and love together. There were no foreigners. Everybody
belonged.'[5] The German lament about the chaos that was Britain
of the Brexit period was about the politics, never the people.

Politics in this new era will, in any case, be messier in all
countries, including in Germany. It will continue to make mistakes. *Langsam aber sicher* . . . slow but sure. That is the German

way. The nosy obsession with rules can instantly antagonize. The reluctance to innovate, to take risks, to throw caution to the wind can have a deadening effect. Yet this punctilious, deliberative approach has provided protection against sudden lurches, navigating the four key moments of its post-war history. It helped the country rebuild after the horrors of the Nazis and embed a new democracy with the Basic Law of 1949. It has been a shock absorber from the protest movement of 1968 to the fall of the Wall in 1989 to the refugee crisis of 2015, to the challenges that Germany has already faced in a decade that has barely begun.

In a television address a few weeks into the COVID-19 crisis, Merkel did something German leaders have rarely done. She invoked the war, but not on this occasion to emphasize guilt: 'There has been no greater challenge to our country since reunification – no, not since the Second World War – that relies so heavily on us all working together in solidarity.'[6] She then spoke grimly of the restrictions on the streets, of the army being called in, of the state monitoring people's whereabouts. 'Let me assure you: for someone like me, for whom freedom of movement was a hard-won right, such restrictions can only be justified as an absolute necessity. They should never be taken lightly, and should only be imposed temporarily in a democracy, but they are vital now to save lives.' For the woman who lived through communism and the Wall, emergency measures did not sit easily.

The default to anxiety and deliberation is, however, a far better insurance policy for the future than the make-it-up-as-you-go-along hubris of those in other countries who think they know better, but do not. As the British architect David Chipperfield put it to me: 'The Germans articulate anxieties that we should all have.' Or this from Martin Rennert, the former president of the Berlin University of the Arts, a Brooklyn Jew who has been in Germany for thirty-five years: 'Even with all the shortcomings,

I admire the way things work out here. The intelligent way in which decisions are taken. That doesn't make the decisions right, but the process reassures.' Or this from Paul Lever, a former UK ambassador to Germany: 'To live in today's Germany, as I was fortunate to do for over five years, is to experience to the full the virtues of European, and Western, civilization.'

Germans still cannot countenance the suggestion that, on many accounts, they *do* do it better. They are alarmed by the very idea that they could possibly teach anyone a lesson. I admit that when I first began to develop the idea, in my mind this was more a proposition to test than a statement of fact. But the more I've looked at how they've addressed their recent history, the way they do politics, the way they do business, the way they manage crises, their attitudes to each other and to the outside world, the more convinced I've become. Especially in these difficult times, other countries would be foolish to ignore Germany's emotional maturity and solidity.

Taken in the round, the Germany of the past seventy-five years is an extraordinary success story. It has established a new paradigm for stability that equivalent countries, such as the US, France and my own, the UK, are for different reasons struggling to achieve. Countries that struggle with the present take comfort from the nostalgia of past glories, real or imagined. Germany, because of its history, cannot.

Germany is Europe's best hope in this era of nationalism, anti-enlightenment and fear. Britain was always seen as a beacon, America too, but both countries have abrogated much of their responsibility to the wider world. Who will represent European values in a fast-changing world? Who will stand up to authoritarian regimes? Who will make the case for liberal democracy? Germany can, because it knows what happens when countries fail to learn the lessons of history.

Acknowledgements

The Germany of the 1980s and 1990s, when I lived there, has been transformed. Over the past couple of years, it has been not just stimulating, but also hugely enjoyable and exciting to spend so much time back in the country.

As I note in the introduction, old friends and new acquaintances were startled when I told them the thesis of the book. The Germans in particular were convinced that the longer I spent there, the more I would be disabused. I allowed the evidence to lead me. I took up the copious offers to introduce me to new people and to invite me to events. I visited places I had not been to before and revisited old haunts.

Many people from all walks of life guided me with their experience, insights and opinions, accommodating me and offering their networks. I couldn't have written the book in the way I did without them.

I apologize in advance if I have omitted anyone.

In the UK, thanks go to: Cathy Ashton, Jonathan Charles, David Chipperfield, Christoph Denk, Alan Duncan, Anthony Dworkin, Nigel Edwards, Jan Eichhorn, Alex Ellis, Dorothy

Feaver, Peter Foster, Susanne Frane, Ulrike Franke, Simon Fraser, Charles Grant, Stephen Green, John Gummer, David Halpern, Nick Hillman, Sian Jarvis, Hans Kundnani, Paul Lever, Neil MacGregor, Michael Maclay, Jürgen Maier, John Major, David Manning, Andrew Peters, Vicky Pryce, Katharina von Ruckteschell-Katte, Nigel Sheinwald, Phil Thomas, Marc Vlessing, Peter Wittig.

In Berlin: Thomas Bagger, Ronan Barnett, Annette von Bröcker, Alastair Buchan, Frank Alva Bücheler, Tobias Buck, Robbie Bulloch, Barbara Burckhardt and Hardy Schmitz, Katy Campbell, Martin Eyerer, Andreas Fanizadeh, Uwe Fechner, Jens Fischer and Heinz Schulte, Marcel Fratzscher, Benjamin Görlach, August Hanning, Anke Hassel, Wolfgang Ischinger, Max Jarrett, Joe Kaeser, Rachel King, R Andreas Kraemer, Rüdiger Lenz, Stefan Mair, Claudia Major, Susan Naiman, Johannes Noske, Tom Nuttall, Philip Oltermann, Hermann Parzinger, Alan Posener, Jana Puglierin, Martin Rennert, Wiebke Reed, Konstantin Richter, Norbert Röttgen, Sophia Schlette, Carina Schmid and Janusz Hamerski, Bettina Schmitz, Ulrich Schmitz, Julie Smith, Rebecca Stromeyer, Jan Techau, Bettine Vestring and Judy Dempsey, Johannes Vogel and Sarah Darwin, Beate Wedekind, Jan Weidenfeld, Thomas Wiegold, Sebastian Wood, Katharina Wrohlich, Astrid Ziebarth.

Elsewhere: Ulrich Wilhelm, Matthias Mühling, Alex Schill, Klaus Goetz (Munich); Antje Hermenau, Helmut Haas, Thomas Weidinger, Alf Thum, Paula Güth (Leipzig); Dirk Burghardt, Marcel Thum (Dresden); Ulrike Kremeier (Cottbus); Hermann Mildenberger (Weimar); Frederik Fischer (Wittenberge); Bettina Leetz (Potsdam); Nick Jefcoat, Rolf Kraemer, Johannes Lindner, Andrej Kupetz, Amanda Diel, Eric Menges (Frankfurt); Andreas Rödder (Mainz); Tina Grothoff, Wolfgang Wähner-Schmitz (Bonn); Tom Bolzen, Roger Brandts, Tim Hörnemann

(Mönchengladbach); Eric Schöffler (Düsseldorf); Johannes Pflug, Martin Ahlers (Duisburg); Manfred von Holtum, Günter Schulte (Aachen); Cihan Sugur (Stuttgart); Markus Schill (Mannheim); Olaf Bartels (Hamburg); Catherine Myerscough (Hannover); Heather Grabbe (Brussels); Andreas Schleicher (Paris).

Special thanks go to the following, who advised me closely throughout and read various versions of the book: Robert and Monika Birnbaum, Stefanie Bolzen, Guy Chazan, Rupert Glasgow, Cornelius Huppertz, Reiner Kneifel-Haverkamp, Benedetta Lacey, Christian Odendahl, Daniel Tetlow and Stewart Wood.

This is my sixth book stretching back twenty-five years. I've been accompanied almost all of the time by Andrew Gordon, as my editor when I was writing *Blair's Wars* and then as my agent for my next three. I'm very grateful for all his work over the years. For the next stage, I'm thrilled to be represented by Karolina Sutton at Curtis Brown. I've hugely enjoyed working with Atlantic and with my editor, Mike Harpley. Thanks to Will Atkinson and the extended team – Kate Straker, Jamie Forrest, Alice Latham, Mike Jones, David Inglesfield and James Pulford – for making sure the assignment was completed so seamlessly amid the COVID-19 crisis. I look forward to working with them more in the future.

In Germany, I'm really grateful to my new agent Michaela Röll. A separate German version of the book was published earlier this year by Rowohlt, and I'm excited to be working with Johanna Langmaack, Nora Gottschalk and Lisa Marie Paesike.

I'm extremely grateful to my research assistant Sam Fitz-Gibbon, who unearthed documents, fixed interviews and advised on the manuscript at every stage. He is an extraordinary talent.

Finally, to my family – Lucy, Alex and Constance – for being at my side for this and all my journeys.

Notes

Introduction

1   Quoted in G. Wheatcroft, 'England Have Won Wars Against Argentina and Germany. Football Matches, Not So Much.', *New Republic*, 12 July 2014, newrepublic.com/article/118673/2014-world-cup-england-have-won-wars-against-both-argentina-germany (accessed 10 September 2019).

2   P. Morgan, 'Mirror declares football war on Germany', *Daily Mirror*, 24 June 1996.

3   M. Sontheimer, 'Gefangene der Geschichte', *Spiegel*, 16 December 2002, spiegel.de/spiegel/print/d-25940368.html (accessed 25 September 2019).

4   D. Woidke, speaking at Chatham House conference, Berlin, 7 November 2019.

5   P. Oltermann, 'Beach towels and Brexit: how Germans really see the Brits', *Guardian*, 30 September 2019, theguardian.com/world/2019/sep/30/beach-towels-and-brexit-how-germans-really-see-the-brits (accessed 30 September 2019).

6   S. Schama and S. Kuper, 'Margaret Thatcher 1925–2013', *Financial Times*, 12 April 2013, ft.com/content/536e095c-a23e-11e2-8971-00144feabdc0 (accessed 5 October 2019).

7   F. O'Toole, 'The paranoid fantasy behind Brexit', *Guardian*, 16 November 2018, theguardian.com/politics/2018/nov/16/brexit-paranoid-fantasy-fintan-otoole (accessed 20 November 2019).

8   Nicholas Ridley, in an interview with Dominic Lawson, then editor

of the *Spectator*. See J. Jones, 'From the archives: Ridley was right', *Spectator*, 22 September 2011, spectator.co.uk/article/from-the-archives-ridley-was-right (accessed 28 October 2019).

9 Quoted in A. Hyde-Price, 'Germany and European Security before 1990', in K. Larres (ed.), *Germany since Unification: The Development of the Berlin Republic*, Basingstoke, Palgrave, 2001, p. 206.

10 H. Young, *This Blessed Plot: Britain and Europe from Churchill to Blair*, London, Macmillan, 1998, p. 359.

11 M. Thatcher, *The Downing Street Years*, London, HarperCollins, 1993, p. 813.

12 D. Auer, D. Tetlow, Guest Blog: More Britons willing to leave UK to escape Brexit uncertainty, 28 October 2019, https://www.compas.ox.ac.uk/2019/brexit-uncertainty-motivates-risk-taking-by-brits-who-decide-to-leave-the-uk-and-theres-usually-no-turning-back/#_ftn1 (accessed 1 November 2019)

13 G. Will, 'Today's Germany is the best Germany the world has seen', *Washington Post*, 4 January 2019, washingtonpost.com/opinions/global-opinions/todays-germany-is-the-best-germany-the-world-has-seen/2019/01/04/abeob138-0f8f-11e9-84fc-d58c33d6c8c7_story.html (accessed 5 October 2019).

1   Rebuilding and Remembering

1 F. Stern, *Five Germanys I Have Known*, New York, Farrar, Straus and Giroux, 2006, p. 425.

2 Ibid., p. 4.

3 A. J. P. Taylor, *The Course of German History: A Survey of the Development of Germany since 1815*, London, Hamish Hamilton, 1945, p. 13.

4 E. Apperly, 'Stumbling stones': a different vision of Holocaust remembrance, 18 February 2019, theguardian.com/cities/2019/feb/18/stumbling-stones-a-different-vision-of-holocaust-remembrance.

5 G. Orwell, 'Creating Order out of Cologne Chaos', *Observer*, 25 March 1945.

6 N. MacGregor, *Germany: Memories of a Nation*, London, Allen Lane, 2014, p. 484.

7 Ibid.

8 Quoted in ibid., p. 484.

9 Quoted in S. Crawshaw, *Easier Fatherland: Germany and the Twenty-First Century*, London, Continuum, 2004, pp. 23–24.

10 J. F. Byrnes, Restatement of Policy on Germany, Stuttgart, 6 September 1946, usa.usembassy.de/etexts/ga4-460906.htm (accessed 15 October 2019).

11 G. C. Marshall, 'The Marshall Plan Speech', Harvard University,
    Cambridge, MA, 5 June 1947, marshallfoundation.org/marshall/the-
    marshall-plan/marshall-plan-speech (accessed 1 November 2019).

12 T. Wurm, H. C. Asmussen, H. Meiser et al., 'Stuttgarter
    Schulderklärung', Evangelischen Kirche in Deutschland, 19 October
    1945, ekd.de/Stuttgarter-Schulderklarung-11298.htm (accessed
    1 November 2019).

13 D. R. Henderson, 'German Economic Miracle', in D. R. Henderson (ed.),
    The Concise Encyclopedia of Economics, Liberty Fund, 2007, econlib.
    org/library/Enc/GermanEconomicMiracle.html (accessed 5 November
    2019).

14 U. Greenberg, 'Can Christian Democracy Save Us?', *Boston Review*,
    22 October 2019, bostonreview.net/philosophy-religion/udi-greenberg-
    christian-democracy (accessed 30 Novmber 2019).

15 H. Lübbe, 'Der Nationalsozialismus im Bewußtsein der deutschen
    Gegenwart', *Frankfurter Allgemeine Zeitung*, 24 January 1983.

16 S. Friedländer, *Memory, History and the Extermination of the Jews of
    Europe*, Bloomington and Indianapolis, Indiana University Press, 1993,
    p. 8.

17 See K. Kuiper, *The 100 Most Influential Women of All Time*, Britannica
    Educational Publishing, New York, NY, 2009, p. 277; S. Kinzer, 'Dietrich
    Buried in Berlin, and Sentiment Is Mixed', *New York Times*, 17 May
    1992, nytimes.com/1992/05/17/world/dietrich-buried-in-berlin-and-
    sentiment-is-mixed.html (accessed 20 November 2019).

18 R. Gramer, 'Sales of Hitler's "Mein Kampf" Skyrocketing in
    Germany – But It's Not Why You Think', *Foreign Policy*, 3 January
    2017, foreignpolicy.com/2017/01/03/sales-of-hitlers-mein-kampf-
    skyrocketing-in-germany-but-its-not-why-you-think (accessed
    19 November 2019).

19 H. Arendt, 'Eichmann in Jerusalem – V', *New Yorker*, 16 March 1963.

20 K. Wiegrefe, 'The Holocaust in the Dock: West Germany's Efforts
    to Influence the Eichmann Trial', *Spiegel*, 15 April 2011, spiegel.de/
    international/world/the-holocaust-in-the-dock-west-germany-s-efforts-
    to-influence-the-eichmann-trial-a-756915.html (accessed 20 November
    2019).

21 F. Kaplan, 'A Match That Burned the Germans', *New York Times*,
    12 August 2009, nytimes.com/2009/08/16/movies/16kapl.html
    (accessed 20 November 2019).

22 W. Brandt, *Erinnerungen*, Propyläen-Verlag, Frankfurt am Main, 1989,
    p. 214.

23 R. von Weizsäcker, Speech during the Ceremony Commemorating the
    40th Anniversary of the End of War in Europe and of National-Socialist
    Tyranny, Bonn, 8 May 1985.

24 J. M. Markham, 'Facing Up to Germany's Past', *New York Times*, 23 June 1985, nytimes.com/1985/06/23/magazine/facing-up-to-germany-s-past. html (accessed 20 November 2019).

25 'Hausbacken, aber erfolgreich', *Spiegel*, 19 November 1990.

26 H. Kohl, speech to the Knesset, Jerusalem, 24 January 1984.

27 E. Nolte, 'Vergangenheit, die nicht vergehen will: Eine Rede, die geschrieben, aber nicht mehr gehalten werden konnte', *Frankfurter Allgemeine Zeitung*, 6 June 1986.

28 M. Stürmer, 'Geschichte in einem geschichtslosen Land', *Frankfurter Allgemeine Zeitung*, 25 April 1986.

29 Quoted in R. J. Evans, *In Hitler's Shadow: West German Historians and the Attempt to Escape from the Nazi Past*, New York, Pantheon Books, 1989, pp. 103–4.

30 H. Engdahl, Permanent Secretary of the Swedish Academy, 'Günter Grass', Nobel Prize for Literature 1999, 30 September 1999, nobelprize. org/prizes/literature/1999/press-release (accessed 10 November 2019).

31 'Zeitgeschichte: "Ein bisschen Spät"', *Spiegel*, 14 August 2006.

32 P. Lever, *Berlin Rules: Europe and the German Way*, London, I.B.Tauris, 2017, p. 45.

33 A. Beevor, 'Letter to the Editor: A Woman in Berlin', *New York Times*, 25 September 2005.

34 W. G. Sebald, *On the Natural History of Destruction*, trans. A. Bell, London, Penguin, 2004, p. viii.

35 J. Banville, 'Amnesia about the Allied bombing', *Guardian*, 6 March 2003.

2 Mutti's Warm Embrace

1 'Mitschrift Pressekonferenz: Podiumsdiskussion mit Bundeskanzlerin Merkel an der Prälat-Diehl-Schule', Groß-Gerau, 30 September 2014, www.bundesregierung.de/breg-de/aktuelles/pressekonferenzen/ podiumsdiskussion-mit-bundeskanzlerin-merkel-an-der-praelat-diehl-schule-845834 (accessed 28 April 2020).

2 Ibid.

3 K. Connolly, 'Angela Merkel: I took a sauna while Berlin Wall fell', *Guardian*, 5 November 2009, theguardian.com/world/2009/nov/05/ merkel-berlin-wall-sauna-1989 (accessed 24 November 2019).

4 'Sauna and oysters: Merkel remembers Berlin Wall fall', The Local (AFP), 8 November 2019, thelocal.de/20191108/sauna-and-oysters-merkel-recalls-berlin-wall-fall (accessed 28 April 2020).

5 Connolly, 'Angela Merkel: I took a sauna while Berlin Wall fell'.

6 Ibid.

7 M. Amann and F. Gathmann, 'Angela Merkel on the Fall of the Wall: "I Wanted to See the Rockies and Listen to Springsteen"', *Spiegel*,

7 November 2019, spiegel.de/international/europe/interview-with-angela-merkel-on-the-fall-of-the-berlin-wall-a-1295241.html (accessed 20 November 2019).

8 R. Pfister, 'The Reckoning: Kohl Tapes Reveal a Man Full of Anger', *Spiegel*, 14 October 2014, spiegel.de/international/germany/helmut-kohl-tapes-reveal-disdain-for-merkel-and-deep-sense-of-betrayal-a-997035.html (accessed 5 November 2019).

9 M. Orth, 'Angela's Assets', *Vanity Fair*, January 2015.

10 Ibid.

11 See C. Drösser, 'Gorbis Warnung', *Zeit*, 13 October 1999, zeit.de/stimmts/1999/199941_stimmts_gorbatsc (accessed 25 November 2019); 'Die Geduld ist zu Ende', *Spiegel*, 9 October 1989, spiegel.de/spiegel/print/d-13497043.html (accessed 25 November 2019).

12 C. Drösser, 'Geflügeltes Wort', *Zeit*, 5 November 2009, zeit.de/2009/46/Stimmts-Brandt-Zitat (accessed 26 November 2019).

13 H. A. Winkler, *Germany: The Long Road West, Volume 2: 1933–1990*, trans. A. J. Sager, Oxford, Oxford University Press, 2007, p. 468.

14 F. Stern, *Five Germanys I Have Known*, New York, Farrar, Straus and Giroux, 2006, p. 470.

15 H. Kohl, 'Der entscheidende Schritt auf dem Weg in die gemeinsame Zukunft der Deutschen', Presse- und Informationsamt der Bundesregierung, Bulletin No. 86, pp. 741–2, 3 July 1990, www.bundesregierung.de/breg-de/service/bulletin/der-entscheidende-schritt-auf-dem-weg-in-die-gemeinsame-zukunft-der-deutschen-fernsehansprache-des-bundeskanzlers-zum-inkrafttreten-der-waehrungsunion-am-1-juli-1990-788446 (accessed 26 November 2019).

16 Interview with Angela Merkel, *Bild*, 29 November 2004. See M. Ottenschlaeger, 'Sind wir noch ganz dicht?', *Zeit*, 9 December 2004, zeit.de/2004/51/Sind_wir_noch_ganz_dicht_ (accessed 27 April 2020).

17 C. Rietz, 'Großbritannien: Fürs Heizen zu arm', *Zeit*, 28 November 2013, zeit.de/2013/49/grossbritannien-heizungsarmut-boiler-energie (accessed 17 November 2019).

18 C. Kohrs and C. Lipkowski, '40 Jahre Grüne: Von der Protestpartei in die Mitte der Gesellschaft', *Süddeutsche Zeitung*, 11 January 2020, sueddeutsche.de/politik/gruene-buendnis-90-parteigeschichte-1.4750533 (accessed 15 January 2020).

19 Rezo, 'Die Zerstörung der CDU', YouTube, 18 May 2019, youtube.com/watch?v=4Y1lZQsyuSQ&t=830s (accessed 20 September 2019).

20 'Birgit Breuel: Frühere Treuhandchefin räumt Fehler ein', *Zeit*, 21 July 2019, zeit.de/politik/deutschland/2019-07/birgit-breuel-treuhand-chefin-fehler-privatisierung-ddr-betriebe (accessed 30 July 2019).

21 T. Buck, 'Lingering divide: why east and west Germany are drifting apart', *Financial Times*, 29 August 2019, ft.com/content/a22d04b2-c4b0-11e9-a8e9-296ca66511c9 (accessed 29 August 2019).

22 S. Neiman, *Learning from the Germans: Race and the Memory of Evil*, London, Allen Lane, 2019, p. 82.

23 Ibid.

24 G. Grass, trans. D. Dollenmayer, 'On Christa Wolf', *New York Review of Books*, 17 January 2012, nybooks.com/daily/2012/01/17/gunter-grass-christa-wolf-what-remains (accessed 10 November 2019).

25 M. Leo, trans. S. Whiteside, *Red Love: The Story of an East German Family*, London, Pushkin Press, 2003, p. 230.

26 Ibid.

27 A. Riding, 'Behind the Berlin Wall, Listening to Life', *New York Times*, 7 January 2007, nytimes.com/2007/01/07/movies/awardsseason/07ridi.html (accessed 30 October 2019).

28 'Germans still don't agree on what reunification meant', *Economist*, 31 October 2019.

3   Multikulti

1 See 'Global Trends: Forced Displacement in 2018', UNHCR, 20 June 2019, unhcr.org/5d08d7ee7.pdf (accessed 10 October 2019).

2 See J. Delcker, 'The phrase that haunts Angela Merkel', Politico, 19 August 2016, politico.eu/article/the-phrase-that-haunts-angela-merkel (accessed 2 February 2020).

3 See 'One in every four German residents now has migrant background', The Local, 1 August 2018, thelocal.de/20180801/one-in-every-four-german-residents-now-has-migrant-background (accessed 30 November 2019); L. Sanders IV, 'Germany second-largest destination for migrants: OECD', Deutsche Welle, 18 September 2019, dw.com/en/germany-second-largest-destination-for-migrants-oecd/a-50473180 (accessed 30 November 2019).

4 S. Boniface, 'It's starting to look like Germany won WW2 in every way bar the fighting', *Mirror*, 7 September 2015, mirror.co.uk/news/uk-news/its-starting-look-like-germany-6397791 (accessed 1 December 2019).

5 Ibid.

6 A. Taub, 'Angela Merkel should be ashamed of her response to this sobbing Palestinian girl', Vox, 16 July 2015, vox.com/2015/7/16/8981765/merkel-refugee-failure-ashamed (accessed 29 April 2020).

7 'Pressekonferenz von Bundeskanzlerin Merkel und dem österreichischen Bundeskanzler Faymann', Berlin, 15 September 2015, www.bundesregierung.de/breg-de/aktuelles/pressekonferenzen/

pressekonferenz-von-bundeskanzlerin-merkel-und-dem-oesterreichischen-bundeskanzler-faymann-844442 (accessed 1 December 2019).

8 K. Richter, 'Germany's refugee crisis has left it as bitterly divided as Donald Trump's America', *Guardian*, 1 April 2016, theguardian.com/commentisfree/2016/apr/01/germany-refugee-crisis-invited-into-my-home-welcoming-spirit-divided (accessed 1 December 2019).

9 Ibid.

10 'Ausgelassene Stimmung – Feiern weitgehend friedlich', POL-K: 160101-1-K/LEV, 1 January 2016, presseportal.de/blaulicht/pm/12415/3214905 (accessed 29 April 2020). See also '"Ausgelassene Stimmung – Feiern weitgehend friedlich"', *Süddeutsche Zeitung*, 5 January 2016, sueddeutsche.de/panorama/uebergriffe-in-koeln-ausgelassene-stimmung-feiern-weitgehend-friedlich-1.2806355 (accessed 2 December 2019).

11 'Germany shocked by Cologne New Year gang assaults on women', BBC, 5 January 2016, bbc.co.uk/news/world-europe-35231046 (accessed 2 December 2019).

12 See Y. Bremmer and K. Ohlendorf, 'Time for the facts. What do we know about Cologne four months later?', Correspondent, 2 May 2016, thecorrespondent.com/4401/time-for-the-facts-what-do-we-know-about-cologne-four-months-later/1073698080444-e20ada1b (accessed 2 December 2019).

13 Ibid.

14 Journalist speaking at 'Brown Bag Lunch: "Populism and its Impact on Elections: A Threat to Democracy?"', Aspen Institute, Berlin, 4 September 2019.

15 T. Abou-Chadi, 'Why Germany – and Europe – can't afford to accommodate the radical right', *Washington Post*, 4 September 2019, washingtonpost.com/opinions/2019/09/04/why-germany-europe-cant-afford-accommodate-radical-right (accessed 20 November 2019).

16 See M. Fiedler, 'Alexander Gauland und der "Vogelschiss"', *Tagesspiegel*, 2 June 2018, tagesspiegel.de/politik/afd-chef-zum-nationalsozialismus-alexander-gauland-und-der-vogelschiss/22636614.html (accessed 3 December 2019).

17 J. Wells, 'Leader of German Anti-Muslim Group Reinstated After Hitler Photo Controversy', BuzzFeed News, 23 February 2015, buzzfeednews.com/article/jasonwells/leader-of-german-anti-muslim-group-reinstated-after-hitler-p (accessed 29 April 2020).

18 'Pegida mobilisiert Tausende Demonstranten', *Süddeutsche Zeitung*, 6 October 2015, sueddeutsche.de/politik/dresden-pegida-mobilisiert-tausende-demonstranten-1.2679134 (accessed 29 April 2020).

19 M. Bartsch, M. Baumgärtner et al., 'Is Germany Lurching To the

Right?', *Spiegel*, 31 July 2018, spiegel.de/international/germany/
german-immigration-discourse-gets-heated-after-footballer-s-
resignation-a-1220478.html (accessed 3 December 2019).

20 C. Erhardt, 'Hasswelle: Kommunalpolitik – Aus Hetze werden Taten',
Kommunal, 25 June 2019, kommunal.de/hasswelle-alle-Zahlen
(accessed 3 December 2019).

21 In an interview with the *Guardian*: P. Oltermann, 'Germany slow to
hear alarm bells in killing of Walter Lübcke', *Guardian*, 2 July 2019,
theguardian.com/world/2019/jul/02/germany-slow-to-hear-alarm-
bells-in-killing-of-walter-lubcke (accessed 3 December 2019).

22 Thomas Haldenwang, speaking at a press conference for the
presentation of the annual Report on Constitutional Protection
(Verfassungsschutzbericht), Berlin, 27 June 2019. See H. Bubrowski
and J. Staib, 'Mord an Walter Lübcke: Versteckt im braunen Sumpf',
Frankfurter Allgemeine Zeitung, 28 June 2019, faz.net/aktuell/politik/
inland/was-der-mord-an-luebcke-mit-dem-nsu-zu-tun-hat-16257706.
html?printPagedArticle=true#pageIndex_2 (accessed 3 December 2019).

23 M. Hohmann, MdB, 'Hohmann: Ein missbrauchter politischer Mord',
25 June 2019, afdbundestag.de/hohmann-ein-missbrauchter-
politischer-mord (accessed 3 December 2019).

24 P. Oltermann, 'Germany slow to hear alarm bells in killing of Walter
Lübcke', *Guardian*, 2 July 2019, theguardian.com/world/2019/jul/02/
germany-slow-to-hear-alarm-bells-in-killing-of-walter-lubcke (accessed
3 December 2019).

25 See M. Eddy, 'German Lawmaker Who Called Muslims "Rapist
Hordes" Faces Sanctions', *New York Times*, 2 January 2018, nytimes.
com/2018/01/02/world/europe/germany-twitter-muslims-hordes.html
(accessed 4 December 2019).

26 J. C. M. Serrano, M. Shahrezaye, O. Papakyriakopoulos and
S. Hegelich, 'The Rise of Germany's AfD: A Social Media Analysis',
SMSociety '19: Proceedings of the 10th International Conference on
Social Media and Society, July 2019, 214–23, p. 3, doi.org/
10.1145/3328529.3328562 (accessed 4 December 2019). See also
J. Schneider, 'So aggressiv macht die AfD Wahlkampf auf Facebook',
Süddeutsche Zeitung, 14 September 2017, sueddeutsche.de/politik/
gezielte-grenzverletzungen-so-aggressiv-macht-die-afd-wahlkampf-auf-
facebook-1.3664785-0 (accessed 4 December 2019).

27 Heute Journal, ZDF, 15 August 2017. See also T. Escritt, 'In
Charlottesville, Germans sense echoes of their struggle with history',
Reuters, 18 August 2017, reuters.com/article/us-usa-trump-germany/
in-charlottesville-germans-sense-echoes-of-their-struggle-with-history-
idUSKCN1AY1NZ (accessed 3 December 2019).

28 See P. McGee and O. Storbeck, 'Fears over far-right prompt Siemens

chief to rebuke AfD politician', *Financial Times*, 20 May 2018, ft.com/
content/046821ba-5c17-11e8-9334-2218e7146b04 (accessed
3 December 2019).

29 Joe Kaeser, @JoeKaeser, Twitter, 20 July 2019, twitter.com/JoeKaeser/
status/1152502196354859010 (accessed 22 July 2019).

30 See K. Proctor and S. Murphy, 'Andrew Sabisky: Boris Johnson's
ex-adviser in his own words', *Guardian*, 17 February 2020, theguardian.
com/politics/2020/feb/17/andrew-sabisky-boris-johnsons-ex-adviser-
in-his-own-words (accessed 17 February 2020).

31 Mesut Özil, @MesutOzil1088, Twitter, 22 July 2018, twitter.com/
MesutOzil1088/status/1021093637411700741 (accessed 6 December
2019).

32 J. Spahn, 'Berliner Cafés: Sprechen Sie doch deutsch!', *Zeit*, 23 August
2017, zeit.de/2017/35/berlin-cafes-hipster-englisch-sprache-jens-spahn
(accessed 6 December 2019).

33 G. W. Leibniz, 'Ermahnung an die Deutschen, ihren Verstand und
Sprache besser zu üben, samt beigefügten Vorschlag einer Deutsch-
gesinten Gesellschafft', *Sämtliche Schriften*, vierte Reihe, dritter Band,
Berlin, Akademie-Verlag, 1986, p. 798.

34 W. Thierse, 'Von Schiller lernen?', Die Kulturnation, *Deutschlandfunk
Kultur*, 3 April 2005.

35 S. Hattenstone, 'Ai Weiwei on his new life in Britain: "People are at
least polite. In Germany, they weren't"', *Guardian*, 21 January 2020,
theguardian.com/artanddesign/2020/jan/21/ai-weiwei-on-his-new-life-
in-britain-germany-virtual-reality-film (accessed 21 January 2020).

36 'Antisemitismus: "Kann Juden nicht empfehlen, überall die Kippa zu
tragen"', *Zeit*, 25 May 2019, zeit.de/gesellschaft/zeitgeschehen/2019-05/
judenfeindlichkeit-antisemit-felix-klein-kippa (accessed 6 December
2019).

37 Ibid.

38 A. Merkel, 'Rede zum zehnjährigen Bestehen der Stiftung Auschwitz-
Birkenau', Auschwitz, 6 December 2019, www.bundesregierung.
de/breg-de/aktuelles/rede-von-bundeskanzlerin-merkel-zum-
zehnjaehrigen-bestehen-der-stiftung-auschwitz-birkenau-am-
6-dezember-2019-in-auschwitz-1704518 (accessed 7 December
2019).

39 E. Reents, 'Morde in Hanau: Böser, als die Polizei erlaubt', *Frankfurter
Allgemeine Zeitung*, 20 February 2020, faz.net/aktuell/feuilleton/morde-
in-hanau-jetzt-ist-der-staat-am-zug-16644270.html (accessed
28 February 2020).

40 'Bundesinnenminister Seehofer: "Wir müssen den Rassismus ächten"',
Bundesministerium des Innern, für Bau und Heimat, 21 February 2020,

bmi.bund.de/SharedDocs/kurzmeldungen/DE/2020/02/pk-hanau.html (accessed 23 February 2020).

4   No Longer a Child

1   See T. Barber, 'Germany and the European Union: Europe's Reluctant Hegemon?', *Financial Times*, 11 March 2019, ft.com/content/a1f327ba-4193-11e9-b896-fe36ec32aece (accessed 10 December 2019); H. W. Maull, 'Germany and Japan: The New Civilian Powers', *Foreign Affairs*, vol. 69, no. 5, Winter 1990/91, foreignaffairs.com/articles/asia/1990-12-01/germany-and-japan-new-civilian-powers (accessed 10 December 2019).

2   Quoted in G. Will, 'Today's Germany is the best Germany the world has seen', *Washington Post*, 4 January 2019, washingtonpost.com/opinions/global-opinions/todays-germany-is-the-best-germany-the-world-has-seen/2019/01/04/abeob138-0f8f-11e9-84fc-d58c33d6c8c7_story.html (accessed 5 October 2019).

3   'Schröder on Kosovo: "The Goal Was Exclusively Humanitarian"', *Spiegel*, 25 October 2006, spiegel.de/international/schroeder-on-kosovo-the-goal-was-exclusively-humanitarian-a-444727.html (accessed 15 December 2019).

4   J. Fischer in a speech to the Green Party Conference, Bielefeld, 13 May 1999. See 'Auszüge aus der Fischer-Rede', *Spiegel*, 13 May 1999, spiegel.de/politik/deutschland/wortlaut-auszuege-aus-der-fischer-rede-a-22143.html (accessed 13 December 2019).

5   See 'Stenographischer Bericht: 186: Sitzung', Deutscher Bundestag, Berlin, 12 September 2001, dipbt.bundestag.de/doc/btp/14/14186.pdf (accessed 15 December 2019).

6   G. Schröder, 'The Way Forward in Afghanistan', *Spiegel*, 12 February 2009, spiegel.de/international/world/essay-by-former-chancellor-gerhard-schroeder-the-way-forward-in-afghanistan-a-607205.html (accessed 15 December 2019).

7   J. Gauck, 'Speech to open 50th Munich Security Conference', Munich, 31 January 2014, bundespraesident.de/SharedDocs/Reden/EN/JoachimGauck/Reden/2014/140131-Munich-Security-Conference.html (accessed 16 December 2019).

8   F. Steinmeier, 'Speech by Foreign Minister Frank Walter Steinmeier at the 50th Munich Security Conference', Munich, 1 February 2014, auswaertiges-amt.de/en/newsroom/news/140201-bm-muesiko/259556 (accessed 16 December 2019).

9   'Schröder lobt Putin erneut', *Spiegel*, 11 December 2006, spiegel.de/politik/ausland/staatsaufbau-schroeder-lobt-putin-erneut-a-453795.html (accessed 15 December 2019).

10 H. Gamillscheg, 'Denkmalstreit in Tallinn eskaliert', *Frankfurter Rundschau*, 28 April 2007.

11 See T. Paterson, 'Merkel fury after Gerhard Schroeder backs Putin on Ukraine', *Telegraph*, 14 March 2014, telegraph.co.uk/news/worldnews/europe/ukraine/10697986/Merkel-fury-after-Gerhard-Schroeder-backs-Putin-on-Ukraine.html (accessed 15 December 2019); 'Der Altkanzler im Interview: Schröder verteidigt Putin und keilt gegen Merkel', *Bild*, 22 December 2017, bild.de/politik/ausland/gerhard-schroeder/vertraut-wladimir-putin-54277288.bild.html (accessed 15 December 2019).

12 'Das "Wall Street Journal" stellt eine unbequeme Frage: Warum gibt es keine Sanktionen gegen Schröder?', *Bild*, 18 March 2018, bild.de/politik/inland/gerhard-schroeder/warum-gibt-es-keine-sanktionen-gegen-schroeder-55137570.bild.html (accessed 15 December 2019).

13 See S. S. Nelson, 'Why Putin's Pal, Germany's Ex-Chancellor Schroeder, Isn't on a Sanctions List', NPR, 18 April 2018, npr.org/sections/parallels/2018/04/18/601825131/why-putins-pal-germanys-ex-chancellor-hasnt-landed-on-a-sanctions-list (accessed 16 December 2019).

14 J. D. Walter and D. Janjevic, 'Vladimir Putin and Angela Merkel: Through good times and bad', Deutsche Welle, 18 August 2018, dw.com/en/vladimir-putin-and-angela-merkel-through-good-times-and-bad/g-45129235 (accessed 18 December 2019).

15 See G. Packer, 'The Quiet German: The astonishing rise of Angela Merkel, the most powerful woman in the world', *New Yorker*, 24 November 2014, newyorker.com/magazine/2014/12/01/quiet-german (accessed 18 December 2019).

16 Ibid.

17 A. Merkel, Lowy Lecture, Sydney, 17 November 2014, www.lowyinstitute.org/publications/2014-lowy-lecture-dr-angela-merkel-chancellor-germany (accessed 19 December 2019).

18 C. Hoffmann, T. Lehmann, V. Medick and R. Neukirch, 'Relations with Moscow Emerge as German Election Issue', *Spiegel*, 29 July 2019, spiegel.de/international/germany/east-german-politicians-see-advantage-in-pro-putin-views-a-1279231.html (accessed 19 December 2019).

19 Ibid.

20 'White Paper 2016: On German Security Policy and the Future of the Bundeswehr', Berlin, Federal Ministry of Defence, 2016, p. 32.

21 S. Thévoz and P. Geoghegan, 'Revealed: Russian donors have stepped up Tory funding', Open Democracy, 5 November 2019, opendemocracy.net/en/dark-money-investigations/revealed-russian-donors-have-stepped-tory-funding (accessed 6 November 2019).

22 See Donald Trump, @realDonaldTrump, Twitter, 9 December 2015,

twitter.com/realDonaldTrump/status/674587800835092480 (accessed 19 December 2019); S. B. Glasser, 'How Trump Made War on Angela Merkel and Europe', *New Yorker*, 17 December 2018, newyorker.com/magazine/2018/12/24/how-trump-made-war-on-angela-merkel-and-europe (accessed 19 December 2019).

23 Quoted in G. Will, 'Today's Germany is the best Germany the world has seen'.

24 I. Traynor and P. Lewis, 'Merkel compared NSA to Stasi in heated encounter with Obama', *Guardian*, 17 December 2013, theguardian.com/world/2013/dec/17/merkel-compares-nsa-stasi-obama (accessed 20 December 2019).

25 R. Hilmer and R. Schlinkert, 'ARD-DeutschlandTREND: Umfrage zur politischen Stimmung im Auftrag der ARD-Tagesthemen und DIE WELT', Berlin, 2013, infratest-dimap.de/fileadmin/_migrated/content_uploads/dt1311_bericht.pdf (accessed 19 December 2019). See also 'Bürger trauen Obama und den USA nicht mehr', *Spiegel*, 7 November 2013, spiegel.de/politik/deutschland/ard-deutschlandtrend-mehrheit-der-deutschen-ist-mit-obama-unzufrieden-a-932455.html (accessed 19 December 2019).

26 J. Borger and A. Perkins, 'G7 in disarray after Trump rejects communique and attacks "weak" Trudeau', *Guardian*, 10 June 2018, theguardian.com/world/2018/jun/10/g7-in-disarray-after-trump-rejects-communique-and-attacks-weak-trudeau (accessed 21 December 2019).

27 Donald Trump, @realDonaldTrump, Twitter, 18 June 2018, twitter.com/realDonaldTrump/status/1008696508697513985 (accessed 19 December 2019).

28 K. Martin and T. Buck, 'US ambassador to Germany backs European right wing', *Financial Times*, 4 June 2019, ft.com/content/3b61a19e-67c7-11e8-b6eb-4acfcfb08c11 (accessed 19 December 2019).

29 J. Poushter and M. Mordecai, 'Americans and Germans Differ in Their Views of Each Other and the World', Pew Research Center, March 2020.

30 G. Allison, 'Less than a third of German military assets are operational says report', *UK Defence Journal*, 21 June 2018, ukdefencejournal.org.uk/less-third-german-military-assets-operational-says-report/ (accessed 22 December 2019). See also T. Buck, 'German armed forces in "dramatically bad" shape, report finds', *Financial Times*, 20 February 2018, ft.com/content/23c524f6-1642-11e8-9376-4a6390addb44 (accessed 22 December 2019).

31 L. Barber and G. Chazan, 'Angela Merkel warns EU: "Brexit is a wake-up call"', *Financial Times*, 15 January 2020, ft.com/content/a6785028-35f1-11ea-a6d3-9a26f8c3cba4 (accessed 16 January 2020).

32 'PESCO: The Proof is in the Field', *European Defence Matters*, no. 5, 2018, eda.europa.eu/webzine/issue15/cover-story/pesco-the-proof-is-in-the-field (accessed 22 December 2019).

33 U. von der Leyen, 'Europe is forming an army', *Handelsblatt*, 1 October 2019, handelsblatt.com/today/opinion/ursula-von-der-leyen-europe-is-forming-an-army/23851656.html?ticket=ST-166577-7jifWCpsKUzfXhWetQov-ap2 (accessed 22 December 2019).

34 P. Köhler, 'China continues German shopping spree', *Handelsblatt*, 25 January 2018, handelsblatt.com/today/companies/international-investments-china-continues-german-shopping-spree/23580854.html?ticket=ST-5042-VvXmnInrGnIliTrJjoIW-ap5 (accessed 28 December 2019).

35 D. Weinland and P. McGee, 'China's Midea makes offer for German robotics group Kuka', *Financial Times*, 18 May 2016, ft.com/content/90f9f7ae-1cd4-11e6-b286-cddde55ca122 (accessed 28 December 2019).

36 S. Mair, F. Strack and F. Schaff (eds.), *Partner and Systemic Competitor – How Do We Deal with China's State-Controlled Economy?*, Bundesverband der Deutschen Industrie, 10 January 2019. See also B. A. Düben, 'The souring mood towards Beijing from Berlin', The Interpreter, The Lowy Institute, 15 April 2019, www.lowyinstitute.org/the-interpreter/souring-mood-towards-beijing-berlin (accessed 29 December 2019).

37 'KfW erwirbt im Auftrag des Bundes temporär Anteil am deutschen Übertragungsnetzbetreiber 50Hertz', Bundesministerium für Wirtschaft und Energie, 27 July 2018, bmwi.de/Redaktion/DE/Pressemitteilungen/2018/20180727-kfw-erwirbt-im-auftrag-des-bundes-temporaer-anteil-am-deutschen-uebertragungsnetzbetreiber-50hertz.html (accessed 29 December 2019).

38 See '"Wir Europäer müssen unser Schicksal in unsere eigene Hand nehmen"', *Süddeutsche Zeitung*, 28 May 2017, sueddeutsche.de/politik/g-7-krise-wir-europaeer-muessen-unser-schicksal-in-unsere-eigene-hand-nehmen-1.3524718 (accessed 30 December 2019).

39 See L. Barber and G. Chazan, 'Angela Merkel warns EU'.

40 J. Lau and B. Ulrich, 'Im Westen was Neues', *Zeit*, 18 October 2017, zeit.de/2017/43/aussenpolitik-deutschland-usa-transatlantische-beziehungen-werte (accessed 30 December 2019).

41 T. Bagger, 'The World According to Germany: Reassessing 1989', *Washington Quarterly*, vol. 41, no. 4, 2018, p. 55.

42 K. Pfeiffer, 'Vortrag von Dr. Kurt Pfeiffer', Aachen, 19 December 1949, karlspreis.de/de/karlspreis/entstehungsgeschichte/vortrag-von-dr-kurt-pfeiffer (accessed 30 December 2019).

43 See L. Barber and G. Chazan, 'Angela Merkel warns EU'.

5 The Wonder

1 Quoted in R. Zitelamann, 'The Leadership Secrets of the
Hidden Champions', *Forbes*, 15 July 2019, forbes.com/sites/
rainerzitelmann/2019/07/15/the-leadership-secrets-of-the-hidden-
champions/#54b7640e6952 (accessed 6 January 2020).

2 See D. R. Henderson, 'German Economic Miracle', in D. R. Henderson
(ed.), *The Concise Encyclopedia of Economics*, Liberty Fund, 2007,
econlib.org/library/Enc/GermanEconomicMiracle.html (accessed
5 November 2019).

3 H. C. Wallich, *Mainsprings of the German Revival*, New Haven, Yale
University Press, 1955, p. 71.

4 'The sick man of the euro', *Economist*, 3 June 1999, economist.com/
special/1999/06/03/the-sick-man-of-the-euro (accessed 6 January 2020).

5 C. Odendahl, 'The Hartz myth: A closer look at Germany's labour
market reforms', Centre for European Reform, July 2017, p. 3, cer.eu/
sites/default/files/pbrief_german_labour_19.7.17.pdf (accessed
6 January 2020).

6 U. Deupmann and B. Kellner, 'Manche Finanzinvestoren fallen wie
Heuschreckenschwärme über Unternehmen her', *Bild am Sonntag*,
17 April 2005.

7 V. Romei, 'Germany: from "sick man" of Europe to engine of growth',
Financial Times, 14 August 2017, ft.com/content/bd4c856e-6de7-11e7-
b9c7-15af748b60d0 (accessed 10 January 2020).

8 See E. von Thadden, 'Sind wir nicht die Reichsten?', *Zeit*, 27 March 2013,
zeit.de/2013/14/europa-reichtum-werner-abelshauser (accessed
30 April 2020).

9 W. Martin, 'Workers at BMW, Mercedes and Porsche can now work a
28-hour week', Business Insider, 7 February 2018, businessinsider.com/
german-workers-can-now-work-a-28-hour-week-2018-2?r=US&IR=T
(accessed 11 January 2020).

10 G. Clark, *Question Time*, BBC One, 23 November 2017.

11 N. Adams, 'UK's Creative Industries contributes almost £13 million
to the UK economy every hour', Department for Digital, Culture,
Media and Sport, 6 February 2020, gov.uk/government/news/
uks-creative-industries-contributes-almost-13-million-to-the-uk-
economy-every-hour (accessed 12 February 2020).

12 'Germany's business barons are finding it harder to keep a low profile',
Economist, 15 June 2019.

13 S. Bach , A. Thiemann and A. Zucco, 'Looking for the missing rich:
Tracing the top tail of the wealth distribution', German Institute
for Economic Research, 23 January 2018, diw.de/documents/
publikationen/73/diw_01.c.575768.de/dp1717.pdf (accessed

15 January 2020). See also F. Diekmann, '45 Deutsche besitzen so viel wie die ärmere Hälfte der Bevölkerung', *Spiegel*, 23 January 2018, spiegel. de/wirtschaft/soziales/vermoegen-45-superreiche-besitzen-so-viel-wie-die-halbe-deutsche-bevoelkerung-a-1189111.html (accessed 15 January 2020).

14 See R. Wearn, '"Drowning" in debt as personal borrowing tops £180bn', BBC News, 20 January 2016, bbc.co.uk/news/business-35361281 (accessed 15 January 2020).

15 'Merkel kritisiert Aufnahmestopp für Ausländer – Dobrindt widerspricht', *Zeit*, 27 February 2018, zeit.de/politik/deutschland/ 2018-02/tafel-essen-angela-merkel-aufnahmestopp-auslaender (accessed 17 January 2020).

16 See '"Wir lassen uns nicht von der Kanzlerin rügen"', *Süddeutsche Zeitung*, 1 March 2018, sueddeutsche.de/politik/debatte-um-essener-tafel-wir-lassen-uns-nicht-von-der-kanzlerin-ruegen-1.3888853 (accessed 17 January 2020).

17 See N. Sagener, trans. E. Körner, 'Minimum wage unlikely to remedy rising poverty in Germany', Euractiv, 20 February 2015, euractiv.com/ section/social-europe-jobs/news/minimum-wage-unlikely-to-remedy-rising-poverty-in-germany (accessed 17 January 2020).

18 See N. Sagener, trans. S. Morgan, 'Child poverty in Germany increasingly the norm', Euractiv, 13 September 2016, euractiv.com/ section/social-europe-jobs/news/child-poverty-in-germany-increasingly-becomes-the-norm/ (accessed 17 January 2020).

19 'Pressemeldung: Paritätischer Armutsbericht 2019 zeigt ein viergeteiltes Deutschland', Der Paritätische Gesamtverband, 12 December 2019, der-paritaetische.de/presse/paritaetischer-armutsbericht-2019-zeigt-ein-viergeteiltes-deutschland (accessed 17 January 2020).

20 H. Morgenthau, 'Suggested Post-Surrender Program for Germany', 1944, Franklin D. Roosevelt Presidential Library and Museum, Hyde Park, NY. Scans of the memorandum can be viewed at docs.fdrlibrary.marist. edu/PSF/BOX31/t297a01.html (accessed 17 January 2020).

21 See 'Ackermann räumt Mitschuld der Bankmanager ein', *Spiegel*, 30 December 2008, spiegel.de/wirtschaft/finanzkrise-ackermann-raeumt-mitschuld-der-bankmanager-ein-a-598788.html (accessed 17 January 2020).

22 M. Hüther and J. Südekum, 'The German debt brake needs a reform', VoxEU, 6 May 2019, voxeu.org/content/german-debt-brake-needs-reform (accessed 17 January 2020).

23 'Sommerpressekonferenz von Bundeskanzlerin Merkel', Berlin, 19 July 2019, www.bundesregierung.de/breg-de/aktuelles/ sommerpressekonferenz-von-bundeskanzlerin-merkel-1649802 (accessed 17 January 2020).

24 S. Wood, 'Whisper it softly: it's OK to like Germany', *Guardian*, 13 July
    2014, theguardian.com/commentisfree/2014/jul/13/germany-world-
    cup-final-football (accessed 17 January 2020).

6   The Dog Doesn't Eat the Dog

1   T. Fontane, 'Richmond', *Ein Sommer in London*, Dessau, Gebrüder Katz,
    1854, p. 75.
2   'In Profile: The Federal Ministry of the Interior', Bundesministerium
    des Innerns, October 2016, bmi.bund.de/SharedDocs/downloads/DE/
    publikationen/themen/ministerium/flyer-im-profil-en.html (accessed
    10 February 2020).
3   See M. Großekathöfer, 'Früher war alles schlechter: Zahl der Vereine',
    Spiegel, 15 April 2017, p. 50; A. Seibt, 'The German obsession with clubs',
    Deutsche Welle, 6 September 2017, dw.com/en/the-german-obsession-
    with-clubs/a-40369830 (accessed 10 February 2020).
4   C. Dietz, 'White gold: the German love affair with pale asparagus',
    Guardian, 14 June 2016, theguardian.com/lifeandstyle/
    wordofmouth/2016/jun/14/white-gold-german-love-affair-pale-
    asparagus-spargelzeit (accessed 10 February 2020).
5   J. Major, 'Speech to the Conservative Group for Europe', London,
    22 April 1993.
6   See 'Mixed Compensation Barometer 2019', Ernst & Young,
    November 2019, p. 4, ey.com/de_de/news/2019/11/gehaltseinbussen-
    fuer-deutsche-vorstaende (accessed 15 February 2020).
7   L. Himmelreich, 'Der Herrenwitz', *Stern*, 1 February 2013, stern.
    de/politik/deutschland/stern-portraet-ueber-rainer-bruederle-der-
    herrenwitz-3116542.html (accessed 17 February 2020).
8   'Kritik an Deutsche-Bank-Chef: Ackermann schürt die Diskussion
    um die Frauenquote', *Handelsblatt*, 7 February 2011, handelsblatt.
    com/unternehmen/management/kritik-an-deutsche-bank-chef-
    ackermann-schuert-die-diskussion-um-die-frauenquote/3824928.
    html?ticket=ST-957390-MTISlcC9d2pPjTw9uzYC-ap1 (accessed
    20 February 2020).
9   See K. Bennhold, 'Women Nudged Out of German Workforce', *New
    York Times*, 28 June 2011, nytimes.com/2011/06/29/world/europe/
    29iht-FFgermany29.html?_r=1&src=rechp (accessed 20 February 2020).
10 J. Hensel, 'Angela Merkel: "Parität erscheint mir logisch"', *Zeit*,
    23 January 2019, zeit.de/2019/05/angela-merkel-bundeskanzlerin-cdu-
    feminismus-lebensleistung (accessed 20 February 2020).
11 See 'The German Vocational Training System', Bundesministerium für
    Bildung und Forschung, bmbf.de/en/the-german-vocational-training-
    system-2129.html (accessed 20 February 2020).

12   See F. Studemann, 'German universities are back in vogue for foreign
     students', *Financial Times*, 22 August 2019, ft.com/content/a28fff1c-
     c42a-11e9-a8e9-296ca66511c9 (accessed 21 February 2020).

13   G. Chazan, 'Oversupply of hospital beds helps Germany to fight virus',
     Financial Times, 13 April 2020, ft.com/content/d979c0e9-4806-4852-
     a49a-bbffa9cecfe6 (accessed 13 April 2020).

14   M. Diermeier and H. Goecke, 'Capital Cities: Usually an economic
     driving force', Institut der deutschen Wirtschaft, 20 October 2017,
     iwkoeln.de/presse/iw-nachrichten/beitrag/matthias-diermeier-henry-
     goecke-capital-cities-usually-an-economic-driving-force-366303.html
     (accessed 21 February 2020).

15   Quoted in R. Mohr, 'The Myth of Berlin's Tempelhof: The Mother of all
     Airports', *Spiegel*, 25 April 2008, spiegel.de/international/germany/the-
     myth-of-berlin-s-tempelhof-the-mother-of-all-airports-a-549685.html
     (accessed 21 February 2020).

16   C. Fahey, 'How Berliners refused to give Tempelhof airport over to
     developers', *Guardian*, 5 March 2015, theguardian.com/cities/2015/
     mar/05/how-berliners-refused-to-give-tempelhof-airport-over-to-
     developers (accessed 21 February 2020).

17   S. Shead, 'The story of Berlin's WWII Tempelhof Airport which is
     now Germany's largest refugee shelter', *Independent*, 20 June 2017,
     independent.co.uk/news/world/world-history/the-story-of-berlins-
     wwii-tempelhof-airport-which-is-now-germanys-largest-refugee-
     shelter-a7799296.html (accessed 21 February 2020).

18   See L. Kaas, G. Kocharkov, E. Preugschat and N. Siassi, 'Reasons for
     the low homeownership rate in Germany', Research Brief 30, Deutsche
     Bundesbank, 14 January 2020, bundesbank.de/en/publications/
     research/research-brief/2020-30-homeownership-822176 (accessed
     25 February 2020); 'People in the EU – statistics on housing conditions',
     Eurostat, December 2017, ec.europa.eu/eurostat/statistics-explained/
     index.php/People_in_the_EU_-_statistics_on_housing_
     conditions#Home_ownership (accessed 25 February 2020).

19   T. Lokoschat, 'Kommentar zur Enteignungsdebatte: Ideen aus der DDR',
     Bild, 8 March 2019, bild.de/politik/kolumnen/kolumne/kommentar-
     zur-enteignungsdebatte-ideen-aus-der-ddr-60546810.bild.html
     (accessed 25 February 2020).

20   See C. Higgins, 'The cutting edge', *Guardian*, 24 November 2007,
     theguardian.com/books/2007/nov/24/theatre.stage (accessed
     25 February 2020).

21   P. Oltermann, 'Katie Mitchell, British theatre's true auteur, on being
     embraced by Europe', *Guardian*, 9 July 2014, theguardian.com/stage/
     2014/jul/09/katie-mitchell-british-theatre-true-auteur (accessed
     25 February 2020).

22 'Open Letter', Volksbühne, Berlin, 20 June 2016, volksbuehne.adk. de/english/calender/open_letter/index.html (accessed 25 February 2020).

23 C. Dercon, speaking at the Goethe-Institut London, video posted on Facebook, 27 April 2018, facebook.com/watch/live/?v=10160588326450 529&ref=watch_permalink (accessed 30 April 2020).

24 N. MacGregor, 'Berlin's blast from the past', The World in 2019, London, The Economist Group, 2018, p. 133, worldin2019.economist.com/ NeilMacGregorontheHumboldtForum (accessed 26 February 2020).

25 S. Hölig and U. Hasebrink, 'Germany', in N. Newman, R. Fletcher, A. Kalogeropoulos and R. K. Nielsen (eds.), *Reuters Institute Digital News Report 2019*, Reuters Institute, 2019, pp. 86–7, reutersinstitute.politics. ox.ac.uk/sites/default/files/inline-files/DNR_2019_FINAL.pdf (accessed 26 February 2020).

7 No More Pillepalle

1 'Information für die Bevölkerung in der Umgebung des Kernkraftwerkes Tihange', Fachbereich Feuerwehr der Stadt Mönchengladbach, October 2018. See also H. Hintzen, 'Neue Broschüre in Mönchengladbach: Stadt erklärt Verhalten bei Atomunfall', RP Online, 8 February 2019, rp-online.de/nrw/staedte/moenchengladbach/moenchengladbach-verhaltenstipps-bei-unfall-im-atomkraftwerk-tihange_aid-36550915 (accessed 1 March 2020).

2 See C. Parth, 'Tihange Nuclear Power Plant: Fear of a Meltdown', *Zeit*, 1 June 2018, zeit.de/wirtschaft/2018-06/tihange-nuclear-power-plant-residents-opposition-english (accessed 1 March 2020).

3 'Cooperation on nuclear safety', Dutch Safety Board, 31 January 2018, onderzoeksraad.nl/en/page/4341/cooperation-on-nuclear-safety (accessed 1 March 2020). See also D. Keating, 'Belgium's Neighbors Fear a Nuclear Incident', *Forbes*, 4 February 2018, forbes.com/ sites/davekeating/2018/02/04/belgiums-neighbors-fear-a-nuclear-incident/#55c658216ca2 (accessed 1 March 2020).

4 See K. Bennhold, 'Impose a Speed Limit on the Autobahn? Not So Fast, Many Germans Say', *New York Times*, 3 February 2019, nytimes. com/2019/02/03/world/europe/germany-autobahn-speed-limit.html (accessed 1 March 2020).

5 Ibid.

6 See 'Abgasaffäre: VW-Chef Müller spricht von historischer Krise', *Spiegel*, 28 September 2015, spiegel.de/wirtschaft/unternehmen/ volkswagen-chef-mueller-sieht-konzern-in-historischer-krise-a-1055148.html (accessed 2 March 2020).

7 J. Miller, 'VW offers direct payouts to sidestep emissions lawsuit',

Financial Times, 14 February 2020, ft.com/content/f41adade-4f24-11ea-95a0-43d18ec715f5 (accessed 14 February 2020).

8 P. Nair, 'Stuttgart residents sue mayor for "bodily harm" caused by air pollution', *Guardian*, 2 March 2017, theguardian.com/cities/2017/mar/02/stuttgart-residents-sue-mayor-bodily-harm-air-pollution (accessed 2 March 2020).

9 See 'DB 2019: Long distance patronage over 150 million for the first time', DB Schenker, 26 March 2020, dbschenker.com/global/about/press/db2019-631574 (accessed 29 March 2020); 'German domestic air travel slump points to increase in "flight shame" and carbon awareness', AirportWatch, 19 December 2019, airportwatch.org.uk/2019/12/german-domestic-air-travel-slump-points-to-increase-in-flight-shame-and-carbon-awareness (accessed 29 March 2020).

10 See 'Fridays for Horsepower: The German Motorists Who Oppose Greta Thunberg', *Spiegel*, 15 October 2019, spiegel.de/international/germany/fridays-for-horsepower-german-motorists-oppose-fridays-for-future-a-1290466.html (accessed 5 March 2020).

11 K. Gutmann, J. Huscher, D. Urbaniak, A. White, C. Schaible and M. Bricke, 'Europe's Dirty 30: How the EU's coal-fired power plants are undermining its climate efforts', Brussels, CAN Europe, WWF European Policy Office, HEAL, the EEB and Climate Alliance Germany, July 2014, awsassets.panda.org/downloads/dirty_30_report_finale.pdf (accessed 5 March 2020).

12 S. Kersing and K. Stratmann, 'Germany's great environmental failure', *Handelsblatt*, 19 October 2018, handelsblatt.com/today/politics/climate-emergency-germanys-great-environmental-failure/23583678.html?ticket=ST-1141019-0RgHHhpypfii593mjbqo-ap1 (accessed 5 March 2020).

13 Ibid.

14 See 'Germany 2020: Energy Policy Review', International Energy Agency, February 2020, pp. 27–8, bmwi.de/Redaktion/DE/Downloads/G/germany-2020-energy-policy-review.pdf?__blob=publicationFile&v=4 (accessed 5 March 2020).

15 See the graph 'Entwicklung des Anteils erneuerbarer Energien am Bruttostromverbrauch in Deutschland', Bundesministerium für Wirtschaft und Energie, March 2020, erneuerbare-energien.de/EE/Navigation/DE/Service/Erneuerbare_Energien_in_Zahlen/Entwicklung/entwicklung-der-erneuerbaren-energien-in-deutschland.html (accessed 31 March 2020).

16 Ibid.

17 *Spiegel*, 7 July 2008.

18 T. Buck, 'Germany unveils sweeping measures to fight climate change', *Financial Times*, 20 September 2019, ft.com/

content/26e8d1e0-dbb3-11e9-8f9b-77216ebe1f17 (accessed
25 September 2019).

19 A. Merkel, 'Neujahrsansprache 2020', 31 December 2019, www.
bundesregierung.de/breg-de/service/bulletin/neujahrsansprache-
2020-1709738 (accessed 10 February 2020).

20 P. Hockenos, 'How to Say Emmanuel Macron in German', *Foreign
Policy*, 8 December 2019, foreignpolicy.com/2019/12/08/robert-habeck-
greens-merkel-emmanuel-macron-in-german (accessed
11 March 2020).

21 P. Oltermann, 'Robert Habeck: could he be Germany's first Green
chancellor?', *Guardian*, 27 December 2019, theguardian.com/
world/2019/dec/27/robert-habeck-could-be-germany-first-green-
chancellor (accessed 11 March 2020).

22 Ibid.

Conclusion

1 'Angela Merkels Erklärung im Wortlaut', *Welt*, 29 October 2018, welt.
de/politik/deutschland/article182938128/Wurde-nicht-als-Kanzlerin-
geboren-Angela-Merkels-Erklaerung-im-Wortlaut.html (accessed
15 March 2020).

2 See L. Barber and G. Chazan, 'Angela Merkel warns EU: "Brexit is
a wake-up call"', *Financial Times*, 15 January 2020, ft.com/content/
a6785028-35f1-11ea-a6d3-9a26f8c3cba4 (accessed 16 January 2020).

3 N. Barkin, 'You May Miss Merkel More Than You Think', *Foreign Policy*,
9 March 2020, foreignpolicy.com/2020/03/09/armin-laschet-merkels-
pro-russia-china-friendly-successor (accessed 9 March
2020).

4 *Face the Nation*, CBS, 15 July 2018. See also 'Donald Trump calls the
EU a foe during interview in Scotland – video', *Guardian*, 15 July 2018,
theguardian.com/us-news/video/2018/jul/15/donald-trump-calls-the-
eu-a-foe-video (accessed 15 March 2020).

5 B. Schulz, 'British Hypocrisy', *Zeit*, 31 January 2020, zeit.de/politik/
ausland/2020-01/great-britain-brexit-alienation-eu-withdrawal-english
(accessed 1 February 2020).

6 'Fernsehansprache von Bundeskanzlerin Angela Merkel', Tagesschau,
Das Erste, 18 March 2020.

Index